CONTINUING PROFESSIONAL DEVELOPMENT FOR TEACHERS

CONTINUING PROFESSIONAL DEVELOPMENT FOR TEACHERS

From Induction to Senior Management

PETER NEIL & CAROL MORGAN

KOGAN
PAGE

First published in Great Britain in 2003

Kogan Page Limited
120 Pentonville Road
London N1 9JN
United Kingdom
www.kogan-page.co.uk

British Library Cataloguing in Publication Data

A CIP record for this book is available from the British Library.

ISBN 0 7494 3741 3

Typeset by Saxon Graphics Ltd, Derby
Printed and bound in Great Britain by Bell & Bain Ltd, Glasgow

Contents

Acknowledgements

The authors are indebted to a number of individuals without whose help, support, advice, expertise and encouragement, this book would not have been written. We are particularly indebted to those from the various jurisdictions who read drafts of individual sections and provided helpful suggestions and corrected misunderstandings:

Sarah Stephens, General Teaching Council for England;
Sue Halliwell, Welsh Assembly Government;
Vivian McIver and Roy Downey, Education and Training Inspectorate, Department of Education, Northern Ireland.

In addition, several other officials at various organizations were most helpful with specific aspects of the work:

Myra Pearson, Grant Gillies and Margaret Russell, General Teaching Council for Scotland;
Maria Boex and Tegryn Jones, General Teaching Council for Wales;
Various officials at the Department for Education and Skills;
Various officials at the Teacher Training Agency;
Philomena McDermott, Western Education and Library Board;
Katherine Raithby, whose help in providing diagrams was invaluable;
Sally Williamson and Charlotte Wootton for their patience and reliability in providing secretarial support.

Finally we would like to thank the vast numbers of teachers who have taken masters and doctoral courses at Queen's and at Bath, who have informed our thinking on a number of areas in the book.

Peter Neil and Carol Morgan
January 2003

Other contributors

Billy McClune (Chapter 6) is currently Lecturer in Education at Queen's University, where he teaches on the science PGCE course and on the Masters level programme on middle management. He was formerly head of science at a grammar school and has many years' experience as a teacher of chemistry and physics. His current research interests include science education and self-evaluation in schools.

Sylvia Gourley (Chapter 7), recently retired Assistant Director of East Antrim Institute of Further and Higher Education, is a trainer on the National PQH programme in Northern Ireland. She is also an NI Threshold Assessor and an Assessor for the MCI Standards in Management at Level 5. She has had many years' experience of management, management development, teacher and counsellor training.

Acronyms

APEL	accreditation of professional experiential learning
APL	accreditation of professional learning
AR	action research
A/AS	advanced/advanced supplementary (level)
AST	advanced skills teacher
BPRS	best practice research scholarship
BT	beginning teacher
CASS	curriculum advisory support service
CEO	chief executive officer
CEP	career entry profile
CLS	critical leadership studies
CPD	continuing professional development
CT	chartered teacher
DENI	Department of Education for Northern Ireland (now DE)
DfEE	Department for Education and Employment
DfES	Department for Education and Skills
EAZ	education action zone
EdD	Doctor of Education
EiC	excellence in cities
ELB	education and library board
EMS	educational management studies
EPD	early professional development
ETI	Education and Training Inspectorate
EU	European Union
FE	further education
GCSE	general certificate of secondary examination
GTC(NI)	General Teaching Council for Northern Ireland
GTCE	General Teaching Council for England
GTCS	General Teaching Council for Scotland
GTCW	General Teaching Council for Wales
HEI	higher education institution
HMI	Her Majesty's Inspectorate
HoD	head of department
HT	head teacher

IBISS	improving behaviour in secondary schools
ICT	information and communications technology
INSET	in-service training
ISI	independent schools inspectorate
ITE	initial teacher education
ITT	initial teacher training
LEA	local education authority
LMS	local management of schools
MA(Ed)	Master of Arts in Education
MBA	Master of Business Administration
MCI	Manager Charter Initiative
MEd	Master of Education
MFR	managing for results
MSc	Master of Science
NAS/UWT	National Association of Schoolmasters/Union of Women Teachers
NCD	non-contact days
NFER	National Foundation for Educational Research
NITEC	Northern Ireland Teacher Education Committee
NPQH	national professional qualification for headship
NQT	newly qualified teacher
NUT	National Union of Teachers
OFSTED	Office for Standards in Education
PANDA	Performance and Assessment document
PAT	Professional Association of Teachers
PDA	professional development activity
PDR	professional development record
PGCE	post-graduate certificate in education
PICSI	pre-inspection context and school indicator
PQH(NI)	professional qualification for headship in Northern Ireland
PSE	personal and social education
QCA	Qualifications and Curriculum Authority
QTS	qualified teacher status
RE	religious education
RgI	registered inspector
SDP	school development plan
SDPM	staff development and performance management
SDPR	staff development and performance review
SEED	Scottish Executive Education Department
SEN	special educational needs
SENCO	special needs co-ordinator
SFR	standard for registration

SL	subject leader
SMT	senior management team
SQH	Scottish qualification for headship
STL	senior teacher leader
TIPD	teachers' international professional development
TL	teacher leader
TST	teacher support teams
TTA	Teacher Training Agency

Introduction

Education appears to be in a constant state of flux. The government's phrase: 'Education, Education, Education', seems to mean 'change, change and more change'. At the sharp end of many of these changes are teachers and managers in schools, who are expected to respond to them, develop initiatives and maintain or raise standards in schools. This time of change is also, however, an exciting time of tremendous opportunity. There are more options for personal and professional development, more chances of gaining promotion and different pathways through the system.

The White Paper on education, *Schools Achieving Success* (DfES, 2001c), sets out the government's vision for the future of our schools. The teachers who are reading this book are the ones who will be in the forefront of developments in schools during the next decade and beyond. You are the colleagues who will be the teachers, managers and leaders facing the challenges and opportunities and you will be the ones who will be making a difference to the education of the young people in our schools during that time.

The term 'continuing professional development' (CPD) may not be interpreted in the same way by different key players in the educational world. Possible areas of different interpretation could include:

- a teacher's own version of CPD, ie how an individual teacher sees his or her professional needs;
- a school's interpretation, such as the policies and arrangements for implementing CPD;
- official regulations and recommendations (in documents from DfES, TTA and GTC);
- other teachers' interpretations, either within your own school or in other schools.

What we hope to do in this book is to clarify the differences between the different interpretations by: offering a wide range of information and opinions; analysing official documents, gathering together research that has focused on teachers' responses to CPD and talking to teachers about CPD issues. In this way we hope to shed light on different CPD routes and maximize the opportunities for professional development. The purpose of the book is to help teachers steer a course from their arrival in their first post through the process of induction, early professional development, towards becoming a subject leader and, perhaps eventually, a headteacher. The book will also be a resource to staff in schools responsible for the professional development of teachers, in supporting them as they weave a course through the relevant documentation. The book maps the journey of the teacher, providing signposts, charting the territory mapped out by others, while giving pointers as to how to proceed in different contexts.

The days when teachers entered their classroom, closed the door and got on with teaching, to be visited only on occasion by inspectors, are, fortunately in most schools, long gone. There is now an emphasis on self-evaluation, reflective practice and continuing personal and professional development. Teachers are now encouraged to take responsibility for their own careers, but with the support and guidance of mentors in schools, colleagues who have the responsibility to ensure that staff, particularly those in their early stages of their teaching, are helped to gain the necessary experience and knowledge. This mentoring or support is designed to help the new teachers to advance to the level within the profession at which they feel they can make the most valuable contribution.

Rationale and sources for this book

In an age where the quick fix and the make-over are ever-present it is important to resist adopting this approach to CPD. Bates, Gough and Stammers in their analysis of the role of central government and its agencies have a sharp vision here; they note that: 'the notion of a "simple" input–output model or a sequential and essentially linear model fails to recognize the complexities of the many agendas that characterize professional development at the different stages of an individual's career' (Bates, Gough and Stammers, 1999: 329).

We would like to suggest that as well as being a complex process, CPD is also a long-term process. In the research by Harland et al into the use of training days in schools, one teacher talks of the unsatisfactory nature of one-off training days and suggests that 'some of the best learning is slow learning' (Harland et al, 1999: 121). In this book we shall encompass both a complex view of professional development and combine long and short perspectives, which acknowledge the benefits of immediate solutions but also the need to work slowly towards goals.

A further frustration that potential CPD organizers may face is the apparent smooth-running positive images that are presented in case studies in government documents. There seem to be assumptions in these studies both that any good practice can be universally adopted and that problems can just be overcome or do not exist. It is less than helpful to be presented with a rosy ideal if your own school has very different problems that are not easily solved. Best practice of course is helpful to hear about, but equally helpful is advice on difficulties and a sharing of realizations about possible necessary compromises. In the descriptions and analyses that follow, we have tried to present an honest picture of some of the situations that do exist; to outline ways that schools have found of succeeding, and to present the kinds of hidden and more obvious problems that can occur.

In collecting information for the book, we have consulted various sources:

- government publications;
- research and development literature;
- professional and research journals;
- handbooks for teachers;
- our own research.

In addition we have conducted interviews with practising teachers and managers, some of which are included in the book as case studies. Questionnaires were sent to teacher educators and these findings have been incorporated. In sifting through all of these sources, we have brought to bear on them experience of working with teachers and student teachers in all the phases covered in the book (induction, EPD, CPD, middle management and senior management). In bringing these sources together, we hope to provide readers with a broad view of the issues and with a starting point for their own development.

Outline of the book

The book is set out in three parts, each focusing on a different stage in the journey:

- getting established;
- preparing for advancement;
- preparing for leadership.

Although we recognize that the contexts in which individual teachers operate differ, there is a certain level of cultural capital that can be gained from the experience of others and can be applied to other educational settings. Across the UK there are different emphases in the different phases, although there is a degree of similarity to the standards and requirements for each of the levels. Reference will be made to the requirements at the various stages in the four jurisdictions; it is beyond the scope of this book, however, to deal in detail with each of the countries. In the past, teachers may have had difficulty accessing or interpreting government regulations because of the 'filtering' systems in schools. In the chapters that follow we present the official guidelines, give key ideas and practical applications and make suggestions for further reading and provide details of relevant Web sites.

Part I

Getting established

1 The new post and induction

Having come through the training process, the trainee will have some idea as to what to expect in the classroom. The experiences of the classroom received during school experience in partner schools during training will have prepared the student exiting the PGCE course (referred to in different parts of the UK as the newly qualified teacher (NQT) (England and Wales), beginning teacher (BT) (Northern Ireland) or probationary teacher (Scotland)), for some of the demands of the teaching job, but taking up full-time, or even part-time employment in a school context, will bring with it some unexpected surprises. We shall use the term NQT throughout except where reference is made to official documents from Scotland or Northern Ireland.

The role of the General Teaching Councils

Each of the four main jurisdictions in the UK has a General Teaching Council, the oldest of which is the GTC in Scotland (GTCS), which was founded in 1965. The GTC in England (GTCE) was established in 2000 and the GTC Wales (GTCW) in 2001. In Northern Ireland the GTC will come into existence in 2003; the developmental work on teacher education has hitherto been undertaken by the Northern Ireland Teacher Education Committee (NITEC), which will hand over this responsibility to the GTC(NI) when it opens. The GTC acts as the gatekeeper to the profession; it is the body responsible for registration of new teachers and its overarching function is to advise on all aspects of the profession, particularly maintaining and raising standards. The GTC is an independent body, answerable to its registered teachers (GTCE, 2001a). It was established following the Teaching and Higher Education Act 1998 with the following remit:

- to contribute to improving the standards of teaching and the quality of learning;

- to maintain and improve standards of professional conduct among teachers; (both of these in the public interest)
- to advise the Secretary of State on the following:
  - standards of teaching;
  - standards of conduct for teachers;
  - the role of the teaching profession;
  - the training, career development and performance management of teachers;
  - recruitment to the teaching profession;
  - medical fitness to teach;
- to establish and maintain a register of teachers (GTCE, 2001a: 24).

The GTCs are responsible for raising the status of teachers and either have produced, in consultation with the profession, a Professional Code for Teachers, or they have distributed a Code for consultation. The Councils will also have a role in matters relating to disciplinary functions.

The role of the GTC in Scotland differs from that of its counterparts. It has responsibility for accrediting courses of initial teacher education (unlike the situation in England where this responsibility rests with the Teacher Training Agency) and the GTCS has generally more legislative powers than the other GTCs.

The main involvement of the NQT with the respective GTC will be seeking registration to teach. The easiest way to consult the regulations at the time of application is to search on the relevant Web site:

GTC (England): www.gtce.org.uk
GTC (Scotland): www.gtcs.org.uk
GTC (Wales): www.gtcw.org.uk

In order to obtain registration it will be necessary for the NQT to pay a fee. If the NQT fails the statutory induction period he or she will be removed from the register. There will be requirements on the school to ensure that a suitable induction programme is provided and the school will have responsibility to confirm that the NQT has successfully completed the statutory induction period. Each Council will have specific regulations for those who have qualified outside the area and leaflets setting out how to apply for registration can be obtained from the relevant GTC. In certain subject areas there are specific requirements which have to be met in addition to the standards before full registration can be granted; it is necessary therefore to check the specific requirements relevant to your subject area and with the relevant GTC as conditions for specific subjects may change. For example, the GTC in Scotland requires teachers of modern languages to have spent at least six months in the country of the languages before they can qualify to teach; this is not a requirement, however, in Northern Ireland at present. In addition to setting out regulations and to maintaining the register, the GTCs are actively involved in promoting teacher development from induction onwards by providing publications and documents to support the process. Some of their policies, recommendations and working papers will be highlighted in later sections of this chapter.

The GTCE has recently launched its second Corporate Plan (GTCE, 2002), in which it sets out its key commitments in relation to each of its corporate objectives:

- providing a professional voice on teaching;
- supporting standards;
- raising teacher status;
- listening to teachers.

The Corporate Plan also details the changes in the GTC's powers following the Education Act 2002. Full details of both the second corporate plan and the Education Act 2002 can be accessed on the GTCE Web site.

Government regulations and recommendations

In all parts of UK education since the late 1990s, professional development of teachers, from initial teacher education and induction through to headship, has undergone unprecedented change. A feature of this development, as a result of devolution, is the diversity of provision in the different parts of the country. The work of the GTC is inextricably linked to the development in the various jurisdictions and each will present its own particular emphases. There are, however, similarities to the process as teachers progress through the system. The general framework which appears to be consistent across the country is as follows:

- initial training;
- induction (first year in post);
- early professional development (EPD) (usually lasting two further years);
- CPD (career long);
- subject leadership/Advanced Skills teacher/Key Stage co-ordinator/SENCO;
- headship, including the National Professional Qualification for Headship (NPQH).

The emphasis at each stage is on the on-going development of the teacher's professional skills and knowledge and certification of competence at particular stages, such as the key stages of head of department or headteacher. What may differ across the UK systems is the terminology. Where there are significant differences in the use of terms, these will be explained.

This section gives a brief overview of some of the important regulations for teacher education in the different parts of the UK. In setting out these according to the various jurisdictions, it is intended to highlight aspects which may be of interest to the wider teaching community. The regulations in one part of the UK may be more prescribed than in others. Where examples from specific areas appear to illustrate good practice, these will be included in the relevant sections.

England

In England, various statutory bodies have a role in teacher education and development. The Secretary of State has responsibility for setting standards of qualified teacher status (QTS) and requirements of programmes leading to the award of QTS. The Teacher Training Agency (http://www.canteach.gov.uk) focuses on initial teacher training but it also provides guidance for induction. The Department of Education and Skills (http://www.dfes.gov.uk/iateach/) has overall responsibility for legislation relating to all aspects of teaching. In particular it sets out guidance on the regulations for induction (DfES, 2001b), which can be found on the Department's Web site in the professional development section. Additional guidance on registering with the GTC in England is available on its Web site.

The Teaching and Higher Education Act 1998 introduced regulations to provide a bridge from the initial teacher education phase to EPD. Precise details of the induction period for NQTs are presented in the DfES Circular 582/2001 (DfES, 2001b) and it sets out the ways in which NQTs should be supported and monitored in their first year of teaching. The induction should take place over three school terms. During the induction year, it is recommended that NQTs have a reduction of 10 per cent of a normal teaching load in order to give them time to devote to induction activities. The Induction Standards which have to be met by the NQT build on those required in the training year. These are listed under the following headings:

- Professional values and practice.
- Knowledge and understanding.
- Teaching.
- Planning, expectations and targets.
- Monitoring and assessment.
- Teaching and class management.
- National test in numeracy.

These standards are currently out for consultation (TTA, 2002). During the process an induction tutor will support the NQT. At the end of the induction year, the

NQT's performance will be judged against the criteria and it will be determined whether or not he or she meets the required standard to be fully passed as a teacher. Normally the period of induction will be one full year, but induction can be completed within a period of up to five years. It is the responsibility of the head-teacher, in conjunction with the so-called Appropriate Body to ensure that induction arrangements are in place and that the NQT has met the Induction Standards. The Appropriate Body is in most cases the Local Education Authority (for those in maintained schools). At the end of the induction period the Appropriate Body will inform the GTCE of the outcome of the induction.

In England, the period following induction is simply referred to as CPD. Whereas the arrangements governing induction are mandatory, there are at present in England no formal requirements governing the years following induction. CPD in England is influenced by the DfEE circular 0071/2001 (DfEE, 2001b), which sets out the Government's CPD strategy. Further details of the CPD strategy can be found at the Web site www.teachernet.gov.uk. The GTCE empha-sizes the fact that teachers are encouraged to develop their professional practice, but that such development must take account of local contexts and professional and personal priorities. It has produced a draft document, the *Professional Learning Framework* (GTCE, 2001b), which is currently out for consultation. This document sets out ways in which teachers can continue to improve their own practice, be involved in learning networks and develop their expertise beyond the school. Many of the aspects highlighted in this document will be dealt with in later sections of the book.

Northern Ireland

The Department of Education in Northern Ireland some years ago developed a three-phase integrated approach to the education and training of teachers. Details of this are found in the Teacher Education Handbook (DENI, 1998a). Originally conceived of as the 3 'I's – that is, initial teacher education, induction and in-service, this has evolved into initial teacher education (ITE), induction and EPD. The unifying strand, which permeates all phases, is the list of competences and core criteria to be acquired by the beginning teacher (BT). The competences are catego-rized in five broad domains:

- Understanding of the curriculum and professional knowledge.
- Subject knowledge and subject application.
- Teaching strategies and techniques, and classroom management.
- Assessment and recording of pupils' progress.
- Foundation for further professional development.

The competences are listed according to the phases in which they are most likely to be developed (A = ITE; B = induction; C = EPD) and the location in which they are to be developed (either the Higher Education Institution on the one hand or the school on the other, on a scale 1–5). In addition to the competences, teachers are required to meet the core criteria which are listed according to five sub-headings:

- Professional values.
- Professional development.
- Personal development.
- Communication and relationships.
- Synthesis and application.

At each stage in the process of professional development, including CPD which will be dealt with in the next chapter, the teacher will continue to develop his or her competence in the various areas of teaching. Full details of the competences and core criteria can be found on the Web site of the Department of Education (www.deni.gov.uk) or on the Northern Ireland network for education (www.nine.org.uk). The second two phases are the ones with which we are concerned in this book. The content of the induction phase is closely defined by the Department of Education (see DENI, 1998a: Section 4). It sets out details of what is considered to be the fundamental aspects of any school induction programme. Following the induction phase, the teachers enter years 2 and 3 which are entitled EPD, a time during which the teachers are engaged in defined professional development activities (PDA). Binding the whole experience of teacher education in Northern Ireland together are partnership links that exist between the higher education institutions (HEIs), the five education and library boards (ELBs), which are the equivalent of LEAs, collectively referred to as the curriculum and advisory support service (CASS) and schools. During each of the phases there is a so-called lead partner. In the initial teacher education phase, for example, the HEIs are the lead partners, supported by the schools and the ELBs; during induction the lead partner is the ELB and CASS service supporting the schools and during the final EPD phase the lead partner is the school, supported by CASS. It is the partnerships working together that are the strength of the teacher education programme. One feature which makes this possible, apart from the goodwill of the partners involved, is the fact that there are advisors and field officers in post for every subject and phase in every one of the five ELBs. Support continues to be provided during the phases post-PGCE, for example the training for teacher tutors organized by the HEIs and the ELBs, both individually and together in partnership. Also during the induction phase and the EPD years, days are organized by the ELBs and CASS for the new teachers to discuss generic and subject specific issues.

A further binding element is the teacher profile, which was originally conceived of as the 'spine' connecting the three phases; this document should accompany teachers on their first few years of teaching. The role of the HEIs in Northern Ireland tends to evaporate after the training year; this was not the original intention of the model of teacher education. The HEIs have a role to play in that they can give credit for the teacher portfolio which can be given CATS points towards a masters module; at this stage, however, they continue to be marginalized in the induction, EPD and CPD phases.

Scotland

The system of induction and CPD in Scotland is currently undergoing significant changes. For details refer to the Web site of the General Teaching Council for Scotland (www.gtcs.org.uk). The year following initial training is now called the induction period (until 2002 it was a two-year probationary period). The period following induction in Scotland is referred to as CPD, therefore there is no EPD in name as such. In order to achieve the full standard for registration (SFR) with the GTCS, the new teacher has to meet the standard under the following headings:

- Professional knowledge and understanding.
- Professional skills and abilities.
- Professional value and personal commitment (GTCS 2002a, 2002c).

During the induction period the probationer teacher should be engaged in an induction programme set up and monitored by the school. At the end of the induction year the induction teacher has to submit an SFR profile to the GTC; this document will contain targets and priorities for development in future years. Failure to achieve the required Standard may result in an extended period of induction or, in exceptional cases, can lead to cancellation of the provisional registration. Full details of the induction programme and the necessary documentation can be found in the publication *Achieving the Standard for Full Registration* produced by the GTCS (2002d). At the time of writing, the content of the CPD years following induction has been issued to local authorities and schools for consultation.

A unique feature of the Scottish system at present is the fact that all teachers in training in 2002 are to be guaranteed a training post in a Scottish school for one year. Places on this scheme are allocated by staff in the GTCS. During this first year the induction teacher will have class contact of 0.7, with 0.3 time allocated for professional development. In addition the Scottish Executive is providing funds for 0.1 time for a supporter (induction tutor) to work with the induction teachers in their professional development. As this is in its first year, there may be changes in subsequent years in the light of evaluation of the project. Questions such as whether the system can cope with the extra staff and how it will impact on existing staff in schools are yet to be answered in the light of experience.

Wales

In Wales the regulations governing induction and early professional development are under development. In 2001, the Welsh Assembly Government produced a paper entitled *The Learning Country*, which indicated its commitment to establishing a framework for teachers' CPD. According to a draft circular issued by the Welsh Assembly Government (Welsh Assembly Government, 2002), all NQTs commencing employment from September 2003 will be required to undergo a supported period of induction which will follow a pilot project on the induction year to be implemented from September 2002. Funding will be available to support each NQT in schools with additional funding allocated to the induction tutor in the school. The Induction standard, which is consistent with the standards required to gain qualified teacher status, is subdivided into four subsections:

- Professional characteristics.
- Knowledge and understanding.
- Planning, teaching and learning and class management.
- Monitoring, assessment and reporting.

Further details of the standard can be found on the Learning Wales Web site: http://www.learning.wales.gov.uk. If the Induction Standard is not achieved by the end of the year, provision can be made for an extension of a further three terms where it is felt that additional focused support would be of benefit to the NQT and would enable him or her to achieve the standard. This is a unique feature of induction in Wales and emphasizes the commitment to support NQTs through their first year of teaching.

The precise regulations that will govern EPD will not be in place until the pilot project of the induction phase has been completed. The first EPD pilot will follow on and be put into place the following year and the second year of the programme in 2004–05. Those NQTs therefore who commence employment from September 2003 will be the first cohort to experience the continuous programme. At present there is no requirement planned to require the NQTs in the EPD phase to complete any formal portfolio of work. Further documentation will be provided to schools in Wales from 2003; it will contain the induction framework and the types of activities which have to be carried out during the induction period. Funding will be made available to schools for EPD on a smaller scale to that in the induction phase, to enable the NQTs and their mentors to have time to focus on professional development. It is being recommended in Wales that the colleague who works with the teachers in years 2 and 3, the mentor, be a different colleague from the one who acted as induction tutor; the reason for this is that the roles are perceived to be different, in that the induction tutor has a formal assessment role to fulfil, whereas the EPD mentor should be more of a colleague supporter.

The aspect of the Welsh and Scottish programmes which may be the envy of others is the level of resourcing to be provided in order to enable the NQT and the induction mentors to carry out the tasks.

An overview of the regulations governing all stages of professional development is presented in Table 1.1.

Induction

This section examines some of the types of induction programme which are either already in place or are recommended in different parts of the UK. As this is the most developed part of the teacher education system, with the exception of the initial training course regulations, more details will be presented on precise regulations than for the other phases in the system.

Across all areas of the UK, and in all school sectors, there are some general principles that underpin the induction period. These aims are stated differently by the various GTCs, but broadly are designed to ensure progression in all areas of the new teacher's professional development. As an exemplar, the aims for induction as set out by the GTC in Scotland are presented in full:

- to develop the new teacher's professional knowledge and understanding of relevant areas of the school curriculum;
- to ensure that [new teachers] have a broad understanding of the principal features of the education system, educational policy and practice and are aware of their own role;
- to encourage them to articulate their professional values and practices and to relate these to theoretical principles and perspectives;
- to develop their ability to plan, implement and evaluate appropriate, coherent programmes of teaching and learning;
- to extend and enhance the range of teaching and learning strategies employed by new teachers;
- to encourage new teachers to work co-operatively with other professionals and adults;
- to develop the new teachers' classroom organization and management skills;
- to consolidate their ability to understand and apply the principles of assessment, recording and reporting and use the evidence of assessment to improve the quality of learning and teaching;

Table 1.1 Overview of the UK system of teacher professional development

	England	Country Northern Ireland	Scotland	Wales
Registration	GTCE	Dept of Educ. /GTC from 2003	GTCS	GTCW
Title of new teacher	NQT	BT	probationer	NQT
1st year	*induction*	*induction*	*induction*	*induction*
Compulsory since	1999	1998	2002	2002 (pilot)
Colleague support	induction	teacher tutor	supporter	induction tutor
Teaching time allocation	10% reduction recommended	8 or 9 days cover	0.7 timetable	10% reduction or 20 days recommended
Criteria	Induction Standards	Competences A and B	Standards for registration	Induction Standard
Years 2 and 3	*CPD*	*EPD*	*CPD*	*EPD*
Colleague support	mentor	teacher tutor	supporter	mentor
Years 4+	*CPD*	*CPD*	*CPD*	*CPD*
CPD initiatives	Sabbaticals Professional bursaries Best practice research scholarships International professional development	School Development Performance Management	Local initiatives Various scholarships and exchanges available	Professional development bursaries Visits and exchanges International visits and exchanges Teacher research scholarships Sabbaticals Professional networks Whole school initiatives
Some promotion prospects	Threshold Advanced skills teacher Subject leader head of department SENCO	Threshold AST (proposed) Teacher leader (proposed) Senior TL (proposed)	Chartered teacher (CT) Assistant principal teacher Principal teacher SENCO	Head of year Head of key Stage Curriculum leader Head of faculty

- to develop their ability to reflect critically on their own learning and development and to take personal responsibility for their own professional learning and development (GTCS, 2002d: 1).

The key features of an effective induction experience in Scotland are that they:

- provide a stable environment for the probationer teacher;
- enable the probationer teacher to meet the Standard for Full Registration;
- are located within a school which has established teachers who will provide support and guidance;
- are located in a school in which staff have a defined responsibility for supporting probationer teachers;
- provide an appropriate support programme taking account of local and national advice;
- are located in a school which has established processes for supporting self-evaluation with probationer teachers and effective monitoring and evaluation mechanisms (GTCS, 2002d: 5).

The guidelines for induction in England (DfES, 2001b) state that the induction programme should have an active role for NQTs and it should encourage them to take increased responsibility for their own professional development. The induction period should:

- provide a programme of monitoring and support tailored to the individual needs of the NQT;
- build on the NQT's knowledge, skills and achievements from the Standards required for qualified teacher status and take account of [his or her] CEP strengths and developmental needs;
- involve the headteacher or induction tutor and the NQT in setting objectives related to the CEP and take account of the school contexts and requirements for satisfactory completion of the induction period;
- involve formative and summative assessments and regular reviews;
- develop the NQT's skills of self-evaluation and provide a sound foundation for CPD (DfES, 2001b: par 39).

The induction period in Wales has certain features, which are summarized below:

- The induction period provides a bridge from ITE and should provide continuity and progression into CPD;
- It is of three terms' duration or FT equivalent; the NQT will have time allocated for professional development;

- An induction tutor, who will have time allocated for the role, will work with the NQT;
- A support and monitoring programme will be devised for each NQT, which will be individually adapted and include half termly reviews and termly assessment meetings;
- Schools are responsible for ensuring that support and monitoring processes are in place;
- LEAs have the responsibility of ensuring that schools do provide monitoring and support;
- At the end of induction the headteacher makes a recommendation as to whether the NQT has met the Induction Standards;
- The Induction Standard describes the characteristics, knowledge, skills and understanding that an NQT should have developed by the end of the induction period (Welsh Assembly Government, 2002: 2).

Common to the interpretations of the induction period by the different jurisdictions is the necessity that the NQTs be given structured input during the year. Different models for an induction programme exist across the UK; three models, namely the English, Northern Ireland and Scottish model will be presented in greater detail.

The induction programme

In England, details of the main elements of a formal induction programme are set out in Circular 582/2001 (DfES, 2001b), from which the main features of the induction programme are cited below:

Monitoring and support (paras. 42–46)

NQTs should have support from a designated induction tutor, whose role it is to provide formative assessment during the process and summative assessment at the end of the induction period. The induction tutor is also required to keep records of the monitoring, support and formal assessment activities and their outcomes.

Observation of teaching and discussion (paras. 47–49)

At intervals of six to eight weeks, NQTs should be observed teaching. These observations should focus on specific aspects of the NQT's teaching agreed in advance of the observed lesson and these aspects should relate to the standards and to the NQT's individual objectives for development. These observations should be followed up by a de-briefing discussion which should enable the NQT to focus on specific objectives for further development. In addition to the induction tutor, some observations may be undertaken by other professionals, such as Advanced Skills teachers and tutors from the HEIs, ie the University teacher education departments.

Professional review (paras. 50–51)

Discussions should take place on a regular basis throughout the year between the NQT and the induction tutor, at least once per term. At these professional reviews, set objectives should be discussed and revised in light of the observations and other experiences of the NQT. They should be in line with the standards and should also take into consideration the needs of the NQT. Records of the agreed targets for development should be kept.

Experienced colleague observation (para. 52)

The NQT should be given opportunities to observe other experienced colleagues teaching. This may be within the NQT's own school or in other training schools, or Beacon Schools.

Other professional development activities (paras. 53–54)

These professional development activities should help the NQT attain the Induction Standards. The activities therefore will differ according to the professional developmental needs of the individual teacher and will depend on the specific school context. It is recommended that the programme of support should enable the NQT to:

- receive information about the school, the specific post and the arrangements for induction, prior to taking up the post;
- receive information about their rights and responsibilities;
- participate in the school's programme of induction for new staff;
- participate in programmes of staff training in the school, eg relating to the national literacy or numeracy strategies;
- know about school policies on child protection, behaviour management etc;
- spend time working with the SENCO;
- receive training or advice from professionals outside the school;
- attend external training events relevant to identified individual.

Summative assessment of the induction period will take place three times during the year. At the first meeting the focus is on the extent to which the NQT is meeting the Standards for the Award of QTS in the school and is beginning to meet the Induction Standards. The second meeting focuses on the progress towards meeting the Induction Standards and the final meeting will determine whether the NQT has met the Induction Standards and the requirements for completion of the induction phase (DfES, 2001b).

The Northern Ireland Teacher Education Handbook (DENI, 1998a) presents one example of what might usefully form part of an induction programme used with the new teachers (BTs). It is set out below:

The induction programme should focus on the general life of the school and it should deal with administrative aspects of the school, the professional development and pastoral needs of the new teacher:

Professional support

- introduction to the school (staff, school buildings, catchment area);
- routines (meetings, assemblies, corridor duty, bus duty, school calendar, regulations for absence);
- ethos and relationships within the school (culture of school, members of a team, governors, staff structure, roles and responsibilities);
- school documentation (general guidelines, policies, schemes of work, lesson planning, examination entries);
- administration (timetable, class records, record keeping, online administration);
- student/classes (class sizes, make-up of classes, special needs provision, pastoral care, child protection);
- areas of responsibility (role of specific members of staff, eg head of department, co-ordinator, form teacher, extra-curricular activities);
- resources (reprographics, user–borrower facilities, library, local teachers' centres);
- roles of key school personnel (school nurse, classroom assistants, technicians, librarian, peripatetic teachers, designated child protection officer, educational welfare officer);
- parental issues (parent/teacher evenings, contacting parents, communication with parents, report writing, meetings with parents).

Pastoral support

- introduction to area (accommodation, travel arrangements, geography);
- salary (point on scale, tax information, payment process);
- social development (clubs, activities);
- union information (range of options, services provided);
- plan time to talk (counselling, needs, fears, problems, health issues, dress code) (DENI, 1998a: 50ff).

The induction programme may be provided as part of a regular meeting one day per week, or it may be a more intensive course towards the beginning of the new teacher's arrival in school. Other activities could also form part of structured school-focused development. One aspect of teaching that takes longer to develop, is the move from evaluation focusing on teaching, to evaluation that specifically targets the learner and the learning which is taking place in the classroom. Some of the subject activities and also general activities suggested below could help to move the new teacher's focus away from his or her own teaching towards the learning which is taking place in the class.

Depending on the focus, some of these activities could be directed by or facilitated by the induction tutor, whereas others would be best carried out by the teacher's head of department.

Support for teaching/learning within subject area

- commenting on the teacher's lesson planning;
- observation of the teacher's lessons;
- team planning of lessons/teaching of lessons;
- peer observation (eg two BTs working together);
- support with setting and marking assessments;
- support for more focused evaluation of lessons.

During the course of the year the activities offered should enable the new teachers to develop their subject teaching expertise, but also to gain a perspective of the wider school.

Whole-school focus

- providing opportunities to observe teaching in other subjects;
- class/student pursuits for a day;
- involvement in devising whole-school policies;
- working with other co-ordinators (eg SENCO, pastoral care staff, literacy/numeracy co-ordinators).

This balance is important in order to facilitate the NQTs' development as expert teachers but also to retain an overview of their role as a team-player in the school as an organization. This is one of the 12 teacher roles outlined in Chapter 4.

Record keeping

Keeping of records of individual teachers' experiences during the induction phase is something for which the induction tutor may have some responsibility. It should be the main responsibility of the NQTs, however, to retain an on-going portfolio of their activities and development, leading on from the career entry profile.

The content of each record will differ according to individual schools, but the broad headings outlined below may provide some broad framework. The design of an induction plan record may be useful. The following five broad headings, based on the model from Northern Ireland (DENI, 1998a: 46ff), could form the basis of a customized induction plan:

- Areas for development (targets). These should be precise and focused.
- Action (including timescale). These should list the actions to be completed and by whom (ie the BT, the induction tutor, the head of department etc).
- Support arrangements (within school and by external agencies).
- Success criteria – what should be achieved at the end of the specified time.
- Monitoring and evaluation – details of the process by which feedback will be given.

A record sheet outlining these areas should contain all details of specific targets set during negotiation with the NQT and agreed with the induction tutor. Other staff should be involved as appropriate and it is vital that all colleagues involved in the process are aware of their commitment to it and their responsibilities for it.

The Scottish model for induction to be in operation from September 2002 presents a three-strand framework of opportunities which might include core experiences, the wider work of the school, experiences outlined in the career entry profile document (ITE profile) and the enhanced planning and preparation time, outlined above. A pack containing detailed guidance has been sent to all schools in Scotland (GTCS, 2002d); it sets out all aspects relating to induction for headteachers and contains all the necessary documentation.

The first area encompasses core experiences, which are those needs identified by previous probationer teachers in the school or by colleagues in schools or in local authorities.

Involvement in the wider work of the school, the second strand of the framework, should provide opportunities for the probationer to:

- team teach with colleagues in other stages or subjects;
- work with learning support teachers;
- work with SEN students;
- participate in a school board meeting;
- meet with other professionals associated with the school.

The third strand allows probationer teachers to achieve their personally identified needs, originally selected from the ITE profile and then by self-evaluation in collaboration with the supporter/mentor (GTCS, 2002d).

The Scottish model presents a suggested time-frame, which provides an overview of the induction year.

August – December

An early meeting between the probationer teacher and the supporter/mentor should focus on the ITE profile and identify a professional development programme. This programme should identify:

- enhanced planning and preparation time;
- core experiences to be done in or out of school;
- specific learning experiences desired by the probationer;
- continued self-evaluation by the probationer teacher;
- weekly meetings with supporter/mentor to discuss concerns, issues etc;
- five observation sessions of lessons with an agreed focus (one of which should be from an independent observer, the others with supporter/mentor) and with feedback provided.

December

- formal review meeting with probationer teacher, supporter/mentor and independent observer. Progress is reviewed, strengths identified and development plan for next phase agreed;
- completion of the Interim Profile for the GTCS;
- discussion with the GTCS of any problems that arise.

January – March

- on-going self-evaluation by the probationer teacher;
- weekly meetings with supporter/mentor;
- three observation sessions with agreed focus and with feedback provided.

March

- formal review (as in December) with support mechanisms for those in difficulty.

April – June

- on-going self-evaluation;
- weekly meetings;
- two observations with agreed focus and with feedback provided.

June

- final formal meeting;
- completion of the Final Profile for SFR and confirmation of full registration;
- procedures in place for dealing with probationer teachers giving cause for concern (GTCS, 2002d: 12ff).

This timetable for induction in Scottish schools illustrates the need for there to be open channels of communication and for there to be frequent meetings and observations arranged to support the NQT. It will not be the case in every school, however, especially outside the Scottish and Welsh systems, for schools to have the luxury of additional time and resources allocated for the task. It is the ultimate responsibility of the headteacher to ensure that induction is completed by staff in their school. The most valuable part of the process, however, will be the on-going discussions with the NQT during the year. How the monitoring and evaluation take place will depend on a number of factors, including the time available for the induction tutor to work with the NQT, the number of NQTs in a school and the workload of the NQTs themselves. It is important, therefore that evaluation takes place both formally and informally during the course of the year. Formal meetings may be set up at regular intervals as well as times for formal observation of the NQTs' teaching. This can be supplemented by informal evaluations of the NQTs' development, such as reviewing lesson plans, assessment records of students' work, homework or class-work completed by students or report cards. The value of the additional informal chats during lunch or break-times should not be underestimated.

The induction file

It is important for the NQT to keep a record of all the activities engaged in during the year, together with an evaluation of them. Targets should be specified and outcomes agreed and evaluated at the end of the year. The following might feature as part of an induction file:

- classes observed;
- details of classes taught;
- lesson plans;
- evaluation of lessons;
- specific activities undertaken with classes;
- meetings attended;
- attendance at courses outside school;
- extra-curricular activities;
- self-evaluation of professional development;
- personal aims (longer term).

Outcome

At the end of the induction year, it is to be hoped that all has gone well and that the new teacher can now be confirmed in post and be fully registered with the respective GTC. Specific forms will have to be completed and submitted to the GTC and the responsibility for doing this has been noted above. If the NQT meets the standards/competences outlined in the documentation, he or she will now be able to be fully registered with the GTC and can be employed in any school in the UK and in many of the EU countries. The teacher now moves into the next phase, termed EPD in Northern Ireland and Wales or CPD in England and Scotland. These will be dealt with separately, although the emphasis from this point in the career of teachers is on the need to seek opportunities for further development, both for their own professional benefit and for the professional benefit of their school.

The following case study will present two sides of the induction process and will present one induction tutor's view of the process and the experiences of an induction NQT in the same school.

The induction year

This case study features an Academy and Sixth Form College, which is a large secondary inner-city school of around 1500 students. It is a recent amalgamation of two schools and, as such, still operates on a split campus.

The induction tutor's perspective

Milly Stevenson is the induction tutor/mentor in the school. This role is a multi-faceted one; it encompasses the role of mentor with student teachers, induction tutor with NQTs and supporter/mentor with teachers during the EPD phase. In the school Milly has responsibility for overseeing the development of 18 NQTs in the induction year and 10 in EPD (with another 10 to take up post next academic year), all of them working on their own individual professional development pathway:

'At times it does seem overwhelming but the teachers at this stage in their career are so keen and motivated that it is great working with them and supporting them.'

From the experience of working with the new teachers, Milly is of the opinion that the induction phase is the more intensive of the two, since the teachers are new not only to teaching, but to the school, its routines, procedures and

Induction Programme

2 complementary prongs

General Induction Programme   Individual Action Plans
(two strands)

In-service days   Workshops   Meetings with induction tutor

All new staff   1. Needs assessment
                                              a) consider possible targets using
Introduced   2. Priority needs addressed

- CEP
- School development plan
- Departmental priorities
- Teaching context (pupils, syllabus etc.)

b) identify and prioritize targets
c) draw up action plan
d) monitor progress
e) interim review
f) summative review
    discussion of possible areas
    to take forward into next phase
    EPD

Induction complete (NQT signed off)

Figure 1.1 Induction programme in case study Academy and Sixth Form College

personnel. An induction programme with two complementary prongs has been developed during the past few years

At the beginning of the school year, all new staff take part in the initial stage of the year – the general induction programme – during which they are introduced to the curriculum of the school, to the routines and procedures and to the pastoral care system of the school. The staff are given details of the roles and responsibilities of the different members of staff and are made aware of who should be contacted regarding specific issues which might arise in their classroom. The heads of year induct the NQTs into their pastoral team at the beginning of the school year, as part of non-contact days.

A second strand of the general induction programme is organized according to the specific requirements of the NQTs. A needs assessment is carried out early on in the year to find out the personal and professional developmental needs of the NQT. Recent areas that have been highlighted by NQTs are: time management, pastoral training, the specific role of the form tutor and extra help with discipline. When these needs have been identified, it is the role of the induction tutor to put in place an individual programme, involving the relevant members of staff. For example, to deal with the issues above, the pastoral team manager conducted a session on the role of the form tutor and organized a session that dealt with positive behaviour strategies in the context of the whole school. The head of maths gave a departmental perspective to the application of discipline procedures within a subject area. These sessions, generally held after school, are given to all the NQTs because it is felt that the issues are of such importance that they all need extra guidance on them. It is also the role of the induction tutor to be aware of aspects that are not highlighted by the NQTs but which have come to her attention either from her experience or from other sources within the school. An example of this gap was the examination system, in particular the supervision of external examinations and the examinations officer in the school was asked to take a session on aspects of the external examinations system. Another area which it was felt appropriate for all NQTs to have experience of was active participation methodologies for teaching; this support was designed to give the teachers strategies and content to develop in the teaching of PSE for which all of them were responsible. The NQTs meet with the induction tutor and the assistant induction tutor regularly in order to discuss their progress and this gives the induction tutor the opportunity to monitor their performance and to deal with specific issues as they arise.

In addition to the two-phase developmental programme, each NQT is required to submit an action plan. This document is devised by the NQT in consultation with the induction staff, and is based on the following: the career entry profile, the school development plan, the respective departmental priorities and takes account of their subject, the classes they teach (years, levels) and their differing roles (eg class teacher, form teacher). At this stage, the targets identified in the CEP can be rather meaningless, since they were devised in vacuum. The priorities identified for the induction year are much more specific and relevant to the context in which the NQTs now find themselves working. Some of the action targets that have emerged have been:

- using ICT;
- dealing with challenging students in RE short-course;
- developing group-work;
- differentiation;
- improving relationships within the form tutor group through drama.

These target areas are all focused on teaching and learning and are finalized in consultation with the induction tutor. The NQTs may raise a number of targets that they feel need to be worked on, but during the negotiation interview these targets are discussed and put in order of priority; it may be that some of the targets have to be dropped. The skill of the induction tutor is in getting the NQTs to prioritize and to get them to establish targets which represent progression from where they are now in their teaching and where they need to be in relation to the Induction Standards. Sometimes the NQTs need to be steered into fitting their targets into the departmental needs or into the school development plan. Occasionally, if the NQT is not focused on the issues, it is necessary for the induction tutor to help them with this progressive focus:

'It is important that the [NQTs have] ownership of the action plan and that they are convinced of the value of working towards the goals that they themselves have set. Sometimes it is necessary to give them direction or to make them see a need that is evident to others but not to themselves. The emphasis has to be on the negotiation of the targets.'

When these action plans have been devised, the next stage is for the induction tutor to identify specific steps which have to be taken by the NQT and others in working through the plan. In the case of the NQT who was working on using drama to enhance relationships within her form group, the following intermediate steps were drawn up:

- learn about the role of drama;
- learn about strategies for using drama;
- learn about group work;

- identify areas of the pastoral teaching programme that could be covered by using drama (eg bullying, human rights);
- draw up a teaching programme incorporating drama;
- assess and evaluate.

The next task for the induction tutor is to identify support mechanisms. This may involve using existing expertise from the staff who can work with the NQT on a specific area. In this case, the head of drama was identified as a critical peer and was asked to work with the NQT. This peer professional relationship is vital not only for the development of the specific area, but because it also helps the NQT to become aware of the need for staff to work together and to learn from each other. This role of the teacher as a team member is highlighted in Chapter 4. The critical peer relationship should be seen as vital support, but it is necessary for the NQT to take responsibility for his or her own professional development and to be in control of the progression of the action plan. An example of the content of an induction action plan as it is used in this school is shown in Table 1.2.

Table 1.2 Induction action plan

Date .... Signed (NQT) .... Signed (Induction Tutor)...............

Completed as an outcome of joint discussion and with reference to the Career Entry Profile

Area(s) for development or targets	Actions (inc. timescale)	Support arrangements	Success criteria	Monitoring and evaluation (inc. portfolio evidence)
To promote more positive relationships with 10R	Carry out needs assessment: identify deficiencies in relationships	Induction tutor to facilitate cover for observation of teaching	Students will record positive comments in evaluation of their experience of learning one unit of work	Completed student evaluation

During the formal summative meetings the success of the development targets is discussed with the NQT:

'Usually there is no disagreement about the outcomes. It is necessary for me to be frank with the NQTs. If they are doing a good job, they know it themselves. Sometimes you get the odd NQT who is good in the classroom but who is not too good at keeping the paperwork. I have to point out to [him or her] the importance of the documentary evidence which is required if we are to sign the induction period off as completed.'

In the EPD phase the role of the induction tutor changes in certain respects to that of mentor but, according to Milly Stevenson, the process is the same. By the time the NQTs have been through the induction phase, they are familiar with the processes of planning, reflecting, evaluating and assessing. There are fewer formal meetings with the induction tutor/mentor but the informal channels of communication are open. During the EPD phase the focus will be more on the learning of the students, and by that time the NQTs will be more confident in their teaching so that they are in a position to change the focus in order to concentrate on the learning processes.

With 28 NQTs whose work requires monitoring, assessing and encouraging through the process, the job of induction tutor/mentor in this school is not an easy one. Milly comments:

'It is difficult with so many at one time, but I am so convinced of the value of the processes that I think it is time well spent with the NQTs. It is encouraging to see them discover the value of reflecting on their practice, especially when they see changes resulting from their actions. I can really see a difference in the new teachers at the end of the induction year and again at the end of EPD.'

The NQT's view

Stephen Adair is an RE specialist who teaches in the same Academy and Sixth Form College, having completed a degree in theology and a PGCE. He was interviewed about his experiences since starting in the school and, in particular, on his views of the induction process and programme. During the first year of teaching, Stephen had the following classes: Year 7; Year 8 (5 classes); Year 9 (5 classes); Year 10 GCSE RE, RE non-exam, ICT non-exam; Year 11 GCSE RE, Short-course RE and he was a form tutor for Year 8 teaching PSE.

Which aspects did you feel unprepared for when entering your teaching career?

Stephen reported that the following aspects in particular caused difficulty: discipline, workload, dealing with a form class, writing reports and parents' evenings.

Workload

'I never realized just how exhausted I would be during the first year.'

Discipline

'The discipline you get during the PGCE tends to be more theoretical and there you are told what you should and should not do. When you are in the class, alone with the students, you become the boss and you have got to think on your feet. A lot of the theory doesn't work in practice, because it depends on the school context in which you are working. It's the practice of teaching that makes the teacher.'

Form class

'I really enjoy working with my form class but I felt a little unprepared for it at the start; by that I mean teaching PSE and dealing with all the administration. It is very time-consuming and the bureaucracy of it all tends to take over.'

Report writing and parents' evenings

'With over 300 reports it's a mammoth task and they all have to be entered into the computerized system. Parents' evenings were difficult, particularly at the beginning. You can imagine what it is like teaching almost 100 students in one year-group; the preparation needed in advance to look at the students' work and to think of comments to make to parents in order to give them an insight into their son or daughter's work in RE was considerable. It also involved spending five or six hours at the actual parents' evening. It wasn't that I didn't enjoy them, but it is quite a daunting task, which the PGCE and school experience did not prepare me for.'

How well aware were you of the requirements of the induction period?

Stephen reported that he was aware during initial training that the next stage was called induction but was less clear as to the content of it. The first awareness he had of it was during the CPD day on the PGCE course when the local advisers came to talk to the RE PGCE group about the requirements for their first post:

'It wasn't until we had the official induction programme from the local authority when they distributed the NQT documentation and went through the various aspects of the induction programme which would be covered during the year.'

How much from your career entry profile did you take on board as targets for this year?

One of the problems of the CEP is that it is written up at the end of the PGCE year when the student teacher is not aware of the school in which they will be working in the following year, so the targets can be rather artificial:

'The things we had discussed at the CEP stage turned out to be rather irrelevant. When you are in the school, you are looking for targets that are not just to do with me as a teacher but that are important for the whole department. I had mentioned A level in the CEP, but that is not a priority for me in this school at the moment.'

What positive experiences did you have of induction?
The advice and support provided by the induction tutor was vital to the process for all NQTs on induction. The important point made to the NQTs was that induction should be seen as a process which was integral to the teaching and not an add-on.

'I have to say that I couldn't have wished for a better school in which to start my teaching. This year was a very positive experience all round. Milly, the induction tutor, gave me important advice. She said that we, as NQTs, had a major job to do finding our feet in the classroom, preparing schemes and lesson plans and to teach, and that we should regard the induction plan as integral to our own teaching context. It was not to be an add-on; our induction action plan should contain targets that we were working on as part of our everyday teaching anyway. The aspect that I chose to work on was the short-course RE, not only because I would be providing evidence for the induction plan which would be of use to me in my teaching but also because it meant that I was making a major contribution to the work of the RE department. It is an advantage being employed in a self-evaluating school. I see myself as a self-evaluating teacher. As part of the induction plan I had to ask the question "How do I make these students more motivated?" I see this as part of my job anyway as this is a question that all teachers should ask themselves at the end of every lesson.'

What support did you receive during your induction?
With 28 teachers plus student teachers in the school, the support of the induction tutor had to be very well managed.

'The support came from several sources; first the induction tutor who set up the meetings, discussed the induction action plan and then devised the plan of targets and support. It was then up to my head of department, Sonia, who was great throughout the year in providing support on a day-to-day basis; she was the person who was most significant to me throughout the induction; she is approachable, encouraging and very supportive. In a way it was a bit like a trinity – the induction tutor, my head of department and me, the beginning teacher – all working together for the benefit of the students. I also got support from the local RE adviser; he had actually been involved in devising the RE short course so I was able to get expert advice from him. Half-way through the year I had a meeting with Milly to discuss interim progress and then again at the end of the year we had the signing-off meeting when induction was finished.'

Were there any aspects of the induction year that you particularly enjoyed?
'On a few days during the year all the teachers in induction were taken to a hotel by the LEA and were given talks and seminars on different topics. It was great to get together with the other teachers from your subject area who are working in different schools and also to meet up with others who were on the PGCE with me.'

What would you regard as less than satisfactory during induction?
'All the new staff were invited to discuss what we felt were our concerns which were not being dealt with in the school induction programme. Some of the things we brought up were dealt with, but there were others which just seemed to get forgotten about; that was a bit disappointing but I realize that you can't deal with everything in one year and I am sure that some of them might be dealt with in the next phase of early professional development.'

Do you think that the induction phase is a good thing?
'Very much so. You feel that you are being supported and guided along the way. There is always someone to ask for help and the atmosphere especially in the department I work in is very supportive. I am a team worker and I feel that I have been able to work to my strengths this year.'

What about the future. Where do you see yourself in five or ten years?
'I have just been made permanent in the job which was initially for one year only. I am thrilled about this. A lot of teachers just want to get on with the teaching at this stage; they think that in three or four years' time they can decide to look for a career path. But I feel that I have to decide now where my career in education is heading. I believe that my strengths lie in the pastoral area and I'd like to be head of year in a few years' time. In the longer term I might consider becoming a special needs co-ordinator. Within the subject of RE, the sky is the limit – subjects such as citizenship and PSE which are developing now will provide other options. It's just up my street.'

This case study gives then a flavour of the processes which the NQT must engage in during induction and raises some of the issues that confront a new teacher during the first year of teaching. It has presented the complementary views of one induction tutor and an NQT who was supported through the process.

Research on induction in Northern Ireland

Other research on the induction phase carried out before the new procedures for induction and EPD came into force in Northern Ireland found that NQTs had the following needs on entering their first post:

- adapting to the ethos and environment of the school;
- classroom and behaviour management;
- motivation strategies;
- familiarity with the pastoral system and whole-school policies;
- role of the form tutor;
- marking and assessment of student work;
- administration;
- supporting GCSE and A level coursework;
- communication with parents;
- managing time and volume of work for planning and preparation (Moran, Dallat and Abbot, 1999: iv).

This research also notes that the NQTs find the most rewarding element of their first year the work with the students. From the overview of the system as it operates throughout the UK and from the case studies, it appears that much is being done in induction to aid the transition to becoming a fully-fledged teacher. It is encouraging to note that the NQTs see the work with their students as the most rewarding thing that they do.

Key points

- There are different regulations and recommendations governing induction, EPD and CPD in the various parts of the UK.
- Many new challenges face the NQT during the first post.
- The induction period is one of many challenges but the NQT is supported throughout the process.

Self study

Key questions

For NQTs:

- Have I devised a suitable action plan for induction?
- What areas do I still need help with?
- How can I develop my expertise in areas outside my subject?

For induction tutors/mentors:

- How can I improve the induction programme for the NQTs?
- Is there expertise in the school that could be used in a support programme for induction?

For senior management:

- How can we provide additional support for the induction tutor/mentor?
- Can additional resources be made available for the induction team?
- Are we doing enough to ensure that the NQTs are supported during their first year in the school?

2 Early and further professional development

The two years following induction are termed early professional development (EPD) in Northern Ireland and Wales. In other parts of the UK all years following induction are referred to as continuing professional development (CPD). In this section we will outline details of the programmes which are specifically related to the EPD phase, ie years 2 and 3 of teaching in Northern Ireland only, since the Welsh proposals will not be piloted until 2003–04. Details of CPD programmes in Scotland and England will be dealt with in the second section.

Early professional development (EPD)

The area of EPD is one which is currently undergoing major development, and the main requirements and differences between EPD practice in the various parts of the UK have been outlined in the previous chapter. This area may change significantly over the next few years and all teachers taking up a position will have to be informed of the regulations in existence at the time in the part of the UK they are working.

A difficulty that may confront the new teacher at this stage may be one of continuity. With many schools initially offering temporary contracts for one year, some teachers may find themselves having to apply for the post they already occupy or to find another school. The situation in Scotland where, all probationer teachers are guaranteed a post, may result in some teachers, on completion of induction, having having to find another school in which to continue their professional development. The process of establishing oneself a second time around should be easier, however, and many new skills will have been acquired during induction. It may be that a teacher who has been employed in one area will be required to undertake specific tasks in order to qualify for full recognition as a fully qualified teacher in another.

EPD in Northern Ireland

The integrated model of teacher education, as outlined in Chapter 1 in the section on Northern Ireland, has been in place for some years. The EPD phase is the third stage of the continuous process and it is designed to build upon the experiences of the new teacher acquired during the induction programme. The focus moves, however, from attention to the actual teaching to concentrating more on the learning which takes place in the classroom, although these two activities are inextricably related. The intention is that the teacher will become more reflective and will analyse his or her classroom practice. All teachers currently in years 2 and 3 are required to complete two professional development activities, or PDAs, one in year 2 and one in year 3. The focus of these PDAs should be on the learning and teaching, specifically curriculum and classroom and/or school management, and should incorporate some element of ICT. Each focused activity should involve the teacher in background reading, reflective thinking and planning and should last 20 hours. In addition to these hours, the teacher is required to engage in a period of teaching, followed up by monitoring, reviewing, discussing, evaluating, writing up the work done in a log, including reflective comments and compiling a portfolio of evidence. During this period the teachers are supported by the teacher tutor, who is the same individual in schools as the mentor and induction tutor. The phases of the process are as follows:

- Year 2 – Select first focus for EPD:
    - carry out activity (identify, plan, consult, implement, monitor, evaluate);
    - review and summarize (complete evidence on portfolio).
- Year 3 – Select second PDA focus:
    - carry out activity (identify, plan, consult, implement, monitor, evaluate);
    - review and summarize (complete evidence on portfolio);
    - complete PDA portfolio.

There are guidelines in the Teacher Education Partnership Handbook (DENI, 1998a: 80) designed to focus the teacher on the processes of planning, reviewing and reflecting.

Planning:

- What do I plan to do?
- Why do I intend to do it?
- What do I hope to achieve?
- What do I need in order to achieve these aims?
- Am I putting the needs of the individual learner first?

Reviewing:

- What kind of evidence should I collect to help me make a judgment about what is happening?
- How will I know if and why I have succeeded, and how will I know if and why I have failed?
- How will I know that the students have learnt what we set out to learn?
- How shall I collect the evidence?

The teachers are encouraged to see reflection on their practice as a collaborative activity, working with the teacher tutor, asking for critical comments, discussing their classroom-based activities and their evaluations with other colleagues. As evidence of student learning taking place, the teachers can collect some of the following:

- lesson plans and schemes of work;
- observations and written assignments of student learning;
- video tapes of teaching;
- lesson observation feedback from critical peers;
- written feedback from peers;
- students' work;
- student feedback/questionnaires.

Following the end of the PDA the teacher is required to formulate his or her own conclusions to summarize the evidence presented. The summary should represent a reflective account of the learning that has taken place and a statement about the teacher's professional values and philosophy of teaching.

This model of EPD has been evaluated and, on the basis of the evaluation, the number of PDAs required was reduced from the originally intended three to two. It may well be that this model will be reviewed again and adapted in light of experience. Some EPD teachers feel that the process is too rigidly defined and that it detracts from their teaching. The authors of the requirements for EPD point out that the original intention of the PDAs was that they should sit at the heart of the EPD teacher's practical classroom work to meet a real classroom need. It is therefore a misunderstanding of the spirit of the PDA if it is seen as an unnecessary add-on. In a minority of cases this misconception has resulted in the PDAs being completed in a rather perfunctory manner. Within Northern Ireland, it is compulsory for all teachers to undertake those two activities. Teachers who have been employed for some years outside Northern Ireland and who want to teach in NI schools may have to undertake portfolio-based activities on EPD. Details of regulations for EPD will be available from the GTC.

EPD in Wales

In Wales a distinction is made between EPD and CPD generally in relation to funding to be provided to schools to encourage professional development following induction. At the time of writing, prior to the introduction of the induction pilot to begin in September 2002, what exactly will constitute development in the EPD phase is still under discussion. It is not intended to produce a separate framework of EPD within years 2 and 3 but it is hoped that EPD will dovetail into the school's performance management arrangements, which is part of the individual professional development. It is also hoped that the EPD will continue in a pilot phase following on from the induction pilot in 2003. The main implication will be for funding to be provided to schools to allow time for the NQT and the mentor to work together during that time. The projects on CPD in Wales will be discussed later in the following section.

CPD initiatives

The rest of this book deals with the many aspects and possibilities of CPD in schools. As with EPD, the regulations for CPD are far from clear-cut. In some areas, documents are in the system for consultation and in others, projects which have been trialled are now being evaluated. There are many exciting possibilities and opportunities in the system. Individual teachers should see it as a priority to explore the different options available within the school and area in which they are working and avail themselves of every opportunity for personal and professional development. In this section some examples of initiatives in CPD in different parts of the UK are presented.

CPD can refer to any developmental activities that take place following the induction period. The GTCE's Professional Learning Framework (GTCE, 2001b) provides a useful navigational tool for the range of activities which can produce professional learning. It can include informal activities, attendance at courses, private study either in the subject area or in education, classroom-based research, pursuing qualifications leading to subject leader, SENCO or NPQH for headteachers. Co-ordinated CPD should ensure that there is some correlation between the professional and personal needs of the individual teacher, and between the needs of the school and the needs of the teacher. There is no longer any prescribed syllabus or format which CPD must take, and with the opportunities open in different arenas and support mechanisms available, teachers should be encouraged to develop their own interests. If teachers plan sensibly, by looking after their own individual professional interests, they will enhance the quality of the teaching and learning taking place in their classrooms and they will benefit the schools in which they are working.

CPD in England

Since the late 1990s various documents from government indicate its commitment to CPD for teachers. The Green Paper entitled *Schools Building on Success* (DfEE, 2001c) followed by the White Paper, *Schools Achieving Success* (DfES, 2001c) both highlight aspects related to the professional development of teachers. In the Strategy Document (DfEE, 2001b: 8–9) the government outline four ways in which they will offer support for CPD (amounting to £92 million from 2002–05):

- £12 million on Best Practice Research Scholarships (BPRS) and Teachers' International Professional Development (TIPD). In the BPRS schemes teachers in England can bid for amounts up to £2,500 to follow up a piece of personal research. Funding will cover the cost of tutor/mentor support and cover (70 per cent) and other costs (consumables, travel etc) and will last for a year. Teachers can apply individually or as a group (up to 15), but not in pairs. About 1,000 scholarships were offered in the first year (2002–03) (DfES, 2002a). Details can be found on www.teachernet.gov.uk/bprs. The TIPD scheme is different. Funding here covers the cost of travel and accommodation for groups of teachers (from a group of schools) to visit schools abroad. Teachers may choose Asia/America (10-day visits) or Europe (5-day visits), or organize an exchange visit (teachers from one school only). Applications here must go through the LEA (Hastings, 2002b). Details can be found on www.britishcouncil.org/education/tipd/index.thtm.
- £30 million on Professional Bursaries. Teachers in England who are in the fourth or fifth year of teaching may apply for £500 to cover the costs of travel or research (Hastings, 2002b). In the Strategy Document it mentions that the scheme is 'being piloted in nine LEAs and associated Excellence in Cities (EiC) areas and Education Action Zones (EAZs)' (DfEE, 2001b: 8). So there may be some preference for teachers in schools in these areas.
- £25 million on sabbaticals. In the first year, funding is restricted to a particular group of teachers: those who have taught for five years in a 'challenging' primary or secondary school. The sabbatical is for six weeks and is worth £6,000 for supply cover with only one sabbatical being allocated per school. The head teacher is responsible for allocation within the school and the allotted time may be shared between two or three members of staff (Revell, 2001).

- £25 million on EPD for teachers in their second and third year of teaching. This scheme is intended to run initially as a pilot scheme with appropriate evaluation from September 2001 in a sample of schools. At the time of writing no information was available on the progress of this scheme.

There are then a range of government and other funding possibilities, some of which may stipulate particular restricted areas of development or research. The opportunities mentioned here for the most part are outside the 'normal' envisaged professional development which is intended to be covered in the statutory five training days allocated to each school and which would form part of each teacher's own professional development plan. However, these opportunities could offer a real enhancement and are funds which are often not fully spent. Hastings (2002b) mentions that 'incredibly, some LEAs fail to take up their full allocation of places' in the TIPD scheme for example.

In terms of teachers' own professional advancement, the government has instituted a new grade of teacher, the Advanced Skills Teacher and a fast-tracking pathway to promotion.

Advanced Skills Teachers (ASTs)

This pathway is designed for teachers who merit advancement but who prefer to remain in the classroom, not wanting to go into school management. ASTs are expected to share their expertise in classroom teaching with colleagues in their own schools and in others, although this scheme appears to be having limited success, as noted earlier in the chapter. Details of how to apply for this status can be found on the professional development of the Teachernet Web site.

Fast Track Teaching Programme

An innovative approach to permit outstanding teachers to move more quickly up the promotions ladder is the Fast Track Teaching Programme, which became available from November 2001 with the first fast track teachers to take up post by September 2002. This programme enables teachers to enter so-called fast track posts; it entails pre-assessment and involves accelerated advancement. Candidates for these fast track posts will take part in an individually tailored programme of professional development, which should allow teachers to develop their own individual career aspirations but at a quicker rate than usual. Some criticism has been expressed at the quality of some of the training courses offered to fast track candidates (Thornton, 2002). It involves a more centrally organized line of progression provided by government and some might think that this was an attempt to get posts filled in less desirable areas or schools. It is suggested that teachers will spend no more than two years in any one post, so that even if a job is unpleasant, the end will always be in sight. As this is a new scheme, it will take time for its success or impact to become visible. Those interested in this route can find additional information on the Web site: www.fasttrackteaching.gov.uk.

It is clear that the government is keen to implement its strategy and is providing funding and establishing initiatives to encourage teachers to take part in a wide variety of schemes, designed to suit different interests and needs. It is adopting a twin track approach by setting up a clear pathway for progression for those who wish to advance and facilitating those who wish to progress more quickly, but also there are the one-off initiatives which should appeal to every teacher at some stage in their career.

CPD in Wales

One of the priorities of the GTC for Wales is CPD of teachers. In 2002 it presented advice to the Welsh Assembly Government in which it pointed to the need for an entitlement for all teachers to have access to high quality CPD. Currently (2002–03) a range of projects exist for which teachers and schools can apply. Each scheme is briefly outlined below, details of which can be obtained on the GTCW Web site or in their publications (GTCW 2001a; 2001b; 2002a; 2002b).

Professional development bursaries

Teachers can apply for up to £500 for CPD. Activities which might be undertaken with the bursary are: attendance at conferences, workshops or seminars; developing innovative approaches to lessons; syllabuses; purchasing specific materials or software to assist with personal development; travel and subsistence and supply cover costs.

Visits and exchanges

For activities relevant to practising teachers in the classroom, a grant of up to £500 per teacher is available to permit activities such as classroom observation between schools, work shadowing in schools, exchanges between similar posts in different schools, mentoring and supply cover costs.

International visits and exchanges

A grant of up to £1,500 is available to support teachers to exchange with schools in other countries to experience good practice or new innovative approaches and methodologies.

Teacher research scholarships

Teachers are being encouraged to involve themselves in classroom-based action research in order to improve their practice. The range of possibilities here is very wide and examples of some recently funded projects include: raising standards, introducing new methods into classrooms, behaviour management, immersion education, working effectively with support workers. Teachers are supported in their research activities by a mentor from another institution such as a university, LEA or research body. Funds of up to £3,000 are available for these initiatives.

Teacher sabbaticals

Financial support of up to £5,000 is available to teachers to enable them to take time off from their school duties for up to half a term in order to engage in activities which will benefit their school on return. Placements, work shadowing, working in another school or conducting a study with an HEI or LEA are examples of the kinds of activities undertaken. Unlike teachers in England, all teachers may apply for sabbaticals, not just those in challenging schools.

Professional networks

Networks are groups of individuals who meet for a common purpose. Funding is available from the GTCW to enable teachers and facilitators to convene meetings to work on specific tasks. Examples of tasks developed are: developing innovative approaches to schemes of work; examining common themes; sharing good practice; developing shared resources.

Whole-school initiatives

A school can apply for a grant to enable a whole-school project to be completed. Examples of suitable activities are: developing cross-curricular policies such as literacy, numeracy, ICT; developing a staff development programme, developing whole-school strategies; developing the Welsh curriculum throughout the school or establishing a student centred approach to learning. A certain sum of money (up to a maximum of £30,000) is available for these initiatives.

Within Wales the options available to teachers is impressive. Funding alone, however, cannot establish a culture of CPD; there has to be commitment from members of staff, from senior management down through the school. When the induction pilot and EPD pilot work their way through the system, it is to be hoped that the NQTs who emerge from 2005 as teachers entering the CPD phase will have been acculturated into a profession which is committed to career-long development.

Evaluation of CPD in Wales

A commissioned research project into the CPD project in Wales has recently been completed (Egan and James, 2002). The researchers sent a questionnaire to all teachers who had participated in one of the CPD schemes and followed up these questionnaires with interviews with a smaller number of participants. Teachers indicated the following benefits to individuals of the CPD schemes:

- the development of individual needs and skills;
- motivational and career factors;
- engagement with good practice;
- time to develop reflective practice;
- work-based learning;
- working collaboratively with other professionals;
- learning and teaching gains (Egan and James, 2002: 15).

One of the successes mentioned was the fact that the activities could be tailored for individual teachers' specific needs and that the strength of the scheme stems from the focus on self-planning and development. The three schemes – bursaries, visits and exchanges and teacher research scholarships provided incentives in motivational terms, for example:

- enthusiasm to consider new perspectives and innovation (visits and exchanges);
- insights for career development;
- increase in status and esteem, having a positive effect on morale and confidence;
- added value from teachers to the project because they felt ownership;
- breaking down professional isolation in particular subjects and geographical areas (Egan and James, 2002: 16).

In terms of benefits to schools, the following were noted:

- improvement in specific skills;
- introduction and evaluation of new teaching strategies;
- curricular enrichment through collaboration between schools or through the production or acquisition of new materials;
- improved continuity and progression on transfer between schools (eg in literacy, numeracy, science) and within schools (Egan and James, 2002).

This evaluation presents a very positive picture of the effect of these pilot projects. It notes only a small number of weaknesses, such as poor outcomes of projects, which do not represent value for money or valuable use of CPD and suggests that quality assurance procedures need to be tightened. In general, however, this report is strongly in favour of the schemes as they operate at present and concludes that the projects have far more strengths than weaknesses. The full report is worth reading and can be found on the GTC Web site.

Research on CPD in England and Wales

Currently a project is being carried out by Manchester Metropolitan University on CPD provision across England to find out what teachers think about CPD and to identify their developmental needs. It is envisaged that 10,000 teachers from all school sectors will be selected to take part in the survey. The findings of the project will inform government on its CPD policy and an update of the progress of the research can be found on the MMU Web site: www.mmu.ac.uk/ioe/ctcpd. The GTCE, the National College for School Leadership and the DfES are jointly funding a research project looking at how schools create and sustain themselves as effective professional learning communities. This project is investigating, over a three-year time-frame, how schools can instigate and sustain a professional learning culture within and between schools and involving the whole professional community that makes a school. The research will report on the main barriers and challenges and aims to identify what really makes a difference. Further details of this project can be obtained from the GTCE.

A recent survey was conducted by researchers at NFER between 2000 and 2001 on the various types of CPD programmes and activities which were being undertaken by teachers in England and Wales (Brown, Edmonds and Lee, 2001). This study was part of the Local Government Educational Research Programme and it was designed to examine the potential role for LEAs in the CPD process. They looked at the experiences of LEAs, schools and teachers and examined examples of innovative practice from across England and Wales. Teachers in schools thought that a CPD activity was effective when:

- it was tailored for the individual teacher;
- it was self-directed mentoring and observation;
- activities were targeted;
- it had a whole-school focus;
- the training/provider was of high quality;
- it was linked with a HEI;
- it included feedback and support;
- funding was available;
- conferences/meetings were involved;
- it was on-going.

These factors are presented in descending order, ie the more teachers mentioned them as factors, the higher they are on the above list. Teachers were asked for more details as to what they considered to be the factors related to effective CPD. Many of them highlighted the importance of the individual's enthusiasm and willingness to better him- or herself to the process of CPD; and they thought that attendance at the specific CPD activity should be voluntary in order for the individual to derive any benefit from it. Another motivating factor, according to the teachers, was professional motivation, that is to say their desire to become better teachers, to develop professionally and to improve their skills. Again this was related to teacher autonomy. Other summary findings of what constitutes effective CPD were as follows:

- Effective CPD should be facilitated by a school ethos that is conducive to professional development and provides a culture of lifelong learning for all. The impetus for this tended to stem from the headteacher.
- CPD should have a challenging and appropriate content, meet needs at all levels (national, school, individual) and evoke ideas for practical implementation. The venue should be accessible and convenient. The delivery style should be varied and include practical demonstrations and interactive activities.
- Adequate non-contact time, resources and supply cover are needed to undertake and consolidate learning (Brown Edmonds and Lee, 2001: 96).

This section has only given a brief overview of a small number of the findings of the research related to the teachers' views on CPD. This report amongst others is discussed in more detail in Chapter 5. Readers are also encouraged to read the whole report which is available from NFER (www.nfer.ac.uk). Egan and James (2002) review other research findings such as Egan and Simmonds (2002), and Friedman, Davis and Phillips (2001), which would provide other comparative data on CPD.

CPD in Northern Ireland

The integrated model of teacher education in Northern Ireland as it stands at present stops after the third year in post, ie the end of EPD, and there is a gap between the end of EPD and the professional qualification for headship which will be discussed in Chapter 7. All schools are also now involved in staff development and performance management (SDPM), which is designed to encourage all schools to focus on their performance and to enable staff to focus specifically in addition on their professional development and on their career. SDPM is designed to:

- enhance the quality of teaching and learning;
- recognize the achievements of teachers;

- support and develop teachers;
- disseminate good practice in and beyond the school (NITEC, 2002: 8).

Proposals have been developed on how to develop a model of CPD which both complements the SDPM arrangements but which also leads on naturally from the EPD phase. It is also intended that the CPD arrangements act as a bridge between the 3 'I's and the qualification for headship. At the time of writing, such proposals were at the recommendation stage only and still under discussion. They will be presented to the new GTC (NI) when it comes into being. These proposals state that the CPD process should follow on directly from early professional development and that it should:

- encourage and sustain the steady growth of the teacher as a reflective practitioner and as an autonomous learner;
- enable teachers to develop their skills and understanding with a focus on the promotion of students' personal, social and academic development;
- involve self-evaluation, goal setting, planning, development work, teaching, external evaluation and review and include school-based action research;
- enable teachers to explore and develop their practices and the professional values and principles that underpin them;
- encourage the use of a professional portfolio (NITEC, 2002).

The report recommends that adequate funding and time should be made available for schools to provide the necessary conditions for teachers to undertake CPD. As a framework for progression, the proposals outline three possible intermediate steps that could be taken on the way towards the Professional Qualification for Headship (PQH (NI)). These are: the Advanced Skills Teacher, the Teacher Leader and the Senior Teacher Leader options. The AST option is designed for teachers who wish to remain in the classroom, the TL option is for those teachers who wish to prepare themselves for leadership roles within the school, specifically head of department and SENCO, for example. The STL role is designed for those who seek senior management positions within the school. In order to qualify for the STL option, some experience of the AST or TL processes will be necessary. It is unclear at this early stage what programmes teachers will have to follow in order to reach these levels; the proposals mention activities associated with the posts, but precise details are not yet available. Teachers will be able to follow the regulations by consulting the Web site of the Department of Education (www.deni.gov.uk) or the site of the GTC (NI) when it becomes operational. At present no formal link is envisaged between the professional aspects of these initiatives and academic qualifications, unlike the situation in Scotland.

CPD in Scotland

In Scotland, regulations for CPD are still in a state of development. This section can only highlight some of the features of a Scottish CPD strategy and point the reader to the relevant Web sites where the most recent proposals and consultation findings will appear. The Sutherland Report, issued in 1997 in Scotland, made some recommendations on CPD for teachers and highlighted the fact that there was no framework to support teacher development (SOED, 1997). The Scottish Executive in 1998 then proposed a national framework for CPD, which incorporated four standards: initial teacher education, full registration, the expert teacher and the Scottish Qualification for Headship. These proposals were issued for consultation and were favourably received by the profession in Scotland. The McCrone Report, *A Teaching Profession for the 21st Century* (SEED, 2000), set the agenda for CPD of teachers in Scotland, the recommendations of which have now been agreed (SEED, 2001a). It has been concluded that a programme leading towards a Chartered Teacher (CT) status would be introduced, progression towards which would be by qualification and that access to the CT programme would be open to experienced teachers who maintained a CPD portfolio. The four standards now in existence in Scotland are: the Standard for ITE, the Standard for Full Registration (discussed under induction), the Standard for Chartered Teacher and the Standard for Headship. A project is currently being funded by the Scottish Executive and carried out by Arthur Andersen and the Universities of Edinburgh and Strathclyde to define the CT standard and to devise a programme of activities which would lead to the CT standard (Chartered Teacher Programme, 2001). Details on the progress of this project and its consultation processes can be found at www.ctprogrammescotland.org.uk.

It appears from the Consultation 2 document that, in working towards CT status, teachers will obtain a masters degree from one of the universities and will also undertake a planned programme of courses. They will emerge therefore with both a professional and an academic qualification. These qualifications will be accredited by the General Teaching Council for Scotland. The CT route is one route through the profession in Scotland, designed for the teacher who does not want to enter into the management stream. Scotland should be congratulated for attempting to make the advanced teachers both academically and professionally qualified in retaining the link with the universities; it is a further step in ensuring the continuity of professionalism in teaching and would be one worth considering by other parts of the UK. For teachers who aspire to senior management, there remains the route through assistant teacher and assistant principal teacher, principal teachers (heads of department), assistant headteacher and deputy headteacher and headteacher/rector. The final Standard is that for the Scottish Qualification for Headship, which will be discussed in Chapter 7.

All teachers across Scotland from this year will have to complete a total of 35 hours per year on CPD activities. These activities will consist of personal, professional, school-focused development activities and attendance at external courses. Teachers will have a CPD record which will accompany them on their career (SEED, 2001b). Further details of these can be found at www.teachinginscotland.com. The providers of CPD activities will have to have courses accredited and approved by the GTCS. The teaching profession in Scotland has always enjoyed relatively high status in the community. By providing a generally accepted route for progression through the teacher's career, the GTCS, in partnership with the Scottish Executive Education Department, the local authorities and teacher organizations can ensure that teachers are encouraged to develop their personal and professional interests throughout their career for the benefit of the whole system.

Research on CPD in Scotland

A recent research project was undertaken in Scotland to investigate the perceptions of new teachers of the CPD proposals. Purdon (2001) sent questionnaires to a 10 per cent sample of newly qualified teachers who were provisionally registered with the GTCS (the total number was 420). The survey questioned those in the sample on aspects of professionalism and sought their attitudes to CPD and to the status of teaching as a profession.

In terms of CPD specifically, the teachers were asked about whether they thought that teachers should be entitled to CPD opportunities beyond the induction period; 96 per cent of the group were in favour of this, stating that entitlement was important to ensure that they did not become 'stale' in their teaching. It was felt by 60 per cent of the sample that providing evidence of CPD should be compulsory in order for teachers to remain members of the GTC. Purdon notes that the new teachers did not appear to give any negative reaction to the fact that they had not been consulted on the possible framework for CPD despite the fact that they would be the teachers who would have to go through the process.

In general the group of new teachers felt that CPD had more to do with accountability rather than with professionalism. Purdon concludes that: 'If Scottish teachers want to avoid going down the road of being regarded as education technicians then open and robust debate, together with an interest and involvement in policy development, must be prerequisites of the professional teacher in 21st century Scotland' (Purdon, 2001: 120).

In Chapters 3, 4 and 5 some of the issues raised in the government regulations and in the research and evaluation documents outlined in this chapter will be discussed in greater detail under the relevant headings.

Key points

- It is clear that there are many similarities between the structures governing EPD and CPD in all parts of the UK.
- Many options for EPD and CPD activities are offered.
- Flexibility is built in to the system to allow for personal goals to be achieved and there is support provided in terms of mentoring and documentation to encourage progression.

Self study

Key questions

For NQTs:

- How I am progressing on my route through EPD/CPD?
- Where do I want to be professionally in five years?
- What steps do I have to take in compiling my career action plan?

For induction tutors/mentors:

- How can I better support the developmental needs of teachers in the school?
- To what extent are NQTs progressing following induction?

For senior management:

- How do arrangements for supporting NQTs during EPD and CPD fit with the school development plan?
- How do the EPD/CPD programmes dovetail with performance management?
- What special interests, expertise do NQTs in the school have which should be nurtured?
- How do we retain good NQTs in the school?

Recommended reading

Nicholls, G (1999) *Learning to Teach*, Kogan Page, London

Part II

Preparing for advancement

3 Personal strategies and collaboration

You can contribute to your own professional development by considering managing your personal circumstances as efficiently as possible and also by seeking to collaborate and network with others. It will be useful to think of collaboration both in terms of the *experience* directly feeding into your professional development; and also of *setting up* and *managing* collaboration for yourself and others as an added professional asset.

Government recommendations

There has been some recognition of teachers' work overload in government publications and initiatives, and of networking with outside agencies and with other teachers. The Green Paper includes sections on 'enabling teachers to teach' and 'streamlining administration' (DfEE, 2001c: 73–74). The White Paper also includes 'workload' as a major issue to be resolved (DfES, 2001c: 55) and refers to the PricewaterhouseCoopers (PWC) report of 2001, which looked particularly at releasing more time for planning, preparation and management (2001: 56) (available on www.teachernet.gov.uk/workloadstudy). Since these two documents were published , there has been a report by the School Teachers' Review Body (May 2002) which recommended reducing working hours from the average 52 to 48 hours – this is returning to 1994 levels (Shaw and Mansell, 2002); recruiting additional support staff; and bringing in contractual requirements to make workloads more manageable (Mansell and Shaw, 2002). In Scotland there is already a 35-hour weekly limit but as yet this has not been accepted south of the border. The two reports mentioned here can be found on www.teachernet.gov.uk/workloadstudy and www.teachernet.gov.uk/teacherspay2002.

To support these recommendations, extra funding was promised to schools (£15 billion from 2002–05), but with stipulations that this money should be spent partly on recruiting assistants rather than extra teachers (Mansell, Slater and Ward, 2002; Mansell and Ward, 2002). Following the PWC report, resources have also been given to a group of schools ('Pathfinder' schools) to investigate ways of cutting workload: laptops, more technology, more teaching assistants, more time allocation for planning (Revell, 2002d). A new £100 million laptop scheme was also launched in 2002 allocating money to schools to distribute laptops. These computers are school property, and there is some expectation that teachers who are allocated a laptop will provide some kind of service in return: training other teachers or sharing ideas and ways of working, for example (Cole and Johnston, 2002).

In the White Paper (DfES, 2001c: 6) there is mention of opening secondary education 'to a new era of engagement with the worlds of enterprise, higher education and civic responsibility'. In the earlier Green Paper, the notion of a wider community is described in more detail: 'The growth of reading opportunities at home and in the community spurred on by dramatic technological change increases the need for educators to work with all kinds of partners' (DfEE, 2001c: 17).

There is much emphasis too on teacher communities sharing practice. (This government emphasis is explored in greater depth in Chapters 2 and 6.) In the Green Paper, teacher–teacher support is seen as part of a broader picture: 'We will encourage those within the education service to learn from each other and to work with ideas from those outside it – parents, communities, the cultural sector and business' (DfEE, 2001c: 17).

Desirable outcomes identified are: overarching benefits for the community as a whole and a broadening of horizons for schools and 'building character': 'The education service can not only learn from experience of change and progress else-where, it can also become a valued possession of society as a whole' (DfEE, 2001c: 17); 'What matters is that all schools break out of isolation and introversion and constantly work with and learn from others, as many already do' (DfES, 2001c: 85); 'Other steps we will take to build character include… developing Creative Partnerships between schools and arts organizations in deprived areas to open up a wider variety of out-of-school learning opportunities' (DfEE, 2001c: 62). Through the National College of School Leadership in Nottingham the government is funding networked learning communities with projects of six schools plus a partner institution with matched funding of £50,000 (Revell, 2002d). The central-ization and proscription of much government rhetoric discussed elsewhere in this book seems mostly absent here.

Stress and time management

It is important to consider personally managing the experiences of teaching and administration in current day-to-day life. In the research and literature on stress and time management there seem to be four areas that are focal:

- knowing yourself;
- keeping a balance between your own life and school life;
- planning activities;
- other strategic behaviour and activities.

Knowing yourself

People react differently to stress and time problems so it can be helpful to recognize your own tolerance levels. Smith and Langston (1999: 177), for example, provide a useful questionnaire to identify if you are the type particularly vulnerable to stress: (their 'A' as opposed to 'B' personality is impatient, ambitious, work-focused). Crawford suggests that 'understanding one's own personal sense of stress is a necessary part of the process that will enable coping mechanisms to develop' (1997: 115).

It can be helpful to identify one's own style of time management. Leask and Terrell (1997: 186) suggest that there are three different organizational styles: 'dealing with tasks one at a time; dealing with tasks immediately; and being able to keep tasks on hold. They also suggest that recognizing your own style will help to manage your own feelings. In order then to manage one's own personal strategies effectively it is helpful to recognize the range of reactions and styles that are possible and where one stands within that range.

Balancing personal and school life

Covey (1992) suggests listing all the different roles in your life (including responsibilities at work, your family, friends and yourself); and then planning activities weekly to make sure that time is spent equally on these different aspects, in other words balancing your life as a person with your responsibilities at school.

Research has shown that working long hours at school is not necessarily productive (Campbell and Neill, 1997; Harris, 1999). The government recognized teachers' work overload and commissioned the investigation by PricewaterhouseCoopers mentioned earlier. The recommendations from this investigation are mainly strategic (discussed further in the section below), but there is acknowledgement here of the high level of current demands in school, which make it difficult to balance home and school life. Covey stresses particularly the counter-productiveness of only working in his notion of 'sharpening the saw'. He cites the example of a man cutting a tree whose saw is becoming increasingly blunt but who claims he has no time to sharpen it. Covey suggests ways of personal 'sharpening' which encompass four dimensions: physical, social, emotional and spiritual, and he suggests creating space for these in a weekly timetable. Bell (1991: 62) cites a teacher attending an INSET careers day as saying: 'I don't have time to plan my time. I'm not sure I know how to.'

This aspect of dealing with stress and time management may be one of the most difficult, particularly if one is working in a climate where there is expected collegiality and conscientiousness, and where the current educational climate focuses on performance and accountability.

Planning activities

There are practical ways of solving time management problems which in turn can help to alleviate stress. It may be that you have established routines that are not effective and it will be helpful to examine these to see if there are more efficient ways of planning and organizing your time.

The following activities can be useful in planning effectively:

- Organize teaching and marking so that this fits in with your own schedule of heavy commitments.
- Work backwards from important dates in the school calendar and write the appropriate planning time for activities.
- Be realistic about how long activities take and plan time accordingly.
- Allocate different kinds of tasks to different times of the day according to when you work best and when circumstances are appropriate (when there are likely to be fewer interruptions, for example).
- Ensure that you have some high quality work time for yourself every day. Revell (2002a) suggests 90 minutes of 'child-free work time in one block, in a place where you can work without being disturbed'.
- Keep an updated list of activities, which you cross off, recognizing that a long list is inevitable.
- Limit times for meetings or cut out unnecessary meetings.
- Divide activities into 'important' and 'urgent' and make sure that there is some time in your week when you can plan strategically. Covey (1992) suggests asking yourself if there is one thing that would make your life easier and then including this in your planning.
- Cut bureaucracy/paperwork as much as you can; throw away unnecessary papers once you have finished with them; consult the government's Web site on cutting red tape: www.dfes.gov.uk/cuttingburdens.
- Use help when it is available. An NFER study showed that some teachers are sometimes too proud, shy or mistrustful to delegate (Ward, 2002a).

A very useful self-evaluative task is to record your activities over the period of a week (or if possible several weeks) and see how these activities match your responsibilities. Smith and Langston (1999: 16), for example, provide a suggested chart of time allocation for management activities: networking – 15 per cent; traditional management – 15 per cent; human resources – 25 per cent; routine tasks – 45 per cent. Harris in her useful workshop manual (1999: 31–34) suggests training tasks which involve reviewing teachers' prioritizing habits and reactive/proactive responses. Ward (2002b) reports on a school in East London where lesson planning is done centrally on computer, giving staff the equivalent of one day off a week.

Strategic behaviour and activities

Stress can come from several sources in a school setting. Crawford (1997) identifies six areas, some of which are due to external circumstances and others which are internal to a school:

- change;
- low perceived status;
- budget cuts/job insecurity;
- time pressure;
- poor student motivation;
- poor working conditions.

Developing appropriate strategies to cope with these will vary according to how much control you have over any situation.

The first three problem areas are more difficult to affect since they depend on the educational climate in general. General lobbying by the teaching profession and unions, however, has resulted in some expressed concern over workload as described earlier. Despite this a 'restricted' government report in 2002 revealed that a 'mountain of paperwork' still existed in schools (Mansell, 2002a). An interesting recent initiative for example (The Time to Teach campaign) calls for a moratorium on government interference and extra allocation of time to teachers to allow for reviewing, reflecting and teaching properly (Palmer, 2001). Where there is little chance to have any influence, Smith and Langston's advice seems pertinent: 'Learn to accept what you can't change' (1999: 173).

Time pressure

The planning strategies mentioned earlier will all be useful in managing time effectively. In addition to planning beforehand it is also useful to consider ways of organizing time as you go along. The following suggestions may be helpful:

- Avoid 'deadline erosion' where you are relying on others to deliver; gentle reminders can be useful.
- Live with an 'interrupted' time frame since this is likely to be the norm, but limit intrusions to a certain period, ie 'manage other people'.
- Change activities so that you are fresh for a task: one suggested cycle, which capitalizes on the stimulus of the new, allows for 5 minutes on each one of a group of tasks in a first round, 10 minutes in a second round, 20 minutes in a third round. In this way all tasks will receive some attention if not be completed fully. This is unlikely though to be helpful if you have a 'serial' organizer style, where one task at a time is completed.

Poor student motivation and working conditions

Unmotivated students can be stressful to teach and here it can be helpful to draw on peer support and we explore this area later in the chapter.

Working conditions can mean the physical environment, the climate in school and relationships with others. While the first two aspects are likely to be best dealt with on a group basis, there may be particular strategies to help deal with 'difficult' colleagues. Smith and Langston (1999: 75ff) identify seven difficult personality types and suggest personal strategies to deal with each type – attackers, egotists, sneaks, victims, negators, super-agreeable people, unresponsive people. They also suggest a list of behaviours which can help to diffuse aggressive situations: for example being open and assertive, being sympathetic, adopting sympathetic body language (1999: 173ff).

Crawford focuses on a more inward reactive stance in her emphasis on 'hardiness': 'Hardy personalities seem to perceive clearly where they are going in life' and know that they are in control and responsible for their behaviour. When new stressors arise these will be seen as opportunities rather than threats (1997: 117). In Chapter 9 where the Ofsted inspection process is explored, one Ofsted official comments on the desirability of 'steeliness' of attitude in a school. This seems to echo Crawford's suggestion of 'hardiness'.

A major source of interpersonal difficulty can relate to communication strategies so it is worth thinking about this in some depth. Smith and Langston again point to useful aspects to be wary of: 'misunderstandings, inappropriate language, both in tone and style, excessive talking and inadequate listening together with a lack of openness can combine to make the spoken word or gesture a fermenting cocktail of frustrations that often explode into unstable interaction and dispute' (1999: 167). In negotiating with others it can also be useful to check expectations (you may be working or providing much more than is necessary), and to turn down requests if you feel that you genuinely cannot do justice to the requested task.

In general, in managing time and stress it will be helpful to look after your health (Covey's 'sharpening the saw'), take care of your diet, exercise and relax. The

Teachers' Benevolent Fund has set up a special helpline (Teacherline) to offer counselling and advice (0800 0562 561, and has published documents relating to fitness and health (DfEE and Department of Health, 2000; Health and Safety Commission, 1998). There is also the Web site www.teachersupport.org.uk. Looking after your voice may be particularly important (Hastings, 2002a). Wolff (2002) has three practical tips for mental health: a one-minute 'time oasis' (sitting down and taking 10 deep breaths); writing tasks on sticky notes, prioritizing them and transferring them to a 'finished' board; and carrying a 'visual symbol' of how you intend to reward yourself in your holidays as a morale booster. Harris suggests that teaching is currently a 'weary profession' (2001) and it is thus important to develop personal strategies both on a practical and on a mental level to help to combat any possible problems.

Collaboration

As well as developing the inner self it is helpful to focus on working with others, developing the interactive self as it were. Collaboration in general is seen as a positive arrangement in educational circles. The prisoner's dilemma is often quoted (Dawkins, 1989; Ruiz and Parés, 1997), which demonstrates that co-operation is the best long-term model; this is also demonstrated by various simulated game theories (Ruiz and Parés, 1997). School improvement literature abounds with recommendations for collegiality. However it should also be noted that collaboration is not always easy either to establish or maintain. Hargreaves and Fullan talk of collaboration, or 'going wider' in their terminology as 'a messy frustrating, conflict-ridden and time consuming business' (1998: 67). They suggest that strong partnerships are founded on:

- perseverance;
- empathy;
- a common focus;
- equity;
- trust.

Farrell, in his in-depth analysis of a peer-support initiative, suggests that the processes in his version of collaboration (in this case in-depth teacher reflection aided by outside critique) may not be suitable for everyone: 'not all teachers are ready to reflect... reflection may not be for everyone' (2001: 373). We can progress this thought from Farrell further and suggest that: collaboration may be of different kinds with different networks and types of support; and collaboration can be pitched at different levels or strengths.

These two ideas are followed up in greater depth later in the chapter. Before moving on to this closer analysis it may be helpful to outline the different kinds of network and peer support that can contribute to professional development.

Networks can be seen as extending out from an individual teacher in seven main possible directions and on two different levels (face to face and online) as indicated in Figure 3.1.

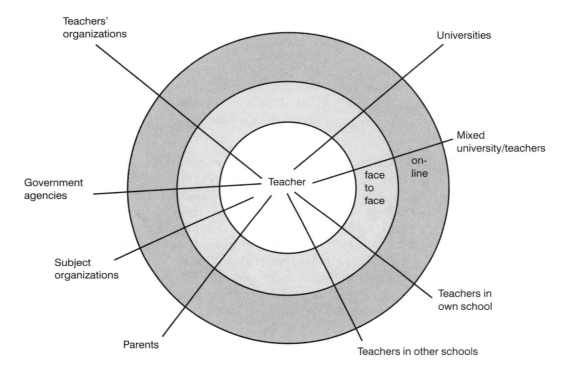

Figure 3.1 Professional networks

The contributions that some of these network partners (government, agencies, subject organizations, universities) can make are also dealt with later in Chapters 5 and 6, where formal organized arrangements with outside agencies are looked at in more depth.

Peer support can be seen to include four major elements and may vary along a continuum from loose/informal contact to structured/formal interaction as shown in Figures 3.2 and 3.3.

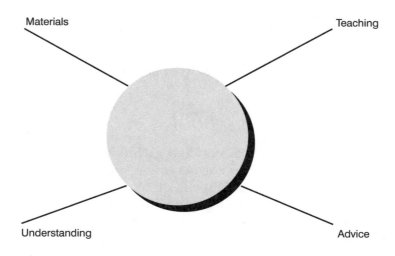

Figure 3.2 Types of support

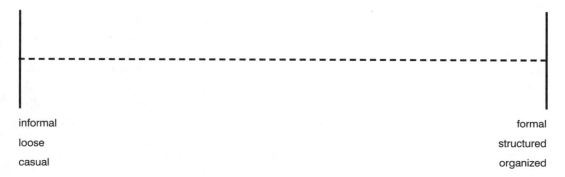

Figure 3.3 Types of contact

In considering networks and peer support within the context of collaboration then, we need to think of *who* is collaborating and *why,* and *how* they are collaborating. It seems then sensible to analyse the value of different kinds of collaboration rather than only advocating a single model.

Networks

Linking back to Figure 3.1 we shall discuss four main groups who can form useful networks for peer support:

- teachers in your own school;
- teachers in other schools;

- 'critical friends' who are working in outside institutions;
- parents.

In addition we shall look at the special role of online networking.

Teachers in your own school

Colleagues of course have always offered each other support in different ways. Researchers have commented on 'the pervasive "ordinary reality" of sporadic and informal exchange' (Little, 1990: 513) and of 'informal contacts between [teachers that] are brief… [with teachers forming] a tight exclusive group with its own jokes and private language' (Haigh, 2001a). Acker (1999), in her study of a primary school with a collaborative culture, cites the following comment from a reception teacher: 'We're willing to work as a team.' There can of course be much stronger contact than informal team spirit. Creese, Daniels and Norwich (1997) describe a particular initiative (teacher support teams or TST) where an in-school team will support an individual teacher's particular problems (with special needs students). This initiative was supported by a three-day training programme at the London Institute of Education and the Creese, Daniels and Norwich book provides a general overview and examples of the tasks and handouts used in those sessions. These authors too comment on the sporadic interchanges typical of school: 'Teachers may often ask each other for advice. However these exchanges typically take place in the context of busy staff rooms in a very short space of time and rarely with any possibility of reviewing the effects of the advice' (1997: 3). Their TST initiative suggests setting up a more structured arrangement with a core team of three teachers (who may at times call in outsiders) who meet on a weekly/fortnightly basis with any teacher requesting support. The team they suggest is the SENCO, a senior teacher and one other teacher. The principle here is based on 'making the most of the knowledge and skills of teachers already in a school' (1997: 6) and is a very focused example of support. Metcalfe (1999) and Wisdom (2001) also mention more structured observation within schools. These initiatives and other examples of robust support are explored in greater depth later in this chapter.

However, collaboration within a school and between colleagues may not be automatic and may not be easy to establish. Lacey alludes to this potential difficulty: 'many teachers feel particularly vulnerable when they are asked to work alongside colleagues as often the demands of the relationship mean that conflict and resistance are endemic' (1996: 68). Acker (1999) also mentions vulnerability, and schools where rivalry rather than collaboration may be pervasive.

Farrell (2001) suggests that it may be very difficult to carry out particular in-depth kinds of support if colleagues are working in the same institution and if there is insufficient 'equality' between the teachers concerned: 'certain constraints may already exist in relation to issues of equality, ownership and ethics… [I] wonder if it is truly possible to have equality with participants within the same institution' (2001: 373). It seems then that there may be a useful role for the outsider and that some types of collaboration are more suited to internal networking than others.

Ruiz and Parés (1997) point to a further influential factor, namely that individual instances of collaboration between teachers are likely to be affected by the presence or absence of a *general* collegial culture within a school (see also Metcalfe, 1999). They compare 'Balkanized culture schools' (with separate competing cultures or colleagues) with more collegial environments. Hargreaves (1994) provides five categories of school subcultures: isolation; collaboration; imposed/contrived collegiality; balkanization; and what he terms a 'moving mosaic' where collaboration is creative and flexible.

A consideration of overall collegiality of a school culture can also raise the question of the usefulness of dissenting or different voices within a group. This can be seen in different ways. As Ruiz and Parés mention in their research, there may be such discontinuity between colleagues as to make collaboration very problematic. However Ruiz and Parés also point out the value of the dissenting voice: 'the heterogeneity of… [a] group… enriches the understanding of… [any] problem and the quality of the discussion' (1997: 243). Ruiz and Parés also provide a useful checklist of supportive factors for successful collaboration:

- small groups;
- short-term objectives;
- free-flowing communication;
- long-term interdependence (1997: 249).

Collaboration within a school may then need careful support and cannot be assumed as automatically present.

Teachers in other schools

In the TST initiative mentioned earlier, use was made of contact between schools to help compare practice and thus provide support. Thus, on the third training day of the programme run by the university, the 14 schools involved worked in mixed school teams in order to be able to share thoughts (see Creese, Daniels and Norwich, 1997).

It can be helpful to set up school 'clusters' where teachers from different schools meet together. This can be particularly useful where a teacher has to operate in relative isolation in their own school. 'Clustering' has been reported particularly with reference to SENCOs and headteachers. Hastings (2001b) for example reports on four new primary heads who work in small village schools in North Leicestershire. The heads pool expertise and provide a much needed support network. They have been described by Ofsted as having 'one of the closest working relationships it has seen' (Hastings, 2001b). The heads report that this cluster 'has helped them develop support structures to make the schools successful – and given them a friendly shoulder to cry on when times are tough' (Hastings, 2001b). As well as the headteachers meeting regularly, the staff from all four schools meet once a month to discuss a variety of matters (teaching strategies, resources, problems, new ideas). They have also recently acquired funding for a shared premises manager and have jointly achieved Investor in People status. Here then is an example of joint collaboration which not only provides the benefits of sharing but which can also exploit economies of scale. Mansell (2002c) also reports on a 'federated' group of headteachers helping to turn around a failing school.

Evans *et al* (1999) carried out a nation wide survey of clustering arrangements for supporting SEN (with data from 93 cluster groups across 45 LEAs in the period 1995–96), with some interesting results. They found that:

- clustering was widespread;
- the majority of clusters comprised 10 schools or fewer;
- there was usually joint management of the cluster;
- clustering tended to be a 'loose' arrangement, not involving the loss of independence for individual schools.

There was no one formula for clusters, indeed Evans and her research team found that 'clusters come in all different shapes and sizes, serve all sorts of purposes, undertake all manner of activities and are managed in all sorts of ways' (1999: 41).

There is though a possible danger, identified by Hargreaves, which could be present in such collaboration, namely that any one individual teacher's perspective may be so limited as to **not** be helpful in any interchange: 'in contexts that restrict professional learning, personal practical knowledge can become personal but also profoundly impractical knowledge' (1996: 16). Any interchange between teachers then is likely to include caveats in evaluating the contribution of others.

It is clear then that the principle of clustering can operate in different ways but that in general there are considerable benefits to be reaped.

Working with a university

One instance of working with a university has already been mentioned, namely the training offered to a group of schools for a specific purpose: the setting up of TSTs (Creese, Daniels and Norwich, 1997). There are also many instances of individuals from universities working with schools in the capacity of a 'critical friend'. This can be either as an integral part of individual action research or on a more general level. This area is explored in greater depth in Chapter 5.

Day (1998, 1999) describes two different ways of providing an outsider's voice: with an individual teacher, and in a more general capacity revealing the usefulness of a dissonant or distant perspective. In his descriptions of helping a single teacher to recognize different conflicting images of his or her own work (Day calls these different 'selves'), Day also mentions the contingent danger that outside researchers may not always understand the perspective of an individual teacher: 'Collaborative researchers... must work with the emotional and intellectual selves of teachers who may have different beliefs, values and practices from their own. They must learn to listen to dissonant voices which may not always be comfortable' (1998: 272). Nicholls also emphasizes the need for both parties in a university/ school partnership to accept 'the differences in the core functions of schools and HEIs' (1997: 36).

In his later book Day talks in more detail about the value of critical friendship and the role of an outside agency such as a university. In his view a critical friend can:

- carry out observations **for** a teacher (saving him or her this task);
- offer a counter-opinion;
- offer comparison with other teachers' practice elsewhere;
- stimulate reflection (Day, 1999).

He does however recognize problematic areas, namely:

- possible adverse reactions from students in the classroom during observations;
- the fact that the time needed for discussion may not always been seen as productive or effective;
- the need for critical friends to be skilled inquirers (observers) with high level communication skills (1999: 101).

Day also points to the fact that 'sharing' with a critical friend may involve 'change' which in turn can be threatening (1999: 102).

A very useful contribution from Day's analysis is his mention of Hubermann's four cycles of learning:

- *the closed individual cycle* – where teachers learn privately;
- *the open individual cycle* – where teachers learn from colleagues in school;
- *the closed collective cycle* – where groups of teachers share collective wisdom;
- *the open collective cycle* – where outsiders are admitted to add a further dimension (1999: 177–79).

Day cites as an example of an 'open collective cycle' the work done by Hopkins and colleagues with a number of schools in order to help with school improvement (the 'Improving the Quality of Education for All' – IQEA – project). In this project university colleagues helped schools in an action inquiry approach through partnership. Revell (2002d) describes a similar network involving seven schools and a university in Bedfordshire.

Underlying many of these critical friendships or open collective cycle learning frameworks is the notion, not so much of providing advice but of identifying or 'naming' aspects of school life which may not have been fully recognized before. Little points to the fact that many teachers may not give their own expertise a label since they operate with 'the taken-for-granted invisible character of "just teaching"' (1990: 525). She suggests that 'teachers may not know what they know, or how to say what they know' (1990: 526). The value of an outsider may be precisely in helping teachers to name things which they 'know' already but have not recognized.

The value then of collaboration with a university may be that it offers the opportunity to network with a distant (possibly dissonant) voice. This can complement the other kinds of networking with closer circles where the emphasis is generally more on sharing.

Working with parents

Networking with parents will of course be an important aspect of school life for teachers and for the senior management team. This may be relatively smooth where there are good home–school relationships; or, as Brookes (2002a) reports, there may be hidden problem areas: he cites proximity of residence, parents being ex-students, many students being related to each other as some unexpected areas of difficulty. Parents though may also be recruited to play a greater role in the school. Wallace (2002) describes a project with a failing school near Sheffield where previously hostile parents became active partners in helping to turn the school around, with extra personnel being funded by the government's 'single regeneration budget' and 'Excellence in Cities' fund. Although unusual, this initiative can serve as a model for positive ways of networking with parents.

Networking online

A further possibility now available to teachers is that of a cyber-network. All the agencies identified earlier (in Figure 3.1) can be contacted online. Outside agencies have Web sites and colleagues in schools can be contacted through e-mail. In addition there are a number of forums that exist online which teachers can tap into. Hargreaves and Fullan talk of the boost that computer technology can offer: 'This enables teachers to interact with each other, about things that matter most to them, day or night, at the touch of a keyboard' (1998; 72).

Information on online forums and the benefits they offer is regularly reported in the *Times Educational Supplement*. For example there is Teacherline, a newly established helpline for teachers with a Web site (www.teachersupport.org.uk). There are two online communities specifically for headteachers and deputy heads: Talking Heads and Virtual Heads (Johnston, 2001; Revell, 2002b). These two communities have been set up by the new National College of School Leadership (NCSL) and can be found on the NCSL Web site; they are 'about networking people together to share practice' (Johnston, 2001). Willard reports on headteachers who use this service 'to get advice or simply off-load the trials of the day' (Willard, 2001). Revell (2002b) also mentions the value of being able to talk directly to policy makers in 'hot-seat' debates. One head admits that: 'Talking Heads was a huge life-saver. For the first six months [of being a head] I went online every day, sometimes for up to an hour' (Willard, 2001). There is a forum for new teachers organized by the *Times Educational Supplement* (www.tes.co.uk/staffroom), which in the words of one of its members 'gives us a voice to express the dissent, frustration and opposition denied us by press and parliament alike' (Andy–91, 2001). Another kind of service offered is that by 'schoolmanager', the online service offered by the Stationery Office (www.schoolmanager.net) which offers publications and a discussion forum for heads. At the time of writing, two publications were available: one on Internet practice and the other on professional development (Holmes, 2001).

Lieberman and Grolnick, in their overview of electronic networking in a US context, cite the following benefits of such contact:

- follow-up contact with friends;
- new contacts;
- contact with experts;
- access to online resources;
- providing teachers with an audience for their work (1996: 16).

They emphasize opportunities to:

- talk;
- learn;
- support.

Online communication offers a broader constituency and the opportunity for free expression.

Selwyn (2000) has carried out extensive research into what actually happens in a cyber forum and his findings can add a useful perspective. He selected the SENCO forum amongst the Virtual Teacher Centres set up by the National Grid for Learning, since this was one of the largest and best established (900 subscribers). He analysed the online exchanges in this forum over a period of two years (3,654 messages in all with 734 threads, or sustained lines of discussion). Selwyn's findings were that the forum did provide useful services but that these were limited, and that the community established was 'artificial' in some sense: 'to claim a sense of community amongst members would be to greatly exaggerate the bulk of online activity' (2000: 771). Selwyn identified four main types of activity in the online exchanges:

- requests for information plus replies;
- swapping experiences and tips;
- complaints about situations in schools;
- celebrations of 'beautiful moments'.

Although these activities are all clearly useful, Selwyn provides other information that throws a somewhat different light on things, for example:

- Over a third of the requests for information remained unanswered, suggesting that while teachers were prepared to be helpful to each other, they were not **always** able or willing to do so.
- There was a hard core of regular responders (26 out of 900) who were keen to provide an answer, whether they knew anything or not. Selwyn speculates that in these cases: 'to be seen answering is sometimes as important as the answer itself' (2000: 760). In other words it is only a small number of teachers who are regularly active in such a network and the motives for answering may be mixed.
- A cyber network does not require the same obligation or commitment as a face-to-face interaction. The teacher who logs on regularly to the TES NQT forum also celebrates this fact: 'the major advantage [is] that no-one knows your name' (Andy–91, 2001). However we can also suggest that anonymity may have some unwanted side-effects.

An interesting additional dimension can be added here from research by Woods *et al*. This team analysed their own practice in working on a book chapter together by e-mail and concluded: 'We can become more involved with the means of communication than the communication itself... E-mail can take over one's life' (1998: 590ff). Ginns *et al*, working in an Australian context, also comment that 'an email awareness needs to develop before people use email confidently for regular communication and sharing of understandings and problem solving' (2001: 127). It is clear from Selwyn's analysis that online networking certainly does offer benefits but that these are limited. He concludes: '[this forum] did not appear to be replacing the staff room's function as an arena in which to unwind and relax' (2000: 772). However for isolated staff there are considerable advantages and an online forum does provide an arena for information exchange and debate.

Peer support

Some of the purposes of networks have already been alluded to (sharing information, discussion/debate). We also mentioned four types of support earlier (see Figure 3.2):

- materials;
- teachers;
- advice;
- understanding.

It is possible to subdivide these types of support and purposes further into two main groups, namely: practical support and emotional/cognitive support. In other words, some reasons for people contacting each other operate on a practical level of helping out. Other contact operates at a deeper level, where there is more challenge to ways of thinking about something, or where there is more emotional engagement.

It is possible to identify these two levels (practical, emotional/cognitive) in descriptions given by other writers on the purposes of networking and kinds of support that are thereby facilitated. Evans *et al*, in the context of their survey of SEN school clusters, identified four reasons for collaboration:

- to exchange information;
- to develop common approaches;
- participation in joint INSET;
- sharing SEN resources (1999: 27).

Here then we could say that there was primarily a *practical* focus.

Creese, Daniels and Norwich (1997) in their description of TST training identify four benefits of the small-scale forum made possible by their suggested in-school networks:

- sharing knowledge;
- expressing and receiving collegial/emotional support;
- an opportunity to air frustration;
- learning new things.

In this more intimate network there is a mixture of both *practical* and *emotional* benefits (1997: 6).

Leach also identifies both emotional and practical benefits in her six named benefits of using ICT:

- acquiring subject information;
- supporting learning;
- supporting teaching;
- providing productivity [organizational] tools;
- providing pedagogical tools;
- providing organizational Intranets for schools (2001: 385–86).

Little (1990) in her description of collegiality identifies four different forms:

- story telling;
- sharing;
- aid/assistance;
- joint work (1990: 512).

Little emphasizes the difference between collegiality that confirms independence – in her view the first three forms – and that which allows for true interdependence – only present in 'joint work' in her opinion. It is also possible though to consider her forms of collegiality as spanning both *practical* and *emotional* concerns. She hints at the difference between purely practical outcomes of collaboration and more challenging cognitive forms when she asks: 'Are we filling potholes, resurfacing the road, or inventing new modes of transport?' (1990: 517). One could suggest that in fact **all** of these activities are useful.

Practical support

We can perhaps identify two main kinds of practical support: materials/activities and teachers.

Materials/activities

In collaborative subject departments teachers are likely to be sharing resources and good ideas for activities. Solomon (2001) quotes a teacher who has provided a free teachers' site (www.primaryresources.co.uk): 'there's a great sense of wanting to share resources to make life easier for all of us.' There have also been moves to set up online arrangements for teachers to get paid for putting their lessons online (Solomon, 2001; Ward, 2001a). Web sites such as www.classroomsupport.com and www.teachingideas.co.uk (primary) have been set up with this aim in mind. One thorny problem here, as yet unresolved, which both Ward and Solomon point out is the question of copyright. It seems that at the time of writing the copyright of teachers' materials may belong to schools. Unions warn teachers to check their legal position carefully before selling their work (Ward, 2001a).

Sharing resources may of course also be problematic. Little (1990) warns that problems can arise if such an arrangement is not seen as reciprocal and Metcalfe, in his developmental work with subject departments in two secondary schools, notes that the 'teachers were quick to point out what they perceived to be the potential threat to the sharing of good practice, if teachers are competing with each other for higher pay' (1999: 455).

Teachers

In the survey of SENCO clusters undertaken by Evans *et al* (1999), teachers were shared across schools in some instances allowing for economies of scale, sharing of equipment and a 'moderated' perspective for the teacher with inter-school experiences. Frost also reports on the sharing of teachers (and resources) in his suggested collaborative community approach to introducing foreign languages into primary schools. Frost suggests that: 'Not only do such arrangements enable schools to share resources such as teachers with expert knowledge and expensive curriculum materials, but they also provide a context for professional learning' (1999: 187).

There may too be situations where two teachers are jointly responsible for a class, with a variety of team teaching arrangements (Morgan, 1998b). In all these cases teachers can offer practical help to each other, whilst taking care that logistical problems do not interfere with the smooth running of the collaboration.

Emotional/cognitive support

In the Elton Report (DES, 1989) emphasis is placed on the benefits of peer support: 'teachers often learn more about classroom skills by talking to each other than by listening to visiting "experts"… Peer support groups can develop the kind of trust and confidence which leads to mutual observation and consultancy which involves watching and commenting on each other's teaching. This is probably the most effective method of classroom skills available' (1989: 76). These comments are helpful in that they point to the idea of different levels of support with a notion of progress, 'leading to' deeper understanding. One could though challenge the lack of appreciation of difficulties that may arise and of the benefits that 'experts' can bring.

One can perhaps talk of 'practical' help 'leading to' help or interaction of a deeper kind. Certainly it is important to recognize that emotional/cognitive support may be a **qualitatively** different experience. While practical collaboration may be problematic (team-teaching for example can call for a high level of sensitivity), in general, teachers who opt to offer and receive practical support will maintain their independence and these arrangements can run relatively smoothly.

Little (1990) talks of the expected environment in a school where 'colleagues will give one another help when asked. Nonetheless, teachers carefully preserve the boundary between offering advice when asked and interfering in unwarranted ways in another teacher's work' (1990: 515).

If teachers choose to collaborate in more developed interactions, such as the open discussions in the TST initiative mentioned earlier or arranging for their teaching to be observed, then the emotional and cognitive stakes are higher. Evans *et al*, in their survey of school clusters, comment that 'individual schools may... be concerned that their own weaknesses and problems may become exposed to others' (1999: 95). In reality they found that sharing often revealed similar problems and brought relief.

Creese, Daniels and Norwich (1997) found that teachers really welcomed the chance to be able to talk through their problems in TST initiatives in some depth and above all to have the **time** to do so (in this project, time was allocated in the timetable to accommodate discussion between the team and the individual teachers). Teachers made the following comments:

> Staff feel now that they do not have to struggle on single handed (1997: 56).

> Teachers feel they are not alone with a problem. More people to share ideas with – more team spirit and sharing of experiences (1997: 56).

> As people get less time to listen to people I think that is one of the main things a TST can do. People can have time and get a chance to talk about something which is bothering them. Sometimes that just helps anyway. You do find people are rushing about so much at the moment that they don't get time to listen (1997: 54).

> Teachers... [are] so busy, doing endless paperwork, it's actually having the time when you can sit down and say 'this child needs talking about'. I think at that very simple level, it's a huge benefit, that it's a specific time when what you're talking about is children's needs and children's learning and how you teach (1997: 54).

Here then there is a recognition of the benefit of having time for serious discussion of important issues for teachers, which may otherwise get drowned out by administrative and organizational claims on teachers' time.

The notion of exploring in more depth can also be realized by peer observation of teaching, as we discuss in Chapter 9. Here the emphasis is developmental and formative, so this should not be the same process as appraisal or inspection (although it may feel similar to the person watched). It may be helpful to think of the observation process happening somewhere along a continuum of possibilities from 'advice' to debate as illustrated in Figure 3.4.

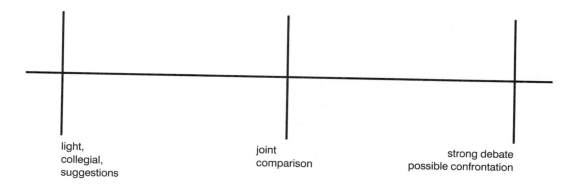

light,
collegial,
suggestions

joint
comparison

strong debate
possible confrontation

Figure 3.4 Peer observation continuum

Wisdom (2001), for example, describes an experiment in a Bristol school where a humanities specialist acts as a staff coach, advising staff on teaching and learning strategies. A variety of techniques is used including videoing lessons, team-teaching and voice training. The coach himself suggests that the 'peer' nature of the support is the most important aspect (harking back to ideas in the Elton report): 'The beauty of it is that it's separate from the culture of performance management... I'm not going to put anything down on paper we haven't agreed' (Wisdom, 2001).

In Metcalfe's description of developmental classroom observation he points out that the process of observation can be extremely helpful for the observer (noted by Mariott in her analysis of observation, see Chapter 9). He notes 'those who observe teaching are likely to feel challenged about their own practice and to learn from the experience of seeing others in action, as well as having to articulate what they have seen' (1999: 455). This experience is also noted by Haigh (2001b) in his description of a 'teacher consultant'. Here then there is much more sense of reciprocal equity.

In a slightly more focused arrangement, Farrell (2001) describes observation of a colleague where both he and the teacher involved analysed seven of her lessons and then compared notes. In this situation he felt that he acted as a catalyst for the teacher, since she was already solving some of her own problems (see also Day, 1998). Their notes in fact were remarkably similar. Farrell does note though that, in this set-up, confrontation was avoided which in turn might have led to a deeper examination or evaluation.

It is just this kind of stronger contact which Day (1998) describes in his work with an individual teacher (coming from an outside, university environment). Day worked with this teacher over a period of a year, observing lessons and discussing his attitudes and approaches. By exploring the teacher's own history and views on how he was teaching and comparing this with his practice, Day was able to reveal the differences between how this teacher felt he ought to teach and how he actually wanted to teach once he was *in situ* (what Day terms his different 'selves'): 'It was the process of collaborative action research which enabled him [the teacher] to "unpick" his different selves and clarify their influence in a way which enabled him, paradoxically, greater choice; and though his teaching itself did not change significantly, his ways of understanding it did' (1998: 270).

These last two examples involved collaboration with a teacher already carrying out action research but this kind of observation need not necessarily only be confined to such situations. We can cite a final example of strong in-depth peer-support where we have teachers seeking to challenge and explore. In this case the setting is a bilingual school where the teaching of all of the curriculum is in German and English – the Vienna Bilingual Schooling First Middle School. There are nine native speakers who regularly team teach with Austrian colleagues and the whole school is committed to a high level of professional development with regular termly INSET focusing on teaching techniques, and also groups within the school carrying out self-evaluation (see Morgan and Feyertag-Pressel, in press). In 1998 the staff used an INSET day to analyse their team-teaching procedures and acted out scenarios from previous lessons, observed and discussed by the whole staff and an outside researcher (see Morgan, 1998b). In 2001 there was a follow-up, more ambitious project to analyse both the language and learning skills taking place in lessons (described in more detail Morgan and Feyertag-Pressel, in press). A working team in the school had put together a grid of different learning skills needed in the curriculum. This grid was given to the staff who then observed 15 examples of lessons, acted out as in the 1998 experiment. The staff and researcher then analysed these lessons in terms of what learning skills were being required as well as the specific content being taught.

In this process teachers became aware of:

- the multiple processes happening in a lesson;
- the skills used in different subjects;
- skills that were being under-developed;
- interesting teacher approaches being used by their colleagues.

In this case there was a high level of trust between the teachers; a high level of co-operation (aided by native speakers who supported a variety of subjects); informed critical evaluation provided by an outside researcher; and an active interest in improvement generated by the working groups within the school and an extremely supportive head and local authority.

In the 'stronger' forms of peer support described here, there may be uncomfortable areas of difference which need to be resolved but these can prove to be really fruitful. Other forms of collaboration may involve a lighter touch but these can be equally beneficial in a different way. Creese, Daniels and Norwich point to the fact that 'teachers are dealing with higher levels of dilemma and tension both in and out of the classroom' (1997: 7). In this kind of climate, having strong networks with teachers and others to provide support is an invaluable aid in both coping with the present and considering future professional development.

Key points

- Time and stress management can be aided by good planning and maintaining a good balance between home life and work.
- Networking can be within school, across schools or with the broader community.
- Networking can serve a variety of purposes and can be online or face to face or through some other medium.
- As well as the clear benefits it offers, there may be other contingent difficulties.

Self study

Recommended tasks

- Keep a record of your activities over two weeks and match this against your responsibilities at school.
- Draw up a list of your roles in and out of school and plan a week's activities which allocates an appropriate proportion to each role.
- Reconsider an area of your life that is stressful and decide if any of the strategies suggested in the chapter might help to alleviate this stress.

Key questions

For the teacher:

- Could I set up or join a network to help my own professional development?
- If already belonging to a network – do I contribute as well as benefit?

For the school management team:

- How might networking help with school improvement issues?
- What implementation problems might there be and how could these be overcome?

Recommended reading

Creese, A, Daniels, H and Norwich, B (1997) *Teacher Support Teams in Primary and Secondary Schools*, David Fulton, London

Evans, J, *et al* (1999) *Collaborating for Effectiveness*: *Empowering schools to be inclusive*, Open University Press, Buckingham

Frost, D (1997) *Reflective Action Planning for Teachers: A guide to teacher-led school and professional development*, David Fulton, London

Nicholls, G (1997) *Collaborative Change in Education*, Kogan Page, London

4 Domains of professional development

As someone who is interested in developing him- or herself professionally, you will no doubt have identified particular areas or domains for this development. This chapter considers a whole range of possible domains, since the picture is not as simple or clear as one might think; we also deal with issues related to choices.

Government recommendations

The government has a clear agenda of linking professional development to improving standards of student performance. In its 2001 strategy document *Learning and Teaching* (DfEE, 2001b) this agenda is endorsed by opinions canvassed during consultation on their Green Paper, *Schools – Building on Success* (DfEE, 2001c): '90 per cent of respondents agreed that professional development should be centred on raising standards in the classroom' (DfEE, 2001b: 10).

It is also clear, as we shall see in Chapter 9, that there will be considerable pressure on schools to be accountable for their CPD programmes and to involve all teachers. In the strategy document, the following statement appears: 'some degree of pressure – to make headteachers accountable for the quality of professional development in their schools… is essential' (DfEE, 2001b: 20). Ofsted will also have a role in monitoring this accountability and this is explored in more detail in Chapter 8.

In the three most recent documents at the time of writing: the strategy document; the Green Paper mentioned above; and the White Paper, *Schools Achieving Success* (DfES, 2001c), there seems to be some tension between two different views of what the government wishes to encourage. On the one hand there is broad encouragement for teachers to develop themselves, and for (successful) schools to have a free hand; and on the other there is a recommended prescribed list of areas for development and a clear indication that choices will be directed.

In the strategy document, the remit of CPD seems open and free: 'By "professional development" we mean any activity that increases the skills, knowledge and understanding of teachers and their effectiveness in schools' (DfEE, 2001b: 3); and in the White Paper there seems a similar sense of choice, with the government talking 'of giving successful schools the freedom they need to excel and innovate' (DfES 2001c: 6). The remit here is extended in general to a school not just to CPD. The Green Paper also talks of 'the excellent practice in a number of schools of placing professional development at the heart of their approach to school development' (DfEE, 2001c: 71); and of building up a workforce with greater skills and understanding: 'people with skills, knowledge, understanding, time and attitudes which enable successful change to occur. In short it is a matter of building capacity' (DfEE, 2001c: 84).

By contrast, there are a number of statements in these three documents that also indicate that a much more prescriptive agenda is being considered. In the White Paper the following appears as one of the four intended objectives for schools: [a] framework of national priorities, underpinned by a system of accountability, inspection and intervention to maintain basic standards' (DfES, 2001c: 6). The strategic document indicates that the government wishes to have a guiding hand in deciding the domains for professional development. One of their proposals is to 'help teachers so they can select the development activities that are likely to have the greatest impact on their teaching' (DfEE, 2001b: 5). The 'help in selection' is backed up by a list of recommended areas, which occur throughout the three documents (relating one presumes to the 'framework of national priorities' identified in the White Paper). These priorities appear to be in four areas.

- *Particular curriculum issues:* literacy, phonics, writing, numeracy cited in the Green Paper (DfEE, 2001c: 76), the Key Stage 3 strategy cited in the strategy document (DfEE, 2001b: 13) and the White Paper (DfES, 2001c: 18).
- *ICT:* mentioned in the strategy document (DfEE, 2001b: 13) and in all three documents in general.
- *Leadership skills:* mentioned in the strategy document (DfEE, 2001b: 16) and the White Paper (DfES, 2001c: 54).
- *Working with particular groups of students:* boys and SEN students cited in the strategy document (DfEE, 2001b: 13) and able students, mentioned in the White Paper (DfES, 2001c: 21). The general descriptions in the three documents describing the recommended domains for development for teachers do not include this final category, but it is a clear priority in terms of examples cited.

These priorities are reinforced by recommendations in other documentation:

- criteria used by Ofsted;
- expectations, for example, that all headteachers will have a NPQH qualification;
- the criteria included in lists of expected standards for NQTs, newly inducted teachers and subject/specialist leaders.

Despite an apparent embracing of a wide remit of possible professional development, the recommended government agenda concentrates on a few areas only. We have attempted in the following sections to take a rather different view, to map the range of areas that **could** be developed professionally, considering these areas/domains in terms of the different roles that a teacher can play.

Different teacher roles

This range of roles was gleaned from conversations with teachers (both personal and in research projects) and from ideas put forward by educationists. The 12 roles identified are:

1. Communicator.
2. Subject expert.
3. Subject teacher.
4. Classroom manager.
5. Pastoral tutor.
6. Administrator.
7. Team member.
8. Manager of other teachers.
9. School member.
10. Representative of a department (year-group/school).
11. Researcher.
12. Deliverer of government policies.

It can be seen that some of these roles are just 'internal' as it were to oneself, although development here is likely also to have repercussions on others in the school (2 and 6); other roles focus on classroom interaction (1, 3, 4, 5, 7); others on functioning within the whole school context (1, 6, 7, 8, 9, 10, 12) and others outside this context (10, 12). The distinctions that will be made in Chapter 9 relating to 'vertical' and 'horizontal' responsibility may be useful to consider here, in thinking of the hierarchical relationships in the classroom or more 'equal' relationships with other adults. The different roles are likely also to entail different responsibilities.

The order in which the roles are presented here does not represent a hierarchy, since this would presuppose allocating greater value say to 'managing' over 'teaching'. Rather, the order represents a widening of the sphere of influence:

self ⇒ students/subject ⇒ systems management + ⇒ world outside school

There have been some attempts to see professional development in 'stages' and this book follows this model to some extent, focusing on the notion of increased responsibility (in terms of constituency). The Davison High School programme, for example, is a model which has received some attention in this connection (Haigh, 2002; Holmes, 2001) and is the first example of best practice shown in the CPD video issued by the DfES (2001a); their CPD programme consists of five stages which the school has devised for its own method of professional development (the 'Expert Trail'), where teachers are rewarded with extra pay after Stage 3. The trail runs as follows:

Stage 1   Concentrating on classroom practice and subject knowledge.
Stage 2   Developing these classroom skills further.
Stage 3   Managing a small team.
Stage 4   Managing a whole school initiative.
Stage 5   Acting as a consultant both inside and outside the school.

The framework chimes to some extent with our own 12-role framework and also with the government's initiatives, with Advanced Skills Teachers for example acting as disseminators (DfES, 2001c: 50).

Higgins and Leat (2001: 60) provide a different kind of mapping which they have evolved from conversations with students on a variety of pre-service and in-service courses at the University of Newcastle. They offer six different models of teacher development showing that conceptualizations overlap with each other to a greater or lesser degree. Their six models (expert/novice; craft knowledge; pedagogical knowledge; subject knowledge; reflection; personal (autobiographical); and socialization) overlap as shown in Figure 4.1.

Here the focus is on the **whole** conceptualization of development as well as domains, although the management roles of a teacher have been omitted altogether.

Day, in his overview of the possible in-service teaching models for Europe, warns against the dangers of a linear view of professional development popular with 'teacher educators, managers and policy makers and researchers… It may be … that conceptualizations of professional development as cyclical or as a linear continuum, although superficially attractive and plausible, are both over simplistic and impractical since they are not based on a teacher-as-person perspective but on a systems managerial perspective of teacher-as-employee' (1997: 40ff). Bates, Gough and Stammers, in their analysis of the impact of government initiatives on

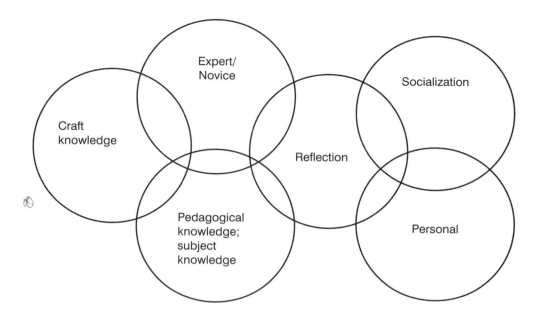

Figure 4.1 Models of teacher development (from Higgins and Leat, 2001: 60)

schools, echo this in their warning of the 'dangers inherent in a top-down national priority-driven, bureaucratically inflexible training structure' (1999: 324). Higgins and Leat (2001: 63) similarly emphasize the need to view the teacher as an individual and they, therefore, argue for a differentiated approach to professional development.

It can be helpful then to separate out different possible domains for development, taking into account that:

- not all teachers will need or want to develop all areas at a particular given time;
- the areas have a flat, horizontal relationship to each other rather than a hierarchical one;
- the areas overlap.

An important footnote here is not only **what** is developed but also **how** it is developed. Reed and Learmonth, writing from a perspective of school improvement, distinguish between 'deep' and 'shallow' school improvement: shallow improvement focusing on short-term quick fixes and deep improvement focusing on long-term learning and understanding (2001: 15ff). This distinction can usefully be transferred to thinking about the individual professional development of teachers. In other words, it can be helpful to think of professional development as a long-term process (as we mentioned in the Introduction) as well as seeing it as necessary interim re-skilling.

Role 1: communicator

This role underpins all of the other 11 roles identified, and perhaps is one that after initial teacher training and induction is assumed as automatically present in teachers. Certainly it may be a sensitive area to discuss in later professional development activities, since the way we communicate is part of our identity and may not easily be open to discussion or change (Morgan, 1998a).

Areas where good communication is vital include:

- teaching, helping and managing students;
- contact with colleagues;
- contact with parents;
- presentations of self or school to outside bodies.

'Good' communication could be described as being:

- clear;
- concise;
- sensitive to the audience;
- in the case of 'presentation', creating a positive impression.

Contact with students

In the role of subject teacher, explored in more detail below, the question of understanding the difficulties encountered by students has been raised. Poulson, in her research on the teaching of literacy in primary schools also comments on the importance of communicating well: '[Effective teachers] were able to present content to students and make conceptual connections between different aspects of language and texts. Their knowledge was functional' (2001: 45). Poulson, in fact, suggests in her article that good skills in communicating subject knowledge are more important than higher levels of subject knowledge itself. (These issues are explored in greater depth in the two sections below on Roles 2 and 3). It is also worth considering that year 7 may be a particularly difficult period for students to adjust to different communicative styles, with the more abstract language of subjects and different conventions of text and teaching styles (Morgan, 1999).

A further point to consider is sensitivity to students from different backgrounds who may have different conventions of speaking and behaving (Brice Heath, 1982). The government's initiatives with the Key Stage 3 strategy and with dealing with different groups of students is an indication that some of these problems areas have been recognized.

Contact with colleagues

In working with other colleagues, either in a team or in taking a more senior role, communication also needs to be clear and sensitive. Grace (2000: 241) in his analysis of the changes in the role of headteachers points to the need for good interpersonal skills, where leadership includes ethical as well as pragmatic considerations. As well as day-to-day contact, there will be occasions when matters need to be reported either verbally or in written form. A problem area here may be switching from the codes of classroom discourse (talking to students) to a discourse among equals and it may be helpful to think of exploring clear ways of communicating with colleagues. (This issue is explored in more depth in Role 10 below).

Contact with parents

Dislocation between schools and parents have been well documented (Crozier, 1999). Some of the problems here may be the kinds of language being used and the concepts which are taken for granted within the school community. Vincent (2001) points to the fact that terms used commonly within a school environment may have quite different meanings for parents. Parkin (2002b) in her report on parental support points out that 'Jargon is a killer for parents'. She also emphasizes the need for clear communication in letters home and the value of phoning home and even arranging a home visit.

Presentation to outside bodies

This last category differs somewhat from the others since here there is a question of presenting oneself or the school in the best possible light (in the event of an Ofsted inspection for example). It may be that outside help is brought in to help a school in this area (this is explored in more depth in Chapter 8) or in order to help 'market' the school effectively.

Although 'communication' is a somewhat nebulous area to explore, it may perhaps be one of the most crucial areas to develop, since it is the engine for many of the vehicles of delivery that are required of a teacher. It is also a domain that can be studied by all teachers in a school.

Role 2: subject expert

It is useful here to draw on two major surveys carried out by the NFER into CPD in schools: a review of LEA support for CPD, mentioned earlier (Brown, Edmunds and Lee, 2001) and a study of non-contact days (NCDs) (Harland *et al*, 1999).

Harland and his team found in their survey of primary middle, secondary and special schools (66 in all) that 'many teachers expressed a heartfelt wish for more time to immerse themselves thoroughly in developments within their own curriculum area, in order to extend their subject-oriented curriculum knowledge and skills' (1999: 133). Subject knowledge is seen as a key area of skills competence in initial teacher training (ITT) but may not always be an area which can be developed extensively at a later stage.

Schulman (1986) provides a useful explanation of the value of subject knowledge (which he terms 'content knowledge'). He distinguishes between 'substantive knowledge' (how the concepts and principles of a subject are internally organized); and 'syntactic structures' (how these concepts and principles belong together in a pattern). For example, he suggests: 'We expect the teacher to understand why a given topic is particularly central to a discipline, whereas another may be somewhat peripheral' (1986: 9).

There is also a difference here between primary and secondary level. Poulson comments on this difference in her analysis of subject versus subject teaching suggesting that the knowledge required to teach primary children effectively may not be the same as the knowledge of the same subject needed at advanced secondary school, or degree level. Poulson goes on to question the 'deficit model' of subject knowledge, 'teachers could not teach what they did not know' (2001: 44), and claims, as mentioned earlier, that the ability to **communicate** knowledge can be more important than higher levels of subject knowledge. Aubrey's study of mathematics teaching in primary schools shows that research in the US revealed **no** correlation between high levels of subject knowledge and achievement (1997).

Even if one accepts Poulson's conclusion that 'teaching a subject clearly' is more important than high levels of subject knowledge (explored in more depth in the next section), it seems understandable that there would be more concerns about subject knowledge at primary level where all subjects have to be covered, rather than at secondary level where teachers generally teach those disciplines they have studied already. If we look at the lists of topics chosen for CPD in surveys by Brown, Edmonds and Lee (2001) and Harland *et al* (1999) it is clear that there is a much greater focus on curriculum and subjects at primary level. In the study activities identified for internal CPD in the 18 case studies in the research by Brown, Edmonds and Lee, schools included the following:

Greater whole-school, subject/specialist focus:	8 (primary), 1 (secondary), 3 (special)
Practical suggestions:	2 (primary), 1 (secondary), 5 (special)
ICT training:	4 (primary), 1 (secondary), 5 (special)

(Brown, Edmonds and Lee, 2001: 88).

Here, then, there was much more focus on subject knowledge at primary level.

In Harland *et al*'s research, the two audits of the number of days spent on different activities in primary and secondary schools show a similar focus on curriculum at primary level: an allocation of 47 days for curriculum at primary level (22 days for English, 7 days Technology, 3.5 days Maths, 3 days Art, 2 days Science, 1 day Geography, ½ day History and PE) and 7.5 days on planning, ie 39.5 days on subjects (1999: 73). This compares with 11.5 days for curriculum issues (half subject, half teaching, no 'days' given here) at secondary level (1999: 70). There is clearly then a higher profile for subject-based CPD in primary schools, influenced of course by the introduction of the Literacy and Numeracy strategies.

The push for better ICT skills has also been part of the government agenda (as cited earlier) although surveys have shown that this has not been particularly successful. Canovan (2002b) reports that Ofsted has criticized NOF training as only enhancing 4 out of 10 schools undertaking the training. Reynolds (2002) also points to the fact that 'most teachers remain unconvinced of the potential of ICT', showing that statistics from 2001 reveal about 60 per cent of teachers not using and not believing in ICT.

There is, though, in some areas, subject-specific CPD taking place as revealed by the figures from Brown, Edmonds and Lee (2001) and Harland *et al* (1999) mentioned above. Beauchamp (1997) and Sekules, Tickles and Xanthoudak (1999) also report on CPD for primary teachers in the areas of art and music. They describe a 'museum experience' for teachers of art at the University of East Anglia with its Sainsbury Centre gallery. Teachers were asked to rethink their experience of art objects, and in so doing it was thought that they would be able to help students with their own aesthetic experiences. Beauchamp (1999) describes the use of taped illustrative music lessons as CPD materials, together with accompanying notes explaining musical terms and definitions.

Subject expertise represents an area where development is likely to have long-term benefits, contributing to the 'vision' and understanding valued by some educationists (Day, 1997). It may be that teachers will have to develop this aspect of their work privately. In secondary schools 'departmental' days could accommodate this area and in primary schools this could be the focus for whole-school training. Because the government's focus is just on selective areas of the curriculum, it may be, as indicated earlier, that tensions here between what teachers would like to do and what they have to do run fairly high.

Role 3: subject teacher

One of the most useful analyses to look at here is that of Schulman (1986) whose work, although it is now quite dated, is still seen as having made a major contribution to the field. Schulman differentiates between three areas of subject knowledge:

- content knowledge (the domain of the subject expert covered in the previous section);
- pedagogical content knowledge (knowing how to teach your subject);
- curriculum knowledge (being familiar with course materials).

All of these three areas may popularly be referred to as 'subject knowledge' (or curriculum).

When it comes to Schulman's second area – pedagogical content knowledge – he sub-divides this further into three areas:

- understanding what makes learning specific topics easy or difficult for students;
- knowing the conception of topics that students (of different ages) are likely to have;
- knowing effective teaching strategies (1986: 9–10).

It is interesting to note here that the understanding of common mistakes or conceptions is a teaching standard which has been dropped from the original list in the TTA's current list of ITT competencies (TTA/DfES, 2001). Banks, Leach and Moon add another interesting dimension, namely that of school knowledge: 'knowing the "school form" of your own subject, how it is interpreted at school level' (1999: 96).

Schulman, thus focuses on the deconstruction of a subject so that it can be transmitted in student-friendly form. Aubrey (1997) endorses this approach both by suggesting that teachers need to know how children build up their subject knowledge (here she is talking about Primary Mathematics), and also understanding that there can be useful recipes: 'classroom processes can be modified and systematized in a form which has utility for teachers' (1997: 16). The government certainly follows this line with their distribution of model lessons as recipes and formulae for teaching, for example the Literacy and Numeracy strategies.

In Harland *et al*'s analysis of non-contact days for CPD, a distinct preference was shown for training which was immediately relevant to teaching practice, in other words relevant to subject teaching: 'In secondary schools, there were many teachers who expressed a determined preference for "departmental" days/sessions because this was when they felt they really came to grips with "the nitty gritty" of teaching' (1999: 93, emphasis in the original). The internal CPD activities listed for primary schools in Brown, Edmonds and Lee's research cite eight demonstration lessons out of 30 activities (with no demonstrations at all for secondary schools (2001: 88). There appears, then, a clear need for help within subject teaching and to some extent this is being met, more it seems at primary than at secondary level. Interestingly, Harland and his team comment on this discrepancy as possibly affecting the measurability of impact in the classroom: 'the lack of opportunities for secondary school teachers to engage in individual practical activity may mean that direct impact on classroom practice is difficult to achieve' (1999: 4).

Locating effective teaching strategies though is only part of what Schulman suggests as helpful pedagogic content knowledge. He also focuses on understanding children's learning. Dadds (2001) points to the importance of avoiding just a recipe model for teaching and of focusing instead on the complexities of the teaching/learning process. She points out that 'learning can only come from the active inner life, moderation and resources of the learner' (2001: 55). Banks, Leach and Moon suggest that students' building up of knowledge may not directly align with the sequencing of knowledge in schools: 'generally learning is far from being linear' (1999: 93). Banks, Leach and Moon also criticize Schulman for not being wide-ranging enough in his concept of 'knowledge', since he views it as something static. Banks, Leach and Moon favour instead a more dynamic view of learning, which is regulated by the context. There could then be a place for CPD which focuses more strongly on learning development, either in general or within the context of particular subjects. Kerschner (1999: 423) notes that opportunities to do this are currently relatively rare.

Another dimension, which could be usefully included in subject-teaching CPD, is that of transforming knowledge into an applied form. Desforges and Lings explore the gap between knowledge and application in their study of learning in the context of the National Curriculum: 'examples of failure to apply skills and knowledge secured in one setting to another are evident in all areas of the curriculum' (1998: 387). They suggest that there is a real need for joined-up thinking which brings together different kinds of knowledge and which recognizes the complexity of the learning process. Here then is an area of subject knowledge where much deeper long-term investigation could be carried out. This domain of CPD may be useful to explore at either departmental or whole-school level, depending on the area chosen. 'Learning in general', for example, could be for the whole school.

Role 4: classroom manager

Harland *et al* (1999), as mentioned earlier, report that teachers preferred non-contact days (NCDs), which they see as directly relevant to improving their practice. In their survey 'provision in classroom management was conspicuously popular' (1999: 93). Given the rising tide of violence in schools and the difficulties with accommodating children from many different backgrounds, it is understandable that classroom management is high on the agenda (and indeed at pre-service level it is one of the main worries for trainees, Morgan and Neil, 2001). One of the teachers in Harland *et al*'s survey of 66 schools, comments: '[the training] gave us some very practical and specific strategies on how to cope with the behaviours and I find that very, very positive. And I think as a school, that was quite good; it made us think about what we were actually doing and what we could do to tackle the behaviour, especially the extreme behaviours' (1999: 123).

Ofsted, too, in its 1993–97 review comments that 'managing students' behaviour in the classroom should be a priority for in-service training' (1998b: 65). However, in Harland *et al*'s survey only five per cent of secondary schools actually included this on their training agenda (1999: 69). In Harland *et al*'s audit of NCDs, only 8.5 days out of 120.5 in secondary schools were dedicated to 'behaviour' (in comparison, for example, with 32 days dedicated to 'departmental issues' (1999: 70). In the audit of primary schools no time was specifically allocated to 'behaviour' as a CPD priority (1999: 73).

It is likely that CPD in this domain will be a whole school concern and that outside expertise may be valuable. There may be special organizations to help in this area, the LEA may provide training days and there is an excellent set of videos by Bill Rogers which is widely used in schools. Different sources for CPD activities are explored in greater depth in Chapter 5.

Role 5: pastoral tutor

In secondary schools, pastoral duties are part of a teacher's responsibility (and, of course, at primary level there is an automatic responsibility as a classroom teacher). Developing this dimension of a teacher's responsibility was seen in Harland *et al*'s research as having roughly the same importance as 'behaviour management': 8 days out of the 120.5 were reported in their audit of secondary schools (1999: 70) with no mention at all in the audit of primary schools (1999: 73).

As with 'behaviour management', it is likely that most of the kinds of topics that are included in pastoral tutoring will be supported best by outside speakers: drugs education/awareness; health education etc. This, too, is a domain which lends itself to whole school treatment.

Role 6: administrator

Teachers becoming good administrators is also of concern to the whole school. The previous chapter, which focused on time and systems management, has covered much of the ground for this domain and CPD could usefully be focused on some of these areas.

It may be that administration is an area where you will wish to develop strategies on your own, through private reading and trying out different administrative techniques. It may also be helpful for a school to bring in an outside expert in this domain to shed some light on a particular system or strategy.

It may also be the case that the headteacher wishes to introduce new administrative systems and that an NCD is used for informational purposes. This was certainly noted in Harland *et al*'s research: 'Many heads saw NCDs as a crucial management and communication tool' (1999: 4). However, there was some negative reaction to NCDs which focused only on information and these were felt less likely to have a positive impact on practice (1999: 7).

There is also some mention in Harland *et al* of 'administration' being a focus for NCDs. In their audits of primary and secondary schools, administrative issues appear in the category of 'Reorientation' days at the beginning of terms (27 days out of 120.5 in secondary and 20 out of 88 days for primary, 1999: 70, 73). Many other topics are also included in this category for both kinds of school.

Harland *et al* (1999) also report that NCDs are sometimes used as an opportunity for joint administrative work (course moderation for example). There were mixed views on the legitimacy of this (since it may be seen by some people as not qualifying as professional development of the administrative role of a teacher). Time constraints in the school year (mentioned in Chapter 3) are such that time earmarked for CPD may sometimes be used in this way for such administrative work. It may also be considered by some people that facilitating an opportunity for staff to be working on the same kind of administrative task together is indeed a kind of informal CPD.

Administration, then, is a key infrastructure process and it can be helpful for a school to have training together here.

Role 7: team member

Every teacher in a school will be working as a team member; either seen globally as a member of the school (dealt with in more detail below in Role 9) or on a more localized level as a member of a subject department (in secondary school) or a year group. CPD activities can be seen as contributing in two ways to this area/domain: with the **experience** of teachers working together as a team; or with individual CPD activities being **shared with** or **disseminated to** other colleagues.

Harland *et al*'s research on NCDs showed that having INSET days was valued as an experience for working collaboratively: 'the opportunity to work with colleagues on departmental issues was a highly valued aspect of NCDs' (1999: 71); 'NCDs allowed all staff to come together to work collectively and contribute their perspective to school level issues' (1999: 99).

John Clarke, head of English in a comprehensive school, cogently presents his view of the experience of being part of a team as follows: 'our training day was a success if, for no other reason than as a team, we had the opportunity to talk and plan with colleagues, share good practice and take decisions on how, together, we would continue to "make a difference". For teaching is a lonely business and as Auden almost said "what will survive of us is collegiality"' (Clarke, 2002).

This positive view of team working is also endorsed by teachers interviewed by Harland and his team, particularly because collegiality improved whole school coherence and provided better liaison across departments and year gaps: 'If we staff do not have time as a whole-staff to discuss together, then you cannot have a team, because we cannot have a common shared vision if we are not ever going to cohere'; '[CPD provided] a focus on that day, for the school to work together… on an issue outside the normal departmental, year group boundaries that people tend to work in' (1999: 100). Interviewees in the research by Brown and her team also voiced similar ideas, particularly teachers in secondary schools: 'In the secondary school, the focus tended to be on team building at departmental level and working within and across departments to develop ideas, not just cascading information' (2001: 89).

Providing time and space then in a busy timetable for members of teams (or the school team) can facilitate informal collegial CPD. It may be also that 'teaming up' with others for joint discussions is not just an internal affair. It can be helpful, for example, for secondary and primary schools to join forces for CPD activities, to help deal with the disjuncture that can occur between primary and secondary schools (Morgan, 1999). Marriott (2001) also describes a joint training day for school staff and governors, which 'helped to build bridges and shed light on each other's proper roles'.

Another possible CPD activity, which can relate to being a team member, is where an individual has undertaken some development work and then involves colleagues in some way. This may be in the form of presentation (which is explored in more detail in Role 10) or may be in the form of sharing and involving others. Miller, Smith and Tilstone (1998a) describe distance learning CPD projects at the University of Birmingham, which are based on just this notion: that other teachers can also benefit from a colleague's individual CPD. Miller, Smith and Tilstone suggest three benefits:

- personal benefits for the student;
- vicarious benefits for others;
- fresh perspectives on school problems.

Thus they comment: 'The opportunity to share the experience of the course with supportive colleagues was important and was identified by some students as a critical part of their learning' (1998a: 112). For the individual teacher then there were two levels of benefit: the initial CPD input and the extension of this through sharing the input with others. Other teachers benefiting can thus be seen as an add-on bonus: '[other teachers] suggested that people at work invariably benefit from their participation in the course' (Miller, Smith and Tilstone, 1998a: 112). The policy of deliberate involvement could also benefit the school: Miller, Smith and Tilstone explain as follows: 'to more explicitly gain support of colleagues than had previously been expected and to use this support in order to take a fresh look at specific aspects of the work of a school including policy and planning, curriculum content and teaching methods' (1998a: 114).

Miller, Smith and Tilstone (1998a) do, however, note that this intra-school collaboration does not always run as smoothly as imagined: some teachers may not have the time to be involved and others may be ambivalent about their role in the involvement. However, the process of sharing or cascading information can be seen as useful, not only pragmatically in terms of using available CPD but also developmentally in terms of the process itself benefiting the growth of team skills.

An endnote here is that schools might like to consider CPD activities focused on reflections on the process of team interaction itself. This is common practice in management training: identifying roles taken and successful strategies for working in teams. Here it would also be useful to bring in some outside expertise. The organization of CPD focused on 'being in a team' could take place as a whole school activity or be divided into subject or year-group teams.

Role 8: manager of other teachers

Training for management is not very likely to be a focus for training days in schools (there is only one mention in Harland et al's research on NCDs, 1999: 70). It is more likely to be part of training by the LEA or local university. NPQH is, of course, now statutory training for heads and the TTA has also produced National Standards for Subject Leaders (1998). In the 81 interviews in the 18 case studies in the research by Brown, Edmonds and Lee only 15 people mentioned CPD related to management or leadership as taking place in school (2001: 25). There may be a lower priority here than in some other areas, although running alongside this there is a high level of prescription from the government.

Harris et al point to the key role that subject leaders and team leaders play in influencing classroom practice (and thus the higher student achievement targeted by the government) and the lack of adequate support: 'there continues to be a lack of adequate and effective training for middle managers' (2001: 85). Middle managers are particularly likely to need training in appraisal and performance management (as mentioned in Chapter 2). Other aspects of management are also mentioned in Chapters 6 and 7 and will need support in terms of development.

Grace (2000) raises an interesting issue in his article on the role of headteachers in the current climate. He contrasts Educational Management Studies (EMS) with Critical Leadership Studies (CLS). The former he categorizes as those proscribed technicist courses (such as NPQH) which encourage headteachers 'to upgrade their management skills but also, more fundamentally, to enhance their relation to modern management culture' (2000: 234). Grace advocates instead a more pluralist humane ethical and emancipatory model (CLS), which would allow for democracy, morality and spirituality. He sees the new managerial discourse of schools fronting a revolution in values: 'Does the emergent "senior manager" of the new order of schooling imply the colonization of schools by marketing and management values?' (2000: 235). There may then be some tension between the prescribed CPD training required by the government and the broader remit of development that some managers may feel drawn to. (This tension is exactly paralleled in the sphere of ITT). CPD training for the management team in a school will by its very nature be selective and may well be most satisfactory if carried out offsite.

Role 9: school member

In Harland *et al*'s audits, school level issues featured as follows: in secondary schools 18.5 days out of 120.5 and in primary schools 9.5 days out of 88 (1999: 70, 73). There is, then, a reasonably high level of priority here, particularly at secondary level.

In Chapter 9 we will examine a possible tension between developmental areas, focused on **school** issues, and developmental areas targeted on **individual** priorities. This is precisely the tension that is picked up in the surveys by Brown, Edmonds and Lee (2001) and Harland *et al* (1999) in their interviews with teachers. Harland *et al* go even further and indicate a three way tension: 'Crucially there was evidence of two main levels of tension: between school needs and national or regional initiatives and, within the school, between "school level" needs and the needs of departments or individual staff' (1999: 5). If we add in the factor that national government initiatives are also likely to impact on the individual this gives us the three-way tension as shown in Figure 4.2.

Harland *et al* usefully summarize what they term 'the marked discrepancy in some schools between the priorities of teachers and those of senior management' (1999: 124). NCDs were seen differently: 'by SMTs in a long-term way focussing on policies and whole school cohesion, and by teachers in terms of direct improvement in their own practice (teaching/learning, classroom management, managerial and pastoral skills) and in terms of focussing on departmental team cohesion and development' (1999: 124–25).

It may be, however, that individual CPD **does** coincide with targets for school development, as will be explored in Chapter 6 and 7. Miller, Smith and Tilstone

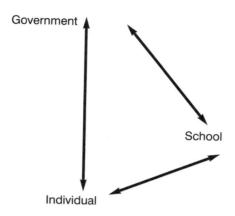

Figure 4.2 Competing priorities for CPD

(1998b) in their research with teachers on a distance education course saw some kind of congruence amongst their teachers: 'all the students believed that the courses would help them in their jobs [...] suggesting that they already saw their own development as part of school development' (1998b: 227). We have already mentioned earlier that individual teachers can provide benefit for others by sharing their CPD experiences, and this can also be seen as contributing to whole school development. Miller, Smith and Tilstone go even further and suggest that 'the greatest impact is generally reported when whole education authorities (LEAs) schools or groups in schools engage in activities, even where an individual is the identified student' (1998a: 112).

Bell (1991) makes a similar, positive comment about involving a whole school: he compares three possible types of CPD:

- an individualistic random model, just learning from other colleagues or courses;
- a school-based and school-focused model looking at specific groups or innovations;
- a school development/professional development model with a much broader policy base leading to greater coherence.

Ideas have moved on in the decade or more since Bell put forward his ideas, particularly in the area of school development. However, it is useful to consider the need to co-ordinate CPD, which is focused on small groups or problem areas within a school, with a broader overall school development plan (SDP).

There can be a place then for both individual issues and school issues in CPD with sometimes, but not always, overlap between the two.

Role 10: Representative

The areas where a teacher acts as a representative are generally those outside the classroom: in contact with other colleagues, with parents and with external agencies of various kinds. The skills needed here link closely to those identified in our first 'role': that of a communicator. Developmental activities can be seen perhaps in two different ways: having the **experience** of presenting (being a representative) to others and being **helped to prepare for interaction** with external agencies, where one is viewed as a representative of the school.

The experience of presenting/being a representative

From time to time individuals will be called upon to act on behalf of a group and to present information to others. In Brown, Edmonds and Lee's research with their 18 case study schools there was some feeling that this experience could be both beneficial and developmental: 'several primary school interviewees considered the process of leading the discussion group or reporting back to staff meetings to be part of their own professional development' (2001: 20). Clarke (2002), mentioned earlier, reports on his own experience of making a presentation on a whole school literacy programme to his colleagues. He sees this as 'a kind of teaching career rite of passage', with decisions having to be made about how to present (PowerPoint and an opening joke being currently popular). These experiences then provide an opportunity for 'learning by doing'.

Preparation for external interaction

The most powerful area of external interaction is that of external inspection. Here you will be judged not only as a person in your own right but also as a representative of the whole school. In Harland *et al*'s audit of NCDs, a proportion of these days were spent on preparing for Ofsted (7.5 out of 120.5 for secondary schools and 8 out of 88 for primary schools, 1999: 70, 73). In Chapter 8 this process is explored in greater detail, thinking not only of how schools need to prepare for inspection, but also of what kind of picture a school may wish to present of itself to an external agency. It may also be helpful in this context to think of interacting with parents, where one's actions are not only those of personal one-to-one interaction but can also be seen as representing the school. In this connection Brookes (2002a) gives some useful advice on coping with aggressive parents.

It seems then that opportunities for this kind of CPD do exist and are appreciated. Acting as a representative can be seen as a role for every teacher in some way and it may be helpful to widen opportunities here as far as possible.

Role 11: researcher

There are conflicting views about this role of the teacher: some (mainly university academics) view broad research as crucial and necessary; others favour only focused practical research (the TTA's *Best Practice Research* initiative, for example); and some in the teaching profession may see research as irrelevant.

Broad research

Many educationists celebrate the usefulness of research. Wikeley, for example, writing in the context of a personal learning planning project for students, comments as follows: 'feedback from the research enabled teachers, with the support of researchers, to reflect on their practice in such a way as to help them plan it more effectively. What it exposed was that some teachers needed time to reflect on the theoretical underpinnings of that practice' (2000: 107).

Kerschner (1999), Day (1997) and Sarland (2001) also concentrate on the notion of research being able to broaden and deepen perception. Kerschner sums up these benefits as follows: 'research can offer a practical way of seeing beyond what is commonly taken for granted in school life, and seeing with "new eyes" […] more widely […] and more deeply […] the processes underlying the surface observations of classroom life' (1999: 426). We hope, too, that the insights from research included in this book have provided some of these deeper and broader insights.

There are, though, some potentially problematic areas with broad theoretical research:

- The research needs time, which may not be readily available to teachers;
- The research may be more personally/privately oriented and thus not fall in with the more collegial kinds of role outlined earlier.
- Such research may be long term and not have the immediate short-term impact seen as crucial in government documentation;
- If the remit is broad, then by its very nature such research may not always fit neatly with specific classroom practice issues;

From one point of view, then, broad research can be seen as valuable, even though it may not immediately align with other current ways of thinking about professional development.

Focused classroom research

A *leitmotif* in government publications is the dissemination of good practice, both within schools and across schools. The contribution of focused research here can be seen with the TTA's award of funding of best practice research. There is pressure here for this research to demonstrably bring about improvement, and this is discussed in more detail in the following chapter.

Such research will be helpful to teachers nationwide who are often facing similar problem areas and constraints within which they work. However, in this area it should be remembered that the TTA has a controlling hand (Dadds, 1998). Only those projects which are approved will be funded. There is also an assumption that there are single best methods, which will fit all contexts.

Reluctance to do research

Hancock explores in some detail his view of why there is reluctance to carry out research in classrooms: 'my impression is that the great majority of classroom teachers shy away from seeing themselves as researchers and they are reluctant to write about their teaching practice' (2001: 119). He points to two main inhibiting factors: general public attitudes (an anti-intellectual and anti-professional stance); and teaching conditions: 'the teaching day has a very crowded skyline [...] teachers' working conditions militate against any activity that is not contributing to the "hands on" work with students' (2001: 122).

There are then clearly some quite different views of the role of research (and the role of the teacher or researcher). It may be helpful here to return to the multiple-model of views of teacher development offered by Higgins and Leat (2001) mentioned in the introduction to this section. Higgins and Leat see reflection as only **one** possible model of development. They point out that 'a reliance on reflective paradigms [...] can leave some teachers and student teachers frustrated by lack of guidance for action' (2001: 62). They argue strongly against a 'one-size-fits-all' approach: 'one approach to teacher development with a set agenda for what needs to be developed is clumsy in the extreme' (2001: 64).

Their championing of a differentiated approach could perhaps then also be transferred to this seemingly contentious area of the role of the teacher as a researcher. In other words different kinds of research (or none at all) may be suitable for different teachers. In Brown, Edmonds and Lee's list of special CPD projects being carried out in schools (2001: 109–15) there seems to be exactly this kind of spread of different types of project taking place.

Role 12: deliverer of government initiatives

It is clear from what has already been covered in this section that there are possible tensions between what schools need to do in terms of CPD in order to fulfil government requirements (as regulated by Ofsted), and between what they may wish to do themselves, although this may not always be the case. In the two surveys on CPD which we have mentioned this disjunction was experienced by many: 'the tension between implementing their own [schools'] priorities within a context of national level priorities is evident' (Harland et al, 1999: 4). Dadds also argues for an 'educative model to replace 'the "delivery" model of teaching [to prescribed external norms] which has characterized the implementation of national curriculum, national testing and school inspection' (2001: 50).

There is no easy answer to resolving this tension. However, as we see in Chapter 8, Ofsted and the government are moving towards a situation where schools' own agendas play a more significant role. It may be then that schools can choose options which more exactly fit their own needs and then be prepared to defend these choices.

Choosing domains for development

In outlining the different possible roles of the teacher in the previous section we hoped to outline a possible range of choices that a school may make in deciding on their own CPD programme. It is clear that there can be demands from different quarters that will make a difference to this choice (governmental, school, individual).

Two further issues might also be of interest in considering the choice of CPD: how a choice is made; and whether individual CPD activities belong together in any way. Harland et al (1999) explore both these issues in some depth so it can be useful to consider the responses from their 66 different schools (more than 100 interviewees). For many, success of a training day related to having had prior consultation with teachers, which they felt:

- increased the likelihood of relevance of topics;
- made teachers feel their opinions were valued;
- gave teachers some sense of ownership (1999: 25).

Consultation could be carried out by questionnaire, through the annual personal staff interview, or at staff meetings. Given the government recommendations that teachers take responsibility for their professional development, such consultation would seem to offer the opportunity for this.

As can be seen in Chapter 9, Brown, Edmonds and Lee's teacher interviews also indicate the value of personal involvement: 'CPD was seen as most effective when teachers were able to choose and direct their own professional development' (2001: iv). Higgins and Leat warn of the dangers of imposition: 'imposed development will be misinterpreted and at best subverted or, more likely, ignored or refused' (2001: 66).

There are clear messages here then about the usefulness of democratic decision-making in the setting up of CPD. Brace (2002) comments on the worth of this approach to CPD, which is currently being proposed in Wales. 'This element of personal choice makes the proposals... different from what already exists... [giving] individual training... [as] an entitlement'.

A further consideration is the overall cohesion of a CPD programme. Harland *et al* found that there was little overall planning for CPD programmes and little attention paid to the cumulative effect of different training activities: 'it would appear from the description of NCDs in this sample [more than 300] that the vast majority were "one-off" events' (1999: 78). There is obviously value in having some follow through with CPD activities, and this is explored in more detail in Chapter 5, but this may be difficult to reconcile with the other varying demands that surround the choice of CPD options.

Harland *et al* (1999) also consider the difficulties of reconciliation. It may be that in providing a diversity of activities, the overall purpose of CPD becomes less clear. They comment that 'where school and staff were at odds over the purpose of NCDs, it impacted negatively on individuals' views of the days' (1999: 5). They also conclude that wide differences in individual preferences mean that there will always be differing levels of satisfaction: 'This gives some indication of how difficult it could be to make NCDs appealing to all staff [...] individuals clearly had diverse expectations of the days and found most value in different types of NCDs' (1999: 115).

There can then be problems of choice on a macro level of deciding which domains of CPD to focus on, in terms of developing particular elements of a teacher's role (as indicated in our 12 roles); there can also be problems on a micro or personal level in terms of making choices which suit the cohort of teachers in any one school. It will also be worth considering that those CPD activities which attract funding and external support may not be the only ones which will be useful to your school.

Key points

- There are many different roles a teacher may play and CPD can relate to any of these.
- There may be tensions between different suggested priorities for CPD from different stakeholders: the government, the school and the teachers.
- Democratic decisions on the choice of CPD are likely to be successful.

Self study

Key questions

For the teacher:

- Which of the many roles that I play needs the most development?

For the CPD organizer:

- Is there a balance between school priorities and individual priorities in the choice of CPD training?
- Is there a balance between government-recommended priorities and our own school priorities in this choice?
- Does the CPD provision cover a range of teacher roles?

Recommended reading

Brown, S, Edmonds, S and Lee, B (2001) *Continuing Professional Development: LEA and school support for teachers*, LEA Research Report, 23, NFER, Slough

Harland, J *et al* (1999) *Thank You for the Days? How schools use their non-contact days*, NFER, Slough

Higgins, S and Leat, D (2001) Horses for courses or courses for horses; what is effective teacher development? in *Teacher Development: Exploring our own practice*, eds J Soler, A Craft and H Burgess, Paul Chapman in association with the Open University, London

5 Sources of professional development

Researchers who have investigated INSET/professional development have come up with varying taxonomies of providers (including who the provider is, where training/development takes place, what happens, and how long the development activity lasts). Thus, Day (1997: 47) talks of seven different kinds of support (short-burst courses, colleagueship, sharing practices, lighthouse [illuminative] experiences, external consultancy, external in-depth intensive courses and external long award bearing courses). Harland *et al* (1999: 26), in locating the provision of school training days, identify five sources (LEA advisers, external consultants, liaison with other schools, pyramid days [with feeder primary and secondary schools] and days jointly organized/funded with other schools). Brown, Edmonds and Lee (2001: 16) give two lists of possible providers given by two different groups in their research on INSET and the LEA. The LEA respondents named 13 providers (one-off conferences, seminars and workshops; non-accredited academic and professional programmes; in school training; action research; visits to other schools; networking forums, in-class support monitoring colleagues and observation). The school respondents answers are identical apart from also including 'mentoring colleagues'.

In the range of sources that we describe in this chapter we have tried to group together particular kinds of training, but also to cover as wide a range as possible of activities that could be deemed professional development (in the spirit of the 12 different roles outlined in the previous chapter). The sources we have identified are:

- private reading;
- private group research;
- in-school activities;
- outside activities in school;
- off-site courses;
- networking with other schools.

Two key features that could also be considered are the questions of coherence and value. Bell, early in the 1990s, comments on the plethora of providing agencies which makes for 'unsystematic and unplanned' provision (1991: 8). Harland *et al* also comment on the fragmented nature of training days with 'little long-term planning' (1999: 1). Ofsted have also criticized CPD courses for being 'uncoordinated, ineffective and poor value' (Canovan, 2002b). The government in its CPD Strategy Document also comments on fragmentation of CPD provision; 'The market for CPD provision is often fragmented and complex' (DfEE, 2001b: 13). But a much higher priority for the government is value for money. The Strategy Document continues: 'Schools get lots of approaches from would-be providers, but it is not easy for schools or teachers to be discerning consumers[sic]. We want to help with this, and also improve the quality and relevance of some of the courses provide[d]' (2001b: 13). To this end the code of practice for providers, *Good Value CPD* (DfEE, 2001a), was produced two months later (discussed in greater detail below). In the Ofsted HMCIS report for 2000/2001 the linking of value for money to higher student achievement is made clear by the following complaint about schools CPD activities: '[the] understanding of the need for financial accountability has not been accompanied by an equivalent insight into the effectiveness of the expenditure in terms of students' achievements' (2002a: section 366).

Perhaps the answer to both these questions (of coherence and value) lies in the located purpose of the professional development. If a school feels that its CPD programme should be seen as a neat and coherent plan that can present a unified picture to the outside world, then clearly planning coherence between individual CPD events is important. The reality, however, may be different. If individual or immediate needs are supported then these may form a more jumbled, less connected picture.

Similarly, with the question of value, the government appears to suggest that, as a centralized body, it can act as a consumer watchdog in terms of monitoring providers and providing recommended guidelines. However, it again depends on the needs of a school. If a school has identified CPD needs that fall outside the recommended priorities laid down by the DfEE, then clearly the value criteria will differ from those laid down in the Code of Practice.

Government regulations and recommendations

The government clearly privileges the knowledge that teachers can give to each other as *the* major source of professional development. In the CPD Strategy Document it makes this very evident:

> For many teachers their image of CPD is still of on-off events or short courses, often away from the school, of variable quality and relevance, delivered by a range of external providers […] But […] we believe there is real value in thinking **first** about creating opportunities within[… teachers'] own schools and through links with other schools, to learn from and with other effective colleagues. Many teachers already know that learning with and from each other and from the evidence of best practice is the most effective way to build their professional skills (DfEE, 2001b: 12, emphasis in the original).

In the nine videoed case studies provided as good examples of CPD by the government, there is universal emphasis on sharing practice within and between schools, either by observing or disseminating (DfES, 2001a).

The routes supported by the government for this teacher-led CPD are:

- Best Practice scholarships (funded);
- professional bursaries (funded);
- Advanced Skills Teachers (given enhanced pay);
- Beacon, specialist and training schools (given extra funding).

Through all four means teachers will be able to spread good practice between schools. The Strategy Document talks of schools and teachers being 'the core of **local and regional networks** for promoting good practice in professional development (2001b: 20, emphasis in the original).

With teachers presented as knowledgeable, there seems to be some idealization of teachers similar to the picture given by Sarland: 'the teacher is some sort of privileged individual without a history or an education or a culture or a set of values of his or her own, who is specifically untainted by the supposedly negative effect of educational theory' (2001: 182). Of course the Strategy Document does also recognize the value of external courses (2001: 12), and the sharing of good practice is without doubt extremely valuable. It does appear though that the scenario the government presents is rather one-sided and also may not entirely reflect the real situation. The scheme, for example, to use Advanced Skills teachers to disseminate skills is not happening according to a 2001 Ofsted report, with fewer than 1,000 such teachers in 2001, less than a tenth of the government's ultimate target (Howson, 2001; Ward, 2002a).

For the government, then, the number one source of professional development is other teachers, whether in teachers' own schools or from other schools. Where schools seek other providers, the DfEE has provided a code of practice, which in their words: 'will provide schools with a clear statement of what they are entitled to expect from external organizations… and guidance on how to secure it' (DfEE, 2001b: 14).

The status of the recommendations is not very clear in this code of practice. On the one hand there is a claim of optionality: 'This Code of Practice is intended to help both partners understand what can and should be expected from outside providers. It does not have the force of law though, of course, schools and providers may enter into a contract if they wish' (DfEE, 2001a: 1). On the other hand the recommendations are framed in absolute terms: 'The provider must put in place procedures whereby the school or individual, with the provider, can evaluate the extent to which provision has been successful in:

a)   improving the opportunities for students to succeed...
b)   meeting the needs of individual teachers including head teachers' (DfEE, 2001a: 1).

The logical outcome of this statement is that **all** CPD must ultimately be measured and seen to be measured in terms of improved student achievement. This is endorsed by Ofsted HMCIS's report for 2000/2001, where the following complaint was voiced: 'Because monitoring arrangements [of CPD activities] were haphazard in most schools, the impact of CPD activities on students' achievements was not widely defined and established' (2002: section 365). In the CPD video of nine exemplary case studies (DfES, 2001a), improvements in student outcomes is emphasized; however it should be noted that the CPD in six of these studies was **already** focused on improving classroom learning: using thinking skills (x 5) and improving mental maths (x 1). This then may conflict with developing some of the roles outlined in the previous chapter.

The Code of Practice does provide a useful checklist of practical organizational features, concerning planning materials, location, equal opportunities and evaluation, which may be helpful to schools when contemplating possible sources of CPD (DfEE, 2001a). However, the prevalence of directives ('must'... 'should'...) perhaps needs to be tempered by the knowledge that this is a set of recommendations only. There may be quite legitimate reasons for adopting different selection criteria and some of these are suggested in the sections below.

Funding possibilities

In Chapter 2, details of government funding schemes were presented. There are additional sources of funding, some of which are listed in this section. Hastings (2002b) in his helpful overview of sabbatical opportunities (significantly the first whole school issue to be presented in the new 'Teacher' supplement launched in the *Times Education Supplement* in April 2002) outlines a range of other funding available to teachers apart from the four schemes already mentioned. These are as follows:

- A range of fellowships for teachers of RE; Farmington Fellowship for one term's research at university (www.farmington.ac.uk).
- Keswick Hall grant (a.m.miller@uea.ac.uk); Hockerill Education Foundation grant (hockerill@surfaid.org); Culham Education Foundation grant (www.culham.ac.uk); All Saints Educational Trust (www.aset.org.uk).
- A range of grants/opportunities for science teachers: Free summer residential courses for science A level teachers at Goldsmiths (www.thegoldsmiths.co.uk); Nuffield Key Stage 2 or Key Stage 3 teacher £1,000 bursaries for travel research or industry visits (www.nuffieldfoundation.org); British Ecological Society grants of £750 for travel, research, or personal projects (www.britishecological-society.org/grants/research/index.php); Amanda Hess environment award for 2–6-day visits to environmental projects in the UK (www.earthwatch.org; Gatsby teacher fellowships of £2,000 to fund an organized project proposal (10 fellowships also for Maths and DT) plus £1,000 for personal use.
- Goldsmith's mid-career refreshment grants of £5,000.
- NASUWT teacher grants of £3,000–£5,000 to union members (telephone Patrick Roach 0121 4536150).
- NUT grants for pairs of teachers of £3,000 for research in thinking skills, run by the University of Newcastle (www.teachers.org.uk). An example of teachers doing such research is on the DfES CPD video (DfES, 2001a, Case Study 5).
- Centre for British Teachers funded projects (www.cfbt.com).
- Churchill fellowships for travel overseas for 4–8 weeks.
- Fellowship in Oxbridge colleges for one term (accommodation and food): Corpus Christi Oxford; St Peters Oxford; Corpus Christi Cambridge; Newnham, Cambridge; Robinson, Cambridge.
- Socrates Comenius 2 funding for European in-service training for languages, history, science, the arts, SEN and IT (www.socrates-uk.net).

Government provision of CPD

As well as funding opportunities for teachers to carry out their own research, the government has also funded its own training programmes and supported the provision of exemplary resource materials. Thus the CPD page in the TeacherNet section of the DfES Web site offers resources (lesson plans, case studies of professional development and of classroom practice and school self-evaluation models). Government sponsored courses for IT training under the New Opportunities Fund (NOF) have been offered by Research Machines. These finished in March 2002. New online courses from the same firm are planned to help English, Maths and Science to use technology better (Revell, 2002c). However, the quality of the NOF computer training has been criticized by Ofsted

(Canovan, 2002a), even though there has been some improvement since 2001 (Johnson, 2002). The National Literacy and Numeracy Strategies have set precedents here with their training and support as the Strategy Document points out (DfEE, 2001b: 26).

Suggested sources for professional development

As we mentioned earlier the sources we have identified are:

- private reading;
- private or group research;
- in-school activities in school;
- off-site courses;
- networking with other schools.

All these activities seem to be possible ways of developing oneself professionally whether this is on a personal or a school level. The different roles identified in the previous chapter may best be met by particular kinds of provision and this will be considered, as well as possible advantages and disadvantages of each type of development activity.

Private reading

As well as the government resources mentioned earlier there are also numerous useful publications available from QCA (www.qca.org.uk) and from the TTA (www.canteach.gov.uk) which teachers and mangers may find useful to access for themselves.

In terms of supporting one's role as a teacher tutor or manager (roles 4, 5, 6 and 8 – see Chapter 4) it may be useful to access relevant journals or books. The weekly *Times Educational Supplement* not only provides useful information on the latest events in the educational world but also contains articles on particular topics (like the one on sabbaticals mentioned earlier), and in their new weekly supplement ('Teacher') you'll find articles on particular teaching and activities, reviews of useful books and information about events.

In terms of keeping up to date with subject knowledge and subject pedagogy there are subject associations and journals which can provide valuable information and support. Some journals are available online and Web sites can also provide useful information, references and resources. The National Foundation for Educational Research (NFER) regularly publishes research related to educational matters (and we have made use of this in this book), and has a newsletter, *Topic News*, which is published biannually, giving updates. The NFER Web site will also be useful to contact here: www.nfer.ac.uk. The government has also launched a new initiative, the Evidence for Policy and Practice Institute (EPPI), which aims to review educational research and produce digests for those in schools (www.eppi.ioe.ac.uk). Reports on their first attempts, however, suggest a lack of concrete findings (Budge, 2002).

The advantages of using private reading as a source of professional development is that development can be targeted absolutely to personal needs; reading can be done at times to fit around other commitments (providing some time is available or is made available) and it need not be costly (if reading materials are obtained online or from libraries).

Disadvantages are that it may be difficult to engage with the reading material without interaction with other people (depending on your personality). It may also be difficult to locate worthwhile sources. O'Hara and O'Hara for example warn against the unreliability of Internet sources where 'the lack of editorial control means that the quality and suitability of material can vary widely' (2001: 65). Foster (1999) in his evaluation of TTA funded research projects in 1996 (16 out of 25 research reports were evaluated) found that research claims often lacked supporting evidence and that there were often problems with clarity of presentation. His conclusion based on this set of projects was one which raised queries: 'it raises doubts about whether shifting funds into teacher-research of the type supported by the TTA would result in an increase in the quality of education research or facilitate the cumulative development of public knowledge about educational practice. Indeed, I think it might well have the opposite effect' (1999: 395). It is hoped that new procedures for the BPRS with close mentoring and evaluation will overcome the problems identified here. Ward (2002b), however, also reports on some concern that using ready-made lessons from government lesson plans (in primary Maths) is killing creativity.

As well as problems identifying valid or useful research, there may also be practical problems in accessing reading material. You may not live near a library (public, college or university) which will have suitable reading material. Even if you do, the libraries themselves may not be user-friendly either in terms of accessing systems or borrowing facilities. However, it is worth persevering here if possible, since in many ways private reading is the cheapest and easiest (if loneliest) form of professional development.

Private or group research

Private or group research will also, of course, involve private reading but here there is much more focus and structured post-reading activity. Doing research can perhaps be divided into three different activities:

- doing personal research on your own;
- doing personal research with guidance/collaboration;
- doing group research.

Personal research on your own

If you carry out research on your own this can be tailored to your own needs (in much the same way as private reading). Tricoglus (2001) provides a very useful protocol for researchers on their own (she writes as a deputy head looking at primary teachers' planning). Her nine-element protocol is as follows:

1. Establish the purpose of your research.
2. Establish the theoretical basis.
3. Know the context.
4. Seek to understand the world from the view of the participants.
5. Know the data.
6. Know yourself.
7. Make the process dialogical (ie talk to your participants).
8. Remain focused on the contradictions.
9. Stimulate a process of continuing critical analysis and enlightened action (2001: 143–48).

Tricoglus sees the value of doing research as relating to authenticity. She comments on the current teaching context: 'Teachers work with increasing prescription of both curricula and pedagogy, but nevertheless strive to maintain their individual identity and values by finding ways to be authentic' (2001: 146). For her, then, private research meets this personal need. Other advantages of research are not only encountering new ideas but also trying these out. This may be in the form of investigating particular situations, others' practice or analysing your own practice in action research.

Ruth Kerschner (1999) sees a similar benefit (in her study of the Effective Learning Project in 30 primary and secondary schools in the Cambridge area). For Kerschner it is a question of ownership: 'Personal research by teachers in school and classroom contexts will help them to gain a sense of ownership of changes in policy and practice and there is then more likelihood that findings will be used effectively' (1999: 438).

There can be, though, a downside to doing research on your own. As with private reading it can be difficult sometimes to operate in isolation. Convery (1998) comments on the difficulties he encountered when doing Action Research. For him there were some difficulties with academic rhetoric. Action Research literature often quotes Schön`s model which differentiates between 'reflection-*in*-action' (thinking and reacting as you are teaching) and 'reflection-*on*-action (thinking afterwards). For Convery 'such categories were not helpful for improving my understanding of classroom decision-making or the planning of sessions' (1998: 197). For him there was never the time for retrospection, but only for 'reflection-*in*-action'. In addition Convery felt the need for outside support. He realized in his own research that he had failed to consider vital aspects (the external contexts of his adult learners) because of his own personal interest in creating situations for these learners to be independent within the classroom. He realized that his personal bias had distorted his enquiry, but that an external observer might have noticed this and have helped him. The external voice might help teachers to come to terms with aspects of their own practice that they might find difficult to acknowledge if they were only working on their own:

> individual teachers are unlikely to make essential changes to their practice if they are not supported and guided through the reflective process [...] for constructive self-critical reflection, teachers need to believe they have the support of others who will sufficiently respect the integrity of their enquiry to enable awkward and uncomfortable self-revelations to be identified (1998: 202–03).

Private research with external support

In Chapter 4 when mentioning the role of the teacher as researcher (role 11) several examples were given of teachers being supported by 'critical friends' at universities. It is common for teachers to consider doing action research (where they evaluate their own practice), and guidance from an external source can be helpful (as Convery noted in the example mentioned earlier).

In the government BPRS scheme a tutor/mentor is a requirement. In the Guidance Document (DfES, 2002a) the government suggest the following: 'A tutor/mentor from higher education of another appropriate organization should support and monitor your research. They should help to critically evaluate the reliability, validity of your findings and support you in writing and disseminating your research report' (2002a: section 11). It is also suggested that tutor/mentors can be found elsewhere (professional associations, subject associations, LEAs research bodies, EiC partnerships, EAZ co-ordinators).

McNiff (1988) describes two Action Research case studies in her book on action research, which may be helpful to read to see what others have done. She also provides some practical suggestions for setting out (start small; plan carefully; set a realistic timescale; involve others; keep others informed; arrange for feedback; organize a writing schedule (1988: 67–71). This, again, is helpful advice.

One potential problem of private research (whether this is with or without external support) is that the teacher, as a researcher (role 11), may explore areas that run counter to school priorities. Elliott (1991) for example, cites an example of a teacher inviting criticisms from students, which was seen in her school as undermining the professional status of all the staff. Here there was a conflict for the teacher–researcher 'between the value of critical openness to students and respect for the professional expertise of colleagues' (2000: 59). It may also be that an area prioritized for research 'does not always have a neat application to classroom practice' (Wikeley, 2000: 97).

Private research, then, can not only enhance development of teachers in their roles as researchers but can focus on teaching or management (Roles 3, 4, 6 and 8). The advantage of external support is that a further critical dimension can be added.

Group research

Research can also be carried out with groups working together. The BPRS scheme, for example, suggests that teachers can apply as a group if they intend to set up collaborative or networked research. (In this case they suggest a co-ordinating organization and a group co-ordinator).

Wilkins (2000) as the Director of Education in an LEA saw setting up group research as a way of overcoming 'a legacy of serious underachievement' in his LEA. Here 11 separate research projects (seven in schools, three in FE colleges and two in the LEA) were set up and supported by the local university and business school. Although there were separate topics there was a general theme (evaluating the input of the LEA). Wilkins saw real advantages in a group approach: 'There was sufficient critical mass to drive forward real changes in professional practice and LEA policy to provide stronger mutual support and to create a team of practitioners able to contribute to staff development programmes on a chosen theme' (2000: 103). For Wilkins, too, there was advantage in using an action research approach, in that this involved intervention (part of the research cycle being to try out new ways of doing something) as opposed to 'most forms of conventional research [which] observe but do not interfere' (Wilkins, 2000: 105).

Another advantage of working in a group is that you may then feel confident enough to challenge some of the traditional conventions of research if these do not fit in with the reality of your experience. Cook (1998), working in a project team considering the effect of action research on organizations (as well as working privately on her own research on parents of special needs children), found that this was the case with her group. Her own experience had been that her research was not as 'neat' as that found in the action research literature. Being in the group meant that she was able to identify with others' experience which matched her own: 'We all had images of AR [Action Research] that we felt we were not "living up to"' (1998: 96). The group members also jointly recognized that there was both a need to have some models to help structure research and also a need to break away from these models (in recognizing, for example, the necessary *messy, creative* stage in doing research).

Another advantage noted by Robertson (2000), in a New Zealand context, where a group of headteachers undertook action research together, was that sharing insights provided a wider perspective: 'As these principals came together they were immediately challenged by the many perspectives on educational issues that were made available at the full group sessions because of the diverse nature of this group. They realized how insular and isolated they had all become in their schools' (2000: 322).

Clearly the remit of group research means that the roles of teachers as a team member (role 7) and a school member (role 9) can be enhanced in two ways: by being part of the research team and benefiting from that collaboration; and by being able to focus on whole school/group problems, bringing different perspectives to bear. A disadvantage of group research can be that personal priorities may be swallowed up by the focus on a whole school issue.

In-school training

We have already seen that this is an option highly favoured by the government and, indeed, there can be many benefits here. Harland *et al*, in their investigation of school training days found that 'input led by a member of the school staff was said to have the advantage that it could be tailored exactly to the needs of the school' (1999: 107). There could also be more chance of follow-up within the school. Here, then, the role of the teacher as school member (role 9) is particularly supported.

In addition, actually running the session, although it will involve extra work, is likely to function as professional development. The experience of Clarke (2002), mentioned in Chapter 4, provides a good example of this.

There can also be the chance on school training days for departments to focus on their own separate priorities (Harland *et al*, 1999: 76). Certainly, as was noted in Chapter 4, Harland *et al* found that in secondary schools there were many teachers who expressed a determined preference for 'departmental' day sessions because this was when they felt they really came to grips with the 'nitty gritty' of teaching (1999: 93).

Internally organized CPD need not just take the form of training days. Colleagues may also support each other in the classroom and of course do so informally in many ways. Beauchamp, in the context of improving music teaching in primary schools, notes this with the presence of a supportive colleague in the classroom: 'The presence of a specialist is a resource which is likely to be used and hence may help to improve music teaching' (1997: 210).

Advantages then of organizing CPD within school is that it is inexpensive; it can focus on the particular and understood needs of the school; sessions can be timed to fit in with school requirements (for example Harland *et al* cite arrangements where equivalent twilight sessions then enable teachers to have a 'training day' off); it can create a good team spirit within the school; and it can also serve as an opportunity for training responsibility for some members of staff. Disadvantages can be that the range of expertise within a school may be limited and that sharing information with professional peers within a school can bring out latent conflicts and tensions (Elliott, 1991: 61).

Inviting experts into the school

One way of overcoming limited experience in a school is to invite in 'experts' from outside. We have already seen that government directions warn against variable provision here and have provided a checklist to help locate and regulate suitable providers (DfEE, 2001a). Their code of practice does recognize the need for 'the teachers and the school... [to] often seek the advice and expertise of outside agencies and quotes these agencies as commercial bodies, local authorities and professional associations' (DfEE, 2001a). The given order of these providers suggests some privileging of private over public agencies.

Harland *et al*'s research suggests that schools see outside speakers as being able to boost teachers' confidence and to improve their skills and knowledge in different areas as well as being able to inspire and motivate (1999: 97). Clearly the question of cost effectiveness comes to the fore in larger schools. An example of bringing outsiders in is the IBISS scheme (Improving Behaviour in Secondary Schools), which operates in the Bristol area. Here teachers and psychologists with proven expertise in managing classroom behaviour come into a school and work either alongside teachers in the classroom or with the SMT or with teachers individually.

Clearly bringing in outside speakers can help to support any of the teachers' roles, not just that of the classroom manager (role 4) as cited here. It is more likely though that the issues covered will be of whole school concern in the interests of economy of scale. Fidler and Atton also note that 'on-site corporate training such as INSET days, can have an advantage in terms of exposing all staff to the same stimulus and also for team building' (1999: 22).

It may be though that an outside speaker is unsatisfactory. Harland *et al* describe the possible frustration that this may cause: 'a poor or patronising speaker could anger staff and lead them to question both the merit and worth of these [training] days' (1999: 97). Carnell and Lodge, in their analysis of support for teachers' learning, also comment on an undesirable passive–didactic model of professional development, which relies on external expertise and one-off training events (2002: 126), preferring instead active involvement of teachers in their own development. The schools in Harland *et al*'s research also emphasized the need for a speaker to be 'classroom aware' (1999: 107).

There needs, then, to be careful planning of how the time with an outside speaker will be spent in school, ensuring that the topics covered really relate to the school's need and that there is sufficient participation in the activities planned for the school staff to feel involved and to voice their ideas. Here the government's code of practice has some useful suggestions: joint decisions (provider and school) on the development activities, after a needs analysis by the school and identification of outcomes; any details from the provider about who will deliver the course, the rationale supporting the input, details of the activities and charges (DfEE, 2001a: 2–3). The 'criteria for success' relating directly to 'improving the opportunities for students to succeed' however, as mentioned earlier, may not always be seen as relevant to every kind of development activity.

Another aspect that needs to be considered when bringing in an outside speaker is the question of cost. A headteacher in an 'excellent' Ofsted-rated school in Preston, for example, hired a team of management consultants (with prices starting at £4,000) to help with team-building skills (Clancy, 2002). Costs will need to be weighed against budgets although here arranging for speakers in joint school ventures may also be a helpful ploy to consider.

Off-site courses

These courses can take two forms: either where members of staff physically/geographically move location; or where a course is run at a distance but transmitted (electronically or by other means) to the participants.

Geographically distant courses

Two features of courses geographically located off-site may make a particular impact: being physically away from the school building may make a difference; course participants are likely to meet up with teachers from other schools.

Bubb and Hoare comment on the time to reflect that is afforded by a break from school (2001: 112). Day talks of a university environment as being 'far removed from the press of school and classroom life' (1997: 44), where, perhaps, some critical distance may be possible. In Harland *et al*'s research on training days it was found that 'evaluations indicated that teachers welcomed the opportunity to train in different environments (eg hotels, teachers' centres) and saw these as valuable experiences. Some maintained that an off-site venue raised the status of these days' (1999: 3).

There can then be real advantages in physically relocating. However, there are also disadvantages. The distance of the location can also mean 'distance' in terms of topic and approach. Bell notes that university courses may be too theoretical and 'based on what the [university] staff ... could and would provide, rather than on any considered analysis of the needs of teachers and their schools' (1991: 6). He also believes that a demand for expertise may be artificially created: 'Courses of this type tend to emphasise the expertise of those outside schools and to deny the legitimacy of the teacher-as-expert. This is almost inevitable and has the spin-off of perpetuating the demand for courses in spite of these often being a mismatch between the needs of teachers and/or their schools and the content of the courses' (1991: 8). Atkinson comments on the possible inappropriateness of language in an off-site course, thinking in particular of her own Masters course in educational management: 'Many participants may have felt alienated by the language [of] management theorists, particularly where it mirrors Ofsted language, which is seen as disempowering teachers' (2000: 468). Bubb and Hoare (2001) also note some other disadvantages including teachers becoming envious of practice in other schools and the practical problems of several teachers being out of school at once and problems associated with travel.

Courses transmitted from a distance

Some of the problems of geographically distant courses may be overcome by teachers using distance learning courses. In the government's code of practice, favourable mention is made of 'new methods such as problem solving groups and consultancies[,] ICT and distance learning [which] are increasingly being used' (DfEE, 2001a: 1). Parkin (2002a) particularly recommends distance learning courses, such as those offered by the Open University (www.open.ac.uk) and NPQH by the National College of School Leadership (www.ncsl.gov.uk) because of their flexibility: 'Teachers need flexible study hours because school and college terms coincide'.

Comiskey and Buckle, in their analysis of Open College courses, point out further advantages: 'improving access for disadvantaged groups ... as well as removal of barriers of price, time and place for all learners' (1996: 56). Teachers in their research particularly welcomed personal contact which was still possible: 'someone with expertise at the end of a telephone' (1996: 62).

Miller, Smith and Tilstone also comment on the usefulness of learning at a distance in that theory can immediately be put into action: 'Activities in course materials can be tried out in daily work and adapted to the needs of a particular context' (1998b: 244). Their own CPD distance-learning course (at the University of Birmingham) uses written/recorded materials, radio, TV, telephone and electronic forms of communication.

However, it may be that distance learning is not ideal for all. Comiskey and Buckle found in their survey of 25 teachers using Open College materials that 'several respondents would have liked more direct face-to-face "instruction" or looked to a return to more conventional "one off" courses' (1996: 62).

Off-site courses thus can provide extra expertise (whether they are geographically distant or are transmitted from a distance) but they may not be a favoured option for all.

Networked learning

Another favourite form of CPD prioritized in government recommendations is the sharing of good practice across schools. In their Strategy Document they also recommend the TTA funded School-Based Research Consortia or professional learning teams where teachers jointly analyse specific lessons, approaches to teaching and learning and students' work (DfEE, 2001b: 12). In the DfES video of nine exemplary case studies (DfES, 2001a) three schools mention working in consortia: case studies 4, 6 and 7.

Abdelnoor (2001) also comments on other forms of 'inter-school co-training [… such as] exchange, coaching and work shadowing'. This sharing could also be extended beyond schools: 'Teachers would share knowledge and skills with parents and paraprofessionals acting as co-trackers with separate, parallel roles'.

The networking activities described in Chapter 3 can also be identified as contributing to this kind of CPD. Holloway and Long (1998) comment on a similar network initiative, their 'shared practice group', where a small number of primary school teachers meet to discuss classroom activities, with an elected facilitator. In their view 'such groups offer a "safe house" where professionals can, indeed, be professionals, a space where they can respect themselves and each other' (1998: 539). Such forums in their view allow for the development of 'collective understandings' (1998: 543).

Melrose and Reed (2000), in a New Zealand context, suggest a particular kind of networking system: their 'Daisy Model' which has a central core group of members, each of whom heads up a 'petal' group. This means that while there is continuity within the core group, sub-groups or 'petals' can 'be discontinued or added to according to the progress of the project' (2000: 163). Such a flexible mould is clearly helpful in terms of coping with changing personnel and sudden demands from an organization.

Teachers networking by telephone or online have already been mentioned in Chapter 3. Ginns *et al* (2001) describe a network of beginning teachers doing action research in Australia who keep in touch by telephone and e-mail in order to 'enhance their professional growth during the first year of teaching' (2001: 112). Lloyd and Draper (1998) also cite a collaborative online community of five schools who exchange information and action-based research in the Learning Interactively at a Distance (LID) project. Such a network they believe establishes collaborating communities.

However, as was noticed in the earlier comments on distance learning, such network communication may not suit everyone. Lloyd and Draper, perhaps rather naively, assume a common delight in computers: 'Technology can be enticing, computers offer a sense of engagement, romance and excitement for some teachers' (1998: 89). 'Some' here is an important caveat. Ginns *et al* (2001), in their Australian context, note that while some teachers are pleased to be part of the network because they are working in isolated regions, others may not have access to e-mail or may not have developed what they term 'e-mail' awareness.

Clearly then there are many different sources of professional development to choose from. Some fall in line with and attract government funding. Many can be used to support all 12 roles of the teacher identified earlier, while others may have more restricted use. There are disadvantages and advantages associated with each type of source, and schools and teachers will need to consider both the purpose of the development activity and the contextual factors at any one particular time in order to make effective judicious choices.

Key points

- Funding is available for CPD but this is in limited areas.
- CPD can be organized in private, within the school, or with contacts outside the school.
- Contact may be face to face or online.

Self study

Key questions

- Has the whole range of sources for CPD been considered?
- What kind of source would best accommodate the identified CPD needs?
- Does an identified source offer 'value for money', not just in government terms of impacting on student achievement, but also in terms of being appropriately organized?

Part III

Preparing for leadership

6 Middle management: the subject leader

Billy McClune

Having come through induction, completed a programme of EPD, and built up a CPD portfolio, some teachers will want to apply for what is commonly referred to as a middle management post in the school. This could be as a head of department in a post-primary school, or a curriculum leader or Key Stage co-ordinator at primary level. The position of department head in secondary education is a well established one. It is a position of responsibility which traditionally focused on the expertise of the subject specialist. In the past it was sometimes seen as a reward for dedication and loyalty, a position which had status and prestige (Marland, 1971). In recent years however, much has changed in schools. Management structures have developed and with them the expectations and responsibilities associated with the role of the head of department have increased. As is often the case in a changing environment, there are those who have found themselves ill equipped and perhaps unsuited for a role in which they were cast (Jones and Sparkes, 1997). The aim of this chapter is to provide an overview of the role of the head of department which will be useful to those who want to prepare themselves for middle management, and to map out their own goals and training needs. Equally it will be relevant to those who are assessing the challenges of a role to which they have recently been appointed. It is hoped however that it will be of value also to more experienced practitioners who wish to review their own performance in this area, helping them to play a role in supporting the professional development of teachers within the department and also informing their own professional development needs. Many of the issues raised will apply equally to those who are heads of Key Stages or departments or curriculum leaders in the primary sector or in special schools.

This chapter should be viewed as a starting point; a first step in subject leadership or a guide to reflective practice enabling individuals to equip themselves better for a middle management role. As such it is not a manual for the head of department but rather a guide from which to start the exploration of a challenging, rewarding and fundamentally important role in the management learning in school.

The role of the middle manager in school has become more clearly defined. As if to emphasize a new order, the terms 'subject leader' or 'subject manager' have replaced that of head of department in many schools. Within the context of this chapter the terms 'head of department' and 'subject leader' will be used interchangeably as generic terms.

The chapter is divided into six broad sections. In the first section, the government recommendations in the form of the Standards for Subject Leaders are examined. The section 'Reference points from the literature' then provides an overview of the some of the themes emerging from relevant middle management and research documents. 'Thinking through the role' is an opportunity to develop a framework within which individuals can explore their own experience. Heads of department must understand the task that they are trying to achieve and the constraints within which they work. The sections on 'Responsibilities of the role' and 'Taking on the role' deal with the key tasks of the head of department role. This section highlights some indicators of both effective and ineffective practice. 'Self awareness' presents an opportunity for self-examination against a pattern of the personal skills and attributes which contribute to effective management of the subject department in the secondary school.

Government regulations

The introduction in 1998 of National Standards for Subject Leaders (TTA, 1998) was one more stage in the recognition of the important role of the subject leader in the life of the school and in ensuring continuity in curriculum provision.

National Standards for subject leaders

Leadership within schools has been under scrutiny in recent years. School improvement has been linked with high standards of leadership at all levels. The Teacher Training Agency (TTA), as authors of the National Standards, expect that the standards will provide a basis for professional recognition. It has been suggested that they may provide for a structured approach to appraisal. They should also be influential in setting targets, helping subject leaders to develop priorities and evaluate progress. In addition these standards could be used to confirm and celebrate success.

By setting out, in a structured way, the basis of professional knowledge and understanding, and the skills and attributes needed by the subject leader, it is important to note that it is the sum of these aspects that defines the expertise demanded of the role. They should not be seen simply as a checklist. They do highlight areas and issues that are important. They do not, however, prioritize nor do they exemplify the principles. National standards need to be interpreted in the context of the school and indeed the subject area.

The National Standards are set out in five parts:

- Core purpose of the subject leader.
- Key outcomes of subject leadership.
- Professional knowledge and understanding.
- Skills and attributes.
- Key areas of subject leadership.

These standards address the knowledge, understanding, skills and attributes that underpin effective subject leadership. The standards set out to: 'define expertise in subject leadership and are designed to guide professional development of teachers' (TTA, 1998: 3). Each of the areas is explained below:

- *Core purpose* provides a definition of purpose that focuses on the role of leadership in student achievement and improving standards both by influencing the quality of teaching and also by securing the effective use of resources.
- *Key outcomes of subject leadership* focuses on results. This section highlights how students, teachers, parents, senior management and the wider school community benefit from effective departmental leadership. The head of department has the potential to influence not only the student's experience of the subject but also the opportunity for parents' effective involvement in and support for their child's learning. The subject leader influences to some degree the classroom practice, working environment and ongoing professional development of teachers within the department. Senior management, in its decision-making role, depends on the head of department to communicate the needs, plans, and priorities of the department effectively.
- *Professional knowledge and understanding* addresses many of the issues common to leadership roles in school, irrespective of the subject area. It provides an opportunity for subject leaders to review their knowledge of key areas and to reflect on their understanding of important issues.
- *Skills and attributes* highlights the leadership, decision making, communication and self management skills which will support the head of department to fulfil his or her role. There is recognition that individuals may need training to

acquire some of these skills, however, for all subject leaders the path of professional development should lead to the development of skills through experience. Skills are not acquired or used in a vacuum and this part highlights the
need for subject leaders to draw on personal qualities to effectively fulfil their
leadership and management roles. Subject leader expertise is demonstrated by
the ability to apply these skills and attributes to the key areas of subject leadership' (TTA, 1998: 7).

- *Key areas of subject leadership* sets out the leadership and management tasks in
  each of four key areas:
  – strategic direction and development of the subject;
  – teaching and learning;
  – leading and managing staff;
  – efficient and effective development of staff and resources.

Within each of these areas are listed the individual tasks which describe many of
the head of department responsibilities. The role of the head of department is,
however, more than the sum of the individual tasks. Subject leadership is complex
and many tasks overlap. The head of department must apply professional
knowledge and understanding, as well as skills and attributes, to bring about the
desired outcomes.

We try to analyse further the National Standards under three themes: expectations, intellectual and personal qualities and areas of leadership.

Expectations

Parts 1 and 2 of the National Standards focus on what the subject leader is seeking
to achieve. The core purpose (Part 1) and key outcomes of leadership (Part 2) offer a
vision of subject leadership. Within the scope of the school and subject aims, the
head of department is required to be both leader and manager. Ensuring effective
use of resources, for example, requires good management. Guiding and motivating
teaching and non-teaching staff is, in the context of a subject department, more of a
leadership than a management task. The goal of leadership, according to the
National Standards, is to secure high quality teaching and improved learning and
achievement. The Standards promote a model of peer evaluation in which the head
of department takes a lead. Within the guidelines, target setting and monitoring
progress is followed by evaluation of teaching. There are often sensitive issues here.
It is perhaps not as unproblematic as might appear from the National Standards.
The extent to which any individual head of department exercises that role within
the department owes much not only to their own skill and relationship with
colleagues but also to the prevailing circumstances in school. The area of
performance management and appraisal is dealt with in more detail in Chapter 9.
Irrespective of how the formal appraisal scheme operates in school, reviewing,

assessing and evaluating the work of the department are core tasks for the subject leader. There are many informal ways in which the head of department observes and evaluates the work of the department and those within it. It is expected that the head of department will have a vision and sense of purpose for the department. It is inevitable that plans will be proposed, and developments initiated arising out of the informal observations, interpretations and judgements that the head of department makes.

Intellectual and personal qualities

Parts 3 and 4 of the standards provide a checklist of the intellectual and personal qualities that the subject leader needs in order to be effective in the role. These are set out in terms of the professional knowledge and understanding (Part 3) and, skills and attributes (Part 4) which are expected of the subject leader.

While all members of the department may be expected to have a sound knowledge of the subject and its place within the curriculum, it is to the head of department that others will look for advice and guidance. The head of department is expected to be confident in dealing with questions relating, for example, to assessment and reporting. He or she should be aware of issues such as the integration of ICT within the subject area and should be engaging with the developments relating to research evidence. It is also expected that the head of department will keep up to date with changes in policy, new emphasis and guidance emerging from local and national developments, for example issues arising from codes of practice in relation to special educational needs. As a manager it is proposed that the head of department is also expected to have knowledge of questions relating to employment law as well as health and safety related issues.

Skills expected of the head of department are listed under the headings leadership, decision making, communication and self-management, as outlined below:

- *Leadership*: the ability to lead and manage people to work towards a common goal;
- *Decision making*: the ability to solve problems and make decisions;
- *Communication*: the ability to make points clearly and to understand the views of others;
- *Self management*: the ability to plan time effectively and to organize oneself well (TTA, 1998: 7, 8).

These skills are used to highlight what the head of department should be able to do. As head of department you will need to assess your own strengths and weaknesses and to seek support and training where necessary.

Alongside these abilities or skills a number of attributes are listed. Effective teachers in leadership roles display these characteristics. Together with personal presence, self-confidence, adaptability and intellectual ability are included reliability and integrity, enthusiasm, commitment and energy. Each head of department will not possess all these attributes in equal measure. Some are naturally gifted while others will have to work hard to develop these features. These personal qualities and attributes are the oil that lubricates the departmental machine as the subject leader facilitates the work of the department.

Areas of leadership

As noted above, the National Standards identify four key areas of subject leadership:

- Strategic direction and development of the subject.
- Teaching and learning.
- Leading and managing staff.
- Efficient and effective deployment of staff and resources.

The professional knowledge, understanding, skills and attributes highlighted previously are applied in these areas. Lists of 'objectives' further elucidate each of these aspects of the subject leader's work. In relation to policies and practices within the department these 'objectives' highlight what is provided, established, developed, monitored and evaluated. They describe what is expected of the head of department in relation to audit, guidance, appraisal and support. Collectively they represent a wide-ranging and daunting list of targets. They will not be achieved overnight, and indeed the extent to which they are applicable is a matter for interpretation within the context of each department. They do, nevertheless, provide a framework within which to analyse the work of the head of department. The National Standards provide a useful setting for assessing one's professional skills and knowledge against the requirements of the qualities required of a head of department. The Standards are also a point of reference from which the head of department can evaluate his or her actions and the principles that inform and guide them. The Standards must be reviewed critically, interpreted and prioritized.

The wide-ranging scope of the Standards may present an unrealistic challenge in some areas. Two points are important here. Firstly, the head of department needs to gather relevant information actively. For most, this will be done by building up a network of contacts and by accessing and organizing written information in the form of bulletins, circulars, discussion documents etc. Secondly, the head of department needs to know how and when to access expert advice in these areas when his or her own knowledge is insufficient. Other levels of management within school share some of the responsibilities.

National Standards also exist for Special Needs co-ordinators in schools. These follow the same pattern as for the subject leader. They are divided into the following five areas:

- Core purpose of the SENCO.
- Key outcomes of SEN co-ordination.
- Professional knowledge and understanding.
- Skills and attributes.
- Key areas of SEN co-ordination.

Full details of the standards can be obtained from the pamphlet for SEN Co-ordinators (TTA, 1998) or from the TTA Web site: www.canteach.gov.uk, or from the Standards Web site of the DfES.

Reference points from the literature

The National Standards bring together some themes in the middle management research literature. In turn they have stimulated ongoing research. The purpose of this section is to draw attention to some of the literature that explores these themes. It is, however, beyond the scope of this text to provide an exhaustive literature review.

Research highlights the changing role of the head of department (Glover *et al*, 1998). This is illustrated by the increasing range and diversity of the tasks expected of the subject leader. Emphasis is also placed on the key role for the subject leader in school improvement. The need for a proactive approach to personal, and departmental, professional development is stressed. Tensions in relation to pressure of time and the need to prioritize different elements of the role are all addressed.

Context

At the outset it is important to underline issues raised by Busher and Harris (1999) and others. The context of departmental leadership differs from school to school. Furthermore, departments subject to the same school management structure vary with respect to culture and organization. Hammond (1999) and Harris (1998) also draw attention to departments at different stages of growth. As a consequence of being at different stages, departments will work out different solutions and improvement strategies to what might on the surface appear to be similar problems. Harris (1998: 277) also makes the point that where there are obstacles that hinder the development of an effective department, there are unlikely to be effective 'quick fix' solutions.

Expansion

Dunham (1978) and Turner (1996) trace the development of middle management in schools. Glover *et al* (1998: 279) point to what they call the 'downward delegation of operational responsibility'. This they believe is the consequence of initiatives which placed greater pressure on senior management. The 1997 Ofsted report on subject management, draws attention to the need for co-ordinated and supportive working between senior and middle management to cope with the increasing demands on all levels of school management. The expansion of the head of department role has, in many cases, led to work overload. This has resulted in increased tension between administrative and leadership related roles, for the individual. Harris, Jamieson and Russ (1995), in highlighting characteristics of effective departments, grouped these under separate headings of effective management and effective teaching and learning. Clearly both of these are elements of the subject leader's job. This tension that exists for many subject leaders is not easily resolved.

Professional development

The need for professional development and training for the subject leader arises out of the expansion of that role. Glover *et al* (1998) and Turner (2000) both address the training of the middle manager. The emphasis is on training for leadership rather than administration. In their study, Glover and colleagues highlight the predominance of school-based management courses which are: 'offered as a basis for understanding increased responsibilities within school but of limited value to those seeking career progression', and they point to the need for 'structured opportunities to reflect on their role' (1998: 289).

Busher (1988), Moran, Dallat and Abbot (1999) and Turner (2000) discuss the professional development needs of teachers in a department. They each address part of the spectrum of professional development needs within a department. These vary from the personal and professional development needs of the newly qualified teacher to the needs of individuals within a stable and established department. While at one extreme the training needs and structure within which to provide support may be obvious, at the other extreme heads of department may need to be made aware of the need to be in Turner's (2000: 299) words, 'proactive in training and professional development of their colleagues'. All are agreed that this has become an integral part of middle management. The subject leader's role in CPD impacts both on the individual teachers and on the effectiveness of the department.

Effective practice

Much of what is written about the role of the head of department flows explicitly or implicitly from recognition of the current prominence of the 'school improvement' agenda (see for example Busher and Harris, 2000). Harris (1998) and Harris, Jamieson and Russ (1995) studied effective and ineffective departments. Hammond (1999) undertook a study of the impact of the head of department on teaching and learning. Both looked to school improvement literature as a basis for assessing departmental effectiveness. These studies, along with others (eg Ofsted, 1997), while recognizing the dangers of a 'one size fits all' approach, point to actions which characterize effective practice. They draw attention to the function of the head of department in developing teaching and learning, and underline the fact that effective heads of department do make a difference.

Thinking through the role

One starting point for thinking about the role of the head of department is to set out the structure in which the head of department works and to explore the relationships that influence and constrain the work. The concept map shown in Figure 6.1 illustrates some of the links between the key features which make up the context in which the head of department works.

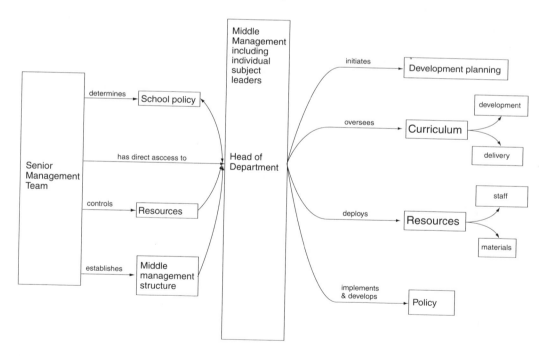

Figure 6.1 A middle management concept map

The links which have been developed are representative but not exhaustive. Indeed, developing a map of elements and links is one way to understand and analyse the uniqueness of each individual school context. While each school has its own distinct set of circumstances, there is sufficient commonality to benefit from some analysis of the model. Thinking through the role, however, is more than mapping out the territory, it also involves thinking about ways in which the features of the model support or hinder the subject leader as he or she pursues the central purpose.

The influence of senior management

At the outset the head of department must hold a clear view of their role in school management. It is your responsibility as head of department to represent the departmental interests and to take the view that at this level no one is more interested in the development of subject than you. If this seems a little too much like self or at least subject promotion, you need to remember that the management structure is established to guarantee that where there are competing interests, each has a voice. Your role is to ensure that your subject area and its contribution to the curriculum are adequately and fairly represented. There can be no justification for some subjects having access to influence or resources that are unwarranted, but in the real world of limited resources difficult decisions may have to be made as priorities are agreed and set. To be effective, the head of department needs to know where and how the role of the subject is shaped, where and how decisions are made and what opportunities exist to influence these. To be effective the head of department needs to be proactive in these areas of management.

Many schools have a hierarchical structure of management (Bush, 1995). Decisions made at senior management level are often acted out through the department structure and in turn influence work in the classroom. In the model represented in Figure 6.1 the influence of the school's senior management on important elements of school structure, school policy, and resources is highlighted. However, the model indicates that senior management also establishes direct links with the head of department. Each of these links is a mechanism through which senior management can influence the role of the head of department.

The effect of school structure

The structure of the school and the place given to subject heads at middle management level will set limits on how the role is to be exercised. For example, the existence or absence of a middle management forum may determine the extent to which department heads have an opportunity to influence one another and also school policy and indeed to speak collectively. However, irrespective of the structure the head of department also has direct access to the principal or other members of the senior management team. The head of department's individual standing, reputation and personal relationships with individuals at this level can be a key factor in how the subject is perceived and how the work of the department progresses. This type of contact and the way in which it develops can have either a positive or a negative impact on the progress of the subject. The nature of these relationships and how they develop should be a key concern of the head of department.

The influence of school policy

Departmental policy must develop in line with school policy, however, not all aspects of school policy impinge directly on the work of the department. While some elements of policy are developed with whole school consensus, other changes are initiated by senior management or external influences. School policy will at times both constrain the freedom of the department head and demand change. All-ability teaching, access to ICT, homework, assessment and record keeping are all areas which may be covered by school policy. The wishes of individual departments in these areas may differ. However it is also the case that teachers in one subject department can have significant influence on practice and in turn on the policy within the school. This may be as a result of going beyond the limits of an existing policy. So, a school-wide homework policy which determines the frequency of homework could be developed in one subject area to demonstrate the effectiveness of a subject policy which, while meeting the basic requirements of school policy, goes further. For example, it may be policy within one department that homework be co-ordinated to ensure consistency and a variety of activity. Guidance may be given on the type of feedback students should receive, developing continuity as students move through the school. Through appropriate management such examples of good practice may influence whole school policy.

In addition, by demonstrating effective practice and policy in new areas the head of department may initiate change at a whole school level by leading through example. Where such development requires resources the head of department may need to access direct links to senior management. However, awareness of management priorities and the external pressures are vital if a bid for additional or at least a relocation of resources is needed.

The control of resources

The control of resources by senior management has significant impact on how the department will function and develop. The quality and quantity of both human and material resources available within a subject area are strongly influenced by senior management. The head of department may have little influence over the appointment of personnel or indeed the overall level of staffing. Aspects of resource provision, both human and material, will be a matter of ongoing negotiation with senior management and the subject leader must demonstrate how the department is making effective use of the resources available while seeking to justify and plan for future development. All material resources involve some level of capital expenditure and are developed over time. All resources, both human and material, have the potential to be used effectively or ineffectively. In relation to human resources, the staffing of the department is an organic resource capable of adaptation.

To work effectively within the management structure the head of department needs to understand the routines and rhythms of the school. Timing is important. Strategic developments which involve even modest expenditure need to be brought forward well before funding is committed to other projects. Changes which may need the agreement of different groups must be planned and approved well in advance. At a more practical level you may need to look for a window of opportunity to raise issues at a time when senior management can give adequate thought to your proposals (eg the period of a school inspection may not be the best time to have the ear of the principal). It is an important skill to know when to take action; when and how to seek support for change. It is important also to anticipate what to expect in terms of support and how to influence the pace of change. The head of department needs to take a long-term view. Ultimately, more is likely to be achieved by co-operative working than by confrontational approaches.

Responsibilities of the post

While recognizing that the head of department is working within some constraints over which he or she has little control, it is also important to emphasize the significant responsibility the head of department has and the autonomy and scope for achievement in a number of important areas.

The head of department is responsible for key elements in the curriculum area. These elements involve: planning for progress; developing and delivering curriculum; the deployment of resources and advancement of department policy. This is the opportunity to revisit the core purpose of the department and to put some flesh on the skeleton.

Development planning

One of the consequences of the new climate of management which exists in schools is the expectation that development planning will be evident at all levels. One task for the head of department may be to produce such a development plan. For some it may seem that this is a bureaucratic exercise to provide an instrument which will facilitate senior management to monitor departmental progress. If the development plan is not embraced by the members of the department and not seen to have an impact on what happens in the classroom then it may well be little more than that. However, without a commitment to planning, the work of a department is in danger of either stagnating or lurching along, a hostage to every new initiative that appears on the educational horizon. Effective planning is only possible if the department has a shared vision. In reality this vision may have to be stated in the most general terms. The English department who can rally around the desire to 'teach the subject well' may start by discussing the availability and the use of appropriate resources on video and CD ROM. Plans for upgrading, developing and sharing resources could then emerge. The Science department staff which must coordinate their work in order to reduce the pressure on resources due to too many classes needing the same equipment at the same time, may agree on the need for an outline scheme to help them co-ordinate their work. This can provide the focus for planning increasingly detailed schemes, which integrate resources and co-ordinate work throughout the year. Alternatively the need to bring departmental practice into line with developing school policy can provide the impetus for further work at departmental level.

Only as the vision is worked out in short-, medium- and longer-term goals can the ownership of and commitment to the goals be negotiated and secured. The strategic importance of such tasks does not, however, guarantee the full co-operation of all the staff. Gaining commitment and building the team are important tasks for the head of department.

While the development plan is important, the subject leader's overview should extend further. The development plan is the outcome of strategic thinking. In an ideal world the head of department would encourage a degree of involvement in such thinking from each member of the departmental team so as to benefit from the various experiences and outlooks.

Curriculum development and delivery

Much has been written about the role of the subject leader in curriculum planning and development (eg Ofsted, 1997; Fleming, 2000). As a starting point to pursuing the core purpose, the head of department needs to have a clear view of the curriculum in the subject area: both the intended curriculum and the curriculum as it is experienced by the students in the school. The subject leader must expect to keep up to date with developments in his or her area of subject teaching. Here the role of the subject expert detailed in Chapter 4 is important. This will include making use of new resources and developments in subject specific methods as well as responding to initiatives emerging from external agencies such as examination boards or those charged with implementing government policy.

The modern language teachers, for example, might explore how they can make effective use of Internet access to French daily newspapers or pick up satellite television broadcasts for native speakers. In many subject areas the introduction of examination at AS level is the latest in a series of initiatives resulting in ongoing curriculum renewal. Syllabus development and new emphases in assessment will require a response from the department. The head of department may also benefit from involvement with appropriate subject specific professional groups as already discussed in Chapters 3, 4 and 5.

Curriculum renewal is often initiated in response to internal evaluation. In recent years following the introduction and expansion of modular courses, departments have evaluated the effectiveness of their traditional teaching approaches in the light of the priorities of a modular curriculum. This author has experience of one science department in which an initiative started with restructuring the teaching scheme to match the modular format of the examination specification. A student self-assessment scheme developed from this. The new scheme was based on units of work within the module and objectives for each unit were translated into student friendly language. The result was an opportunity to involve students in systematic self-assessment in relation to short periods of study. In addition, the feedback from examination boards of modular results has enabled the department to highlight particular strengths and weaknesses in their teaching of topics on the course.

The strategic value of curriculum development

In the absence of appropriate development the curriculum will become outdated. Development of the curriculum is a recognition of the need to respond to changing external circumstances and also the need to constantly monitor the effectiveness and appropriateness of students' experience within the subject. In response to external and internal changes and the availability of new resources, curriculum renewal will be an ongoing task. It should also be a task which is part of development planning. The strategic importance of curriculum development is in ensuring that the department is making the appropriate response to changing circumstances and making appropriate use of developing resources.

Deployment of resources

The importance of giving careful thought to deploying resources lies in the need to ensure that they are used effectively. The most significant resource in any department is the staff: it is important to gain maximum benefit from their skills and expertise. In addition, staff are more likely to sustain effective work if they have a challenging and fulfilling working environment. This includes, but goes beyond, allocation of teachers to classes. In some schools and departments human resources includes both teaching and support staff. To ensure that development and progress are sustained, the energy of the staff needs to be directed into key areas and the workload needs to be shared equitably. There is clearly a link here to development planning but the deployment of resources is also an exercise in staff development. One aim is to ensure that staff expertise and experience are expanded, and people have the opportunity to explore new areas and develop new skills and expertise.

The use of resources is something for the head of department to think about carefully. In order to provide appropriate material resources and to plan for adequate access to shared resources such as centrally accessed ICT facilities the strategic use of material resources must be planned for. These issues ought to be discussed at the departmental meeting. Understanding and agreement need to be sought and, where necessary, decisions taken. Issues relating to the management of human and material resources will be addressed later.

The purposeful deployment of material resources can contribute to efficient and effective use of materials. The thoughtful deployment of human resources can lead to personal and departmental development ensuring that the department will profit from individual strengths.

Department policy

As with development planning it may be that there are those who think of this as a bureaucratic exercise. Certainly it may be the case in many schools that the head of department is required to produce a number of policy statements to provide documentary evidence for internal or external inspection. However, the purpose and the strategic importance of policy development ought to be shared with all staff. It is often the case that policy statements are required in a number of areas to mirror or expand on whole school policy in, for example, homework, assessment, record keeping.

Some departments will require subject-specific policy. In subjects such as science, home economics and technology, for example, safety policy or guidance on the use of equipment and apparatus and the supervision of practical activities will be necessary. It is unlikely that the head of department will have difficulty in persuading staff that such policy is relevant to the classroom and, in some of the latter examples, the policy will be important for their own and, the students' protection. A policy statement is an opportunity for a department to address in very specific terms what they are doing and why they are doing it. What is important however, is to generate ownership and commitment both to the policy and to the development of the policy. The process which a department goes through is no less valuable than the product they produce. The opportunity to share ideas and views and the opportunity to talk about and agree on good practice is what is important.

Policy statements are also important for new or temporary members of staff. As well as providing guidance for experienced teaching support staff, they also provide a point of reference for senior management, parents and students as appropriate.

A word of warning, it is important to decide what the key policy areas are so that the department does not become overburdened with policy statements. It may be necessary to prioritize these and to revisit and refresh statements as they become dated. Finally, it is important to be concise. A brief and clearly written statement is more likely to be accessed and acted upon.

Taking on the role

The purpose of this section is to provide an outline or checklist of key tasks for the head of department. These could be grouped under four headings: planning and development tasks, logistics, human resource management and external relations. This section is concerned specifically with the question: What does a head of department do?

Planning and development tasks

The planning and development tasks are of strategic importance and, in that respect, have been dealt with in the previous section. They centre on guiding departmental policy. This policy will relate to the specific interests of the subject but must also be seen to be an interpretation of school policy and to respond to and reflect developments from external agencies.

The head of department should:

- identify key areas where departmental policy is needed;
- compile a record of the policy statements and ensure that where appropriate each member of the teaching and non-teaching staff, has a copy;
- provide a copy of the policy file to senior management, whether they ask for one or not;
- make sure that anyone working in the department, eg temporary teachers and student teachers, has a copy of the policies;
- keep the policy file under review. (Make a note of work to be done, assess the size of the task, set priorities and plan the work. Avoid the temptation to write the policy yourself and give it to everyone as a *fait accompli*).

When addressing planning and development it will be important to identify the challenging areas for your department. Don't shy away from them, but don't try to start with the most difficult. Establish a format for policy writing and presentation, eg a single A4 sheet with key points and information on how to access additional guidance as needed. If appropriate, allocate sub groups to develop policy and be prepared for a number of drafts to ensure ownership by the department as a whole.

Logistics

This section highlights the tasks which relate to the organization of material resources and the management of 'projects'. In some subjects, particularly those with a significant practical component, the organization of apparatus, chemicals, equipment and other consumable supplies is a significant task involving considerable expenditure on an annual basis. For all departments however, there are ongoing projects resulting from planning decisions and the need to ensure an adequate supply of text books, CD ROMs, video and other resource materials is of central importance. In many departments, provision of or adequate access to appropriate ICT facilities is also a concern, though this varies from school to school and between subjects.

Material resources

There are two issues. One is to ensure that the appropriate resources are available in school in adequate quantities and the second is to manage the storage, access, distribution and effective use of all the resources within the department. The care and effective management of the resources already available are essentially matters of good house-keeping. Systems need to be in place to ensure that resources can be traced and accounted for. The head of department needs to take responsibility for access to resources. A resource inventory is useful, with materials available centrally or their location identified, rather than hidden in a cupboard where only a few people know of their existence.

The provision of adequate resources has implications for funding and is part of the head of department's strategic role. Securing funding may be a matter of timing. The head of department needs to identify internal and external deadlines which will be placed on the release of funds. With deadlines identified, the next priority is to target dates for drawing up lists of wants and needs. These 'wish lists' should be clearly linked to identified needs and expected use. There will be conflicting interests. One element of departmental management discussed later is that of consensus management and the value of collective decision making will be seen in this process. Review resources if possible with the help of non-teaching support. Match resources to the existing and anticipated needs of the curriculum. Identify resources which need to be replaced. Evaluate new resources. It is unlikely that the budget will be adequate for all you want. In any consultation process you may undertake, allow sufficient time for department members to put forward their view and make a case for resources they want. It is in the nature of effective departments that they engage in collaborative decision making and involve staff in taking responsibility for a wide range of tasks. Some key points to note under logistics are:

- Make an inventory of resources.
- Store materials in accessible places.
- Have a system for tracking departmental assets.
- Identify needs.
- Plan requisitioning in good time, avoid pressure points within the school year.
- Identify deadlines and set time scales to meet these.
- Engage staff in setting priorities.
- Set priorities in line with agreed department development.
- Where appropriate, plan to make a special case to senior management.

Project management

This includes the management of schemes of work. It is unlikely that a newly appointed head of department would find themselves in the unfortunate position of a department with no documented scheme. However, the development of the department will undoubtedly involve stages of review and renewal that may range from minor adjustment to an existing element, to major revisions of whole areas of the curriculum. Whatever the need it is always possible to break the task into a number of 'projects'. This could be referencing new resources in the geography GCSE scheme of work, the English department writing active learning lesson activities to focus on the impact of the media and advertising following a school-based staff development day, or it could be the development of an entirely new scheme to cater for a new AS specification in mathematics. These projects may involve one or two people acting on behalf of the whole group or may require the entire department working together. It is unlikely that a department will be so small that some sharing of work cannot be achieved. Tasks must be specific, and ideally should be agreed by the whole group before being delegated. Finally, projects, however small, should be given a timescale so that they can be monitored, completed and the department can move on. Schemes of work are only one of a number of such tasks which require to be managed. Others would include developments in assessment of oral English, end of topic tests in the science department, project work in technology, or planning for fieldwork in geography. The important points in project management are:

- Divide the work into manageable 'projects'.
- Share the workload.
- Set realistic work loads.
- Set realistic time targets.
- Monitor progress.
- Evaluate the outcome.

Human resource management

This represents what is perhaps the greatest challenge for the head of department. The combination of the individual personality and personnel management skills of the head of department, along with the mix of personalities within the group mean that each department is unique. There are, however, some guidelines which can be helpful. The head of department must keep two things in mind. Firstly, the nature of the management structure within the department will almost certainly be different from the overall structure of the school. While the majority of schools operate within a hierarchical system of management, effective subject departments are often characterized by a collegiate approach (Bush, 1995). Secondly, the purpose of management needs to be clear.

The context of departmental management

The subject department is made up of professionals who enjoy a high degree of autonomy. In thinking about the management of peers and fellow professionals the term 'subject leader' is particularly helpful. The head of department exercises a leadership role within a collegiate system which has a number of unique constraints.

The professional status of teachers means that they accept responsibility within the classroom. Teachers expect to exercise their own decision-making in certain areas and will not necessarily agree to a majority view. Teachers may, for example, take very different views on the extent and nature of support which students should receive with coursework or they may differ as to the value they place on the use of text books. You cannot in every situation impose a majority view. It is essential to distinguish between those situations where it is important to secure agreement and compliance and those where this is not necessary. There is currently some degree of autonomy which means that teachers do not as a rule experience the work of their colleagues in the classroom and they do not see one another teach, although as we can see from Chapters 3 and 4 there is increasing emphasis on peer observation and support. Furthermore, performance management and appraisal are becoming more widely accepted, as shall be discussed in Chapter 9. Classroom teaching reflects the personality of the teachers and the class and cannot be prescribed, although some government recommendations would lead in this direction. It should be the aim of the subject leader to celebrate individuality, while at the same time ensuring that good practice in classroom teaching is shared so that the delivery of the subject as a whole is improved.

Members of the department while coming together because of their subject expertise may have varied responsibilities in other areas of the school and may as a result have different levels of status. The head of department may not be the most senior figure within the group which they have the responsibility to lead. There may be sensitivities within the department and issues between members of the group which arise from outside. The subject leader needs to know the staff, identify strengths and weaknesses and potential areas of difficulty and co-ordinate the work of individuals so that they keep the focus on the central task of the group.

The purpose of management

One of the aims of management at this level is to work towards developing an effective team that in turn provides for effective teaching and learning in the subject area. A second aim of management should be to facilitate personal development among the members of the group.

Building an effective team

The team will be most successful if the different skills available within the department are used effectively and if the members of the team work co-operatively and in support of one another. While recognizing the strengths and weaknesses within the team the head of department must be careful to balance the needs of the department as a whole and at the same time guard against too much of the burden of work falling on too few willing or conscientious members.

In a project to review or develop some aspect of the teaching scheme, the subject leader might arrange for a teacher with flair and imagination in the classroom to work alongside another whose teaching styles are more traditional and predictable so that they could complement one another. The teacher who has a reputation for attention to detail and getting the job done on time might be a key player of the group working on topic tests or the end of year examination and marking schemes.

CPD

Personal development of the members of the group, while a responsibility of the individual, ought also to be of concern to the head of department. One practical step towards this is through thoughtful delegation of responsibilities and the provision of opportunities to tackle different types of task. Individuals can be encouraged to gain experience and develop new skills. Where people may be reluctant, support may be needed to get the job done. This is better than taking the job back to give it to someone else or doing it yourself. Here then as head of department you will be directly inputting into the CPD of your department members.

It is important to note that heads of department must not neglect their own personal development. The experience of departmental management will be a significant element in this but you should also seek opportunities to develop skills and gain experience through involvement in whole school and out of school interests. The routes and sources suggested in Chapter 5 could be helpful here.

Departmental meetings

While the members of the department may meet on a daily basis and interact informally, often to discuss their work and subject-related issues, staffroom meetings and conversations in passing are no substitute for time dedicated to the business of running the department. The departmental meeting represents a key instrument for communication and decision making.

It is important that members of the department recognize the value of the forum and are encouraged to make a commitment to it. Some guidelines for departmental meetings can help. Departmental meetings should be organized for a convenient and if possible an agreed time; they should be time-limited. Set a time limit and stick to it – if the business cannot be completed, prioritize and if necessary arrange another meeting. If possible find relaxed and comfortable surroundings, a little refreshment and a short time to unwind before the meeting, especially at the end of the school day; this is likely to put everyone in a better frame of mind. In respect of the business of the meeting some points are noteworthy, the meeting should be:

- Focused – an agenda should be circulated prior to the meeting, making the purpose of the meeting clear. (If there is no important business there should not be a meeting!).
- Planned – staff should be given plenty of notice of the meeting. If possible dates should be set well in advance at the start of the term or even the year. It is often helpful to choose a regular day and time. The agenda should be used as a reminder a few days in advance of the meeting.
- Realistic – the agenda should not be too crowded.
- Organized – a record of the meeting should be taken and the minutes should be circulated promptly. These should contain details of what was agreed, and the names of the staff who have responsibility to deal with them.
- Regular – a department which meets only infrequently will find it difficult to build a sense of mutual understanding, or ownership of decisions.
- Genuine – along with a commitment to meet regularly there needs to be a genuine exchange of views.

Much of the atmosphere and ethos of the department meeting depends on the personality and skill of the head of department and on the relationships that are being developed within the group. The department meeting is the place where collective decisions ought to be taken, where the direction of the department can be negotiated and the development of the subject planned. The head of department needs to prepare for and persevere with the department meeting and ought not to expect overnight success. There will from time to time be obstacles which need to be overcome. These can in themselves be valuable learning experiences.

External relationships

There are many relationships to be developed beyond departmental boundaries. The subject department is one type of administrative unit, but within the structure of the school there are many opportunities for individuals to be involved with a number of different units or groupings. Some teachers work within more than one subject area. The structure of school may involve teachers in working groups relating to special needs teaching or discipline for example. The pastoral care structures within school will involve teachers from all subject areas as year heads and form tutors. Members of staff will be interacting with one another at different levels and in different contexts; however, there are occasions on which the subject leader must be the representative of the department. He or she is the representative not only within the school between departments, at management level, and at times with governors but also to external bodies such as advisory services, examining bodies and those involved in the inspection process.

Whole school perspective

In general the head of department needs to be alert to the impact which discussions and decisions in one area of the curriculum may have on the teaching and delivery of their subject. The head of department needs to think through the wider effects of changes in what might seem to be unrelated areas. These could relate to changes in curriculum time, reallocation of resources, and interpretation of guidance or directives from outside agencies. In these circumstances you need to consider how to make an appropriate response which represents the interests of the department and the contribution which your subject makes to the curriculum. You will need to articulate clearly how real or proposed changes might affect your ability to deliver the current curriculum, while at the same time demonstrating that you have a grasp of the whole school perspective. The head of department who has established good working relationships with colleagues and senior management and a reputation for sound and reasoned judgement, is likely not only to represent the subject area effectively but will also make a valuable contribution to the school as a whole. A reputation for ill-considered reactions and a tendency to self- or subject promotion at the expense of the general good is likely to diminish the impact of any case you may wish to make, no matter how worthy or well founded.

In fulfilling the representative role, a sound understanding of wider educational issues and thinking and the ability to apply this effectively to the particular circumstances of school and subject area will be an advantage. An understanding of the decision-making processes within school and an awareness of how to influence these is important. If things do not always go your way, and it is unlikely that they will, then the ability to respect the authority and responsibility of others and to move on will be helpful strategies.

In general the same principles apply in terms of relationships with external bodies. Seek to gain a sound understanding of the subject within the wider curriculum. Engage with curriculum and subject specific issues and developments. Demonstrate willingness to establish links and relationships outside school and broaden your perspective. Begin to establish networks of contacts and make a contribution outside the boundaries of your own school. The principles of establishing a reputation for awareness and sound judgement still apply.

Self-awareness

The skills, personal qualities and attributes of the head of department play an important part in any effective department. Organizational, communication and team-building skills are all essential. Like a three-legged stool, these three elements are all important if the structure is to stand. It may be that after reflection and self-analysis or as a result of painful experience, the head of department recognizes his or her strengths in some areas and deficiencies in others. Self awareness and a degree of humility are key attributes which will help heads of department know where to concentrate extra effort and when to rely on the strengths of those around them to compensate for their own limitations.

Organizational skills

The head of department needs to have a good level of personal organization. There is a core of routine tasks, things to do in the right way at the right time. There needs to be sufficient attention to detail and it is important to reject casual attitudes to administration. You do not have to enjoy the administration but a competent, careful and conscientious approach is essential.

In addition to routine administration there is the organization of targets and goals. You need to focus personally and to keep others focused on projects which move the work of the department forward. It is easy to become busy and indeed to take comfort in routine administration as a way of avoiding some more difficult organizational tasks which have developmental potential. The head of department must not neglect this aspect of organization and your skills should be directed towards keeping the group focused and working together.

Communication skills

A subject leader cannot run an effective department without a degree of organization, but no amount of organization will be effective if there is a lack of appropriate communication, and this is identified as a key role in Chapter 4. This is a two-way process. Heads of department needs to be as good at taking in as they are at giving out information. There needs to be a steady supply of information. Tasks need to be assigned, action needs to be taken, and deadlines need to be set. People are all different and you need to allow for these differences and respect the professional integrity of the group to get the job done adequately and on time. If you like to work to a deadline and leave tasks to the last available opportunity, don't assume that this way of working will suit your colleagues, so give plenty of notice of work to be done. Similarly if you like to be organized well in advance of any deadline don't be over-anxious if some of your colleagues don't follow your lead. Let people choose their own style of working.

Communication is more than finding an efficient way of passing on information. Communication needs to be ongoing, for example talking to people finding out their views, their worries and expectations, seeking to understand their concerns. At times communication needs to be formal and written, such as in the passing of action points from the department meeting. However, the value of informal moments, words of encouragement and appreciation, thoughtful recognition of a contribution, enlisting help, and valuing expertise all contributing to building relationships should not be overlooked.

Team-building skills

This is perhaps the most challenging task for the head of department. In a very real sense the 'team' may not exist. As with most working environments the group have not chosen one another; personalities and interests may not be compatible so while some groups may appear to have a natural affinity and seem to work together effortlessly, a look beneath the surface often reveals a significant effort and skill at team building. Some key tasks the head of department needs to address are:

- Aim to understand the dynamics of the group.
- Identify individual roles within the group.
- Be prepared to confront difficult issues.
- Encourage participation and value each contribution.
- Be positive and lead by example.

In addition to the day-to-day discourse, the head of department needs to present the department with a challenge and through words, actions and attitudes translate his or her vision for the department into reality. A key element of any effective department is the sense of community and the willingness to work together as a team with a common goal. This depends in part on the ability of the head of department to communicate respect for individuals and the contribution they can make to the work of the department. It is also the case that to earn credibility as a leader a head of department needs to protect individuals in situations where they are vulnerable. A willingness to engage with the pastoral care needs of the department is another way in which team building is facilitated.

Key points

- The National Standards for Subject Leaders provide a useful framework within which to assess the role of the head of department.
- The role of the head of department is complex and the way in which it is interpreted and worked out is a consequence of many interacting parts.
- Guidance is given on some of the responsibilities and tasks which might be required of all those in a middle management role.
- Links are made between effective heads of department and school improvement.

Self study

Key questions

For the teacher:

- How does my profile match up with the Standards for subject leader?
- What can I do to gain the necessary expertise for the post of subject leader?
- What can I do in CPD to enhance my prospects of promotion?
- Are there areas of responsibility I could seek to develop?

For senior management:

- Am I making sufficient use of the talent in the school?
- Are there areas of responsibility which could be given to other colleagues?
- Are staff aware of how they can become subject leaders?
- Does the school have supportive mechanisms following induction to mentor staff?
- How am I managing CPD for maximum effect to staff?

Recommended reading

Busher, H and Harris, A (1999) Leadership of school subject areas: tensions and dimensions of managing in the middle, *School Leadership and Management*, **19** (3), pp 305–17

Busher, H and Harris, A (2000) *Subject Leadership and School Improvement*, Paul Chapman, London

Fleming, P (2000) *The Art of Middle Management in Secondary Schools*, David Fulton, London

Fleming, P and Amesbury, M (2001) *The Art of Middle Management in Primary Schools: A guide to effective subject, year and team leadership*, David Fulton, London

Harris, A (1998) Improving ineffective departments in secondary schools, *Educational Management and Administration*, **26** (3), pp 269–78

Ofsted (1997) *Subject Management in Secondary Schools: Aspects of good practice*, Ofsted, London

7 Senior management

Peter Neil and Sylvia Gourley

The job of headteacher is one of the most fundamental to the success of a school. This has been recognized by government, and various initiatives have been introduced to improve the level of leadership of schools. In recent years schools performing badly in league tables have either been closed or have been taken over by LEAs or business consortia. Headteachers of failing schools have even been threatened with dismissal and their schools with transferral to the management of a successful headteacher. There is no question therefore about the high level of responsibility attached to this post and it is perhaps not surprising that some challenging schools have been without a permanent headteacher for some time. The government has raised the profile of school leadership with the establishment in 2000 of the National College for School Leadership (NCSL) in Nottingham and with the introduction of National Standards for Headship and the National Professional Qualification for Headship (NPQH).

In discussing the National Standards for Headship and the NPQH, it is acknowledged that there are differences in provision and standards in the various jurisdictions. It is also accepted, however, that the requirements are broadly similar to the extent that it will suffice to present the general framework and to refer to individual differences, where appropriate. What the following sections intend to do is to provide a flavour of the Standards for Headship and of the programmes designed to enable aspiring headteachers to achieve the qualification.

Government regulations and recommendations

National Standards for headship exist in all four jurisdictions. The National Standards for England are set out in the DfES publication 0195/2000 (DfES, 2001d). They set out the knowledge, understanding, skills and attributes required of a headteacher and are subdivided into five parts:

- core purpose of the headteacher;
- key outcomes of headship;
- professional knowledge and understanding;
- skills and attributes;
- key areas of headship.

The National Standards for headteachers state that the core purpose of the head-teacher is: 'to provide professional leadership for a school which secures its success and improvement, ensuring high quality education for all its students and improved standards of learning and achievement' (DfES, 2001d: 4).

As the leading professional in the school working with the Governing Body, the headteacher provides vision, leadership and direction for the school and ensures that the school is managed and organized to meets its aims and targets. The head-teacher, in the context of the National Standards, is responsible for the continuous improvement in the quality of education; for raising standards, for ensuring equality of education for all; for the development of policies and practices and for ensuring that resources are efficiently and effectively used to achieve the school's aims and objectives. The headteacher also secures the commitment of the wider community to the school by developing effective networks with, for example, other local schools, the LEA, HEIs, employers, the careers service and others. Furthermore, the headteacher is responsible for creating a productive, disciplined learning environment and for the day-to-day management, organization and administration of the schools and is ultimately responsible to the Governing Body.

The Standards list the key outcomes of headship. The personification of this core purpose will be a senior, strategic manager who is managing a school where excellence reigns in all aspects of school life, leading to a school where:

- there is a positive ethos, reflecting a commitment to high achievement, effective teaching and learning and good relationships; staff, governors and parents have confidence in the leadership and management of the school; staff and governors recognize their accountability for their tasks and the school's success and contribute fully to the development and successful implementation of school policies and practices; the life of the school and the curriculum effectively promote students' spiritual, moral, cultural and physical development and prepare them for adult life; effectiveness is kept under rigorous review, and links with the wider community contribute to students' attainment and personal development.
- efficient and effective use is made of staff, accommodation and resources; financial control and administration are effective and the carefully costed development plan is focused on improving educational outcomes; good value for money is provided (DfES, 2001d: 5).

The school where the above exists will also have an enormous impact on students, teachers, governors and through ever-increasing circles into the community. The key outcomes contain details of what will be expected of the students, the teachers, the parents and the governors in a school in which effective leadership is evident.

Professional knowledge and understanding of various aspects, drawn from sources both within and outside education, are required by the effective head-teacher. The following are listed as examples:

- What constitutes quality in educational provision, the characteristics of effective schools and strategies for raising students' achievement and promoting their spiritual, moral, social and cultural development and their good behaviour;
- Strategies to achieve effective teaching in literacy, numeracy, ICT;
- Using comparative data to establish benchmark and set targets for improvement;
- The curriculum and assessment;
- Political, economical, social, religious and technological influences which have an impact on strategic planning;
- Leadership styles and practices;
- Management, including employment law, equal opportunities legislation;
- National policy framework;
- Statutory framework for education;
- Governance at national, local and school levels;
- The contribution that evidence from inspection and research can make to professional and school development.

Under skills and attributes the following groups of skills are listed:

- Leadership skills;
- Decision-making skills;
- Communication skills;
- Self-management skills;
- Attributes (DfES, 2001d: 7ff).

The final section of the Standards lists the five key areas of headship as follows:

- Strategic direction and development of the school.
- Teaching and learning.
- Leading and managing staff.
- Efficient and effective deployment of staff and resources.
- Accountability.

The five key areas are underpinned by a specific body of knowledge, a bank of skills and a set of attitudes which define the role.

The Scottish Standard for headship details the key purpose as follows: 'To provide the leadership and management which enable a school to give every student a high quality education and which promotes the highest possible standards of achievement' (University of Edinburgh, 2001: 5). The Scottish Standard for headship emphasizes that the success of any school is critically linked to the leadership of the headteacher. Emphasis is also placed on the vision of the headteacher which must be articulated to all stakeholders: 'The headteacher must articulate a vision and give direction to the school which will lead to effective learning and teaching' (University of Edinburgh, 2001: 5). Focus on the climate and ethos of the school will create an environment which will engender a positive response to change. The headteacher must systematically review all aims, plans, policies and procedures which translate the vision into an everyday reality. The headteacher is in addition accountable for the quality of education which takes place within the school and through the application of continuous improvement leading to the raising of standards.

In addition to defined professional values, the Scottish Standard outlines the key functions performed by headteachers in order to achieve this key purpose of headship:

- managing learning and teaching;
- managing people;
- managing policy and planning;
- managing resources and finance.

The rationale for the professional behaviour of the headteacher is described as follows:

- to hold, articulate and argue for professionally defensible educational values;
- to act as a model of a leading professional within the school, committed to their own learning and developing their practice;
- to have up to date knowledge and understanding of educational development and of the management issues relevant to that (University of Edinburgh, 2001: 6).

In addition to the professional values and management functions, the Scottish Standard sets out the interpersonal and intellectual abilities which underpin the competent senior manager:

- Interpersonal abilities
  - demonstrates confidence and courage;
  - creates and maintains a positive atmosphere;
  - inspires and motivates others;

- communicates effectively;
- empathizes with others;
- values and works through teams.
- Intellectual abilities
  - seeks and uses information;
  - thinks strategically;
  - judges wisely and decides appropriately;
  - identifies and solves problems;
  - shows political insight (University of Edinburgh, 2001: 11f).

In Wales the National Standards contain five key areas:

- strategic leadership and development of the school;
- teaching and learning;
- leading and managing staff;
- efficient and effective deployment of staff and resources;
- accountability (NPQH/CPCP, 2001: 1).

In Northern Ireland the National English Standards are used and adapted to reflect the local context.

The above section has given some insight into the national standards required for headship. There are broad similarities in the Standards in all parts of the UK, with some differences in nomenclature and emphasis. The following section outlines the requirements of the courses leading to the qualification for headship.

NPQH

The NPQH is the qualification for headteachers and is the benchmark for entry to headship. The programme has been designed to prepare candidates for the rewarding role of leadership and the training is focused on development needs, although as pointed out in Chapter 4, this is not universally accepted as the definitive model for everyone (Grace, 2000). The NPQH offers challenging and relevant training, including online learning, school-based assessment and visits to successful schools. There are various routes through NPQH depending upon the training needs of an individual. There are many similarities in the programmes offered by the various jurisdictions (NPQH in England, NPQH/CPCP in Wales, PQH(NI) in Northern Ireland and SQH in Scotland). It is not necessary to describe each of the programmes in depth, as the details of each are available on the respective Web pages, details of which are given at the end of this section. In the discussions that follow, examples will be taken from aspects of the different courses throughout the UK.

At the time of writing, the government is proposing that the NPQH should be mandatory for headteachers by April 2004 and the document is out for consultation (DfES, 2002b). This means that all those applying for headteacher posts from that time will either have to hold the PQH or be registered on a course leading towards the qualification. The NPQH in England (now run by the NCSL) was introduced in 1997 as a means to improve teachers' knowledge and skills for the job. It was reviewed in 1999 and restructured. According to the Government, the NPQH is now more streamlined and more accessible and it:

- is underpinned by the National Standards for Headteachers;
- draws on the best leadership and management practice inside and outside education;
- is practical, challenging and up to date;
- is focused on school improvement;
- sets rigorous standards, while building on previous achievement and proven ability;
- is based on supported self-study, suitable for busy professionals;
- uses e-learning, including online discussion communities, to maximize learning opportunities for candidates;
- provides a benchmark of achievement against the National Standards for Headteachers from which new headteachers can develop their leadership and management capabilities whilst doing the job (DfES, 2002b: 12).

There are three distinct routes to the qualification:

- Access – for those with relatively limited experience in senior management roles. This route takes up to two years to complete.
- Development stage – for candidates with senior management experience and achievements. This can take up to one year to complete.
- School-based assessment – for candidates who can demonstrate significant achievements against the National Standards. This route can be completed in the minimum time of six months.

The first two routes require the candidates to undertake four modules: strategic direction and development of the school; teaching and learning; leading and managing staff; and efficient and effective deployment of staff and resources. Candidates select some or all of the modules, based on their previous experience and achievements. When they can demonstrate that they meet the Standards, they proceed to a closing assessment or final stage which comprises a two-day residential at the NCSL.

The PQH in Northern Ireland is run by the Regional Training Unit (RTU, undated); the accredited trainers and assessors, many of them serving headteachers and managers from outside education, are trained by the RTU to meet the national standards. The limited pilot of the course began in 1999 with 73 practising or aspiring headteachers from all backgrounds and from all types of schools. PQH(NI), is intended for all those with potential for headship, as indeed are the other national qualifications. A typical candidate might be a deputy head, senior teacher or Key Stage co-ordinator, who already takes responsibility for a range of activities within a school and whose next application might be for headship. People may apply from outside the teaching profession, for example inspectors, advisers or former teachers. Candidates in this category, however, require the support of a school to enable them to carry out their school improvement task, an assessed aspect of the programme. All those applying for the course must have qualified teacher status.

The new model of PQH, introduced in 2002, has a strong focus on online learning but incorporates taught sessions of the old model, in order to allow the participants an opportunity to network. Mentoring is an added feature of the new model. Candidates have an online mentor available for discussion and to give direction.

The programme is designed to meet the differing needs of aspiring heads in different phases, types and sizes of schools. Candidates are expected to undertake practical school-based tasks, directly related to the National Standards for Headteachers and which require an understanding of the application of headship and management. Consistency and quality are monitored by the RTU and funding is provided by the unit. Existing headteachers have responsibilities within the PQH programme for their own staff who apply for the course. They are involved, for example, by:

- encouraging suitable colleagues to apply for the PQH;
- supplying references for applicants;
- discussing the application with applicants;
- helping candidates to evaluate their work in terms of the National Standards;
- identifying achievement and expertise in the key areas of headship;
- helping candidates to prepare their action plan for training and development;
- giving candidates opportunities to develop and demonstrate their achievement in relation to the Standards.

The model in Scotland for the SQH comprises four Units, each of which provides elements of taught and workplace learning and it accredits prior learning:

- Unit 1. Introduction to the SQH requirements, outline of the Standard.
- Unit 2. Managing Core Operations, covering the two key functions from the Standard: managing learning and teaching and managing people. It

incorporates work-based projects and extensive reading. It also deals with the interpersonal abilities outlined in The Standard.

- Unit 3. Managing School improvement covers the two key areas: managing policy and planning and managing resources and finance. It also deals with the intellectual abilities outlined in The Standard.
- Unit 4. School Leadership which pulls together the main themes on leadership and management.

As with the other courses, it is possible for experienced managers to complete the model in a shorter timescale, by omitting Units 2 and 3.

The NPQH/CPCP in Wales was revised in 2001 and consists of three stages: application and selection; training and development; school-based and final assessment. The training and development phase comprises contract visits to the workplace by a tutor, four training days focusing on specific aspects of the key areas, development guides and workshops. It is possible to complete the training and development within one year and candidates have a further eight months to complete the school-based and final assessment (at the NPQH centre).

Benefits of the NPQH have been found to accrue both to schools and to candidates. School improvement projects are a major part of the programme and candidates must show how they have contributed to school improvement. The NPQH course helps candidates in their current jobs as well as preparing them for headship. A significant number of teachers have successfully completed the training for the NPQH and many have since been promoted.

Informal feedback received from candidates who successfully completed the programme (by one of the authors who has been a trainer on the NPQH) seems to suggest that candidates found that their training and development needs which had been identified through the initial diagnostic assessment were met by the end of the programme. They were challenged by the taught sessions and benefited from the opportunity to share and network with colleagues. Networks which were established during the course existed beyond the life of the NPQH training. They found the feedback given to them by the trained assessors as useful in contributing to their ongoing professional development. Those involved in the programme identified the following as particularly significant:

- excellent training materials;
- comprehensive treatment of the five key areas;
- networking;
- use of a variety of methods of training and assessment;
- flexibility and learner-centred approach;
- reflection on best practice;
- increased confidence.

The above section has given some details of the qualification for headship as it is interpreted by the various jurisdictions within the UK. The qualification gives less attention to theory, research and the academic literature, emphasizing the acquisition of measurable competence (Bush and Foreman, 1998). It is regrettable that the training of school leaders could not have been more firmly rooted in the academic domain by articulating it with masters or doctoral programmes of University Schools and Departments of Education. Some might suggest that this was a great opportunity missed and that it emphasizes a residual perceived tension between theory and practice. For a detailed discussion of the NPQH the reader should access the article by Bush and Foreman from the Web site of the University of Leicester: www.le.ac.uk/se/centres/emdu.

Since the regulations and recommendations have changed quite significantly over a short period of time and are likely to change again in the future, if you aspire to become a headteacher you should consult the various Web sites or documentation to find the precise details of the area in which you want to work as a headteacher. This will ensure that you are fully *au fait* with the requirements at the time of application for a programme. The respective Web site addresses are as follows:

England: www.ncsl.org.uk
Northern Ireland: www.class-ni.org.uk
Scotland: www.scotland.gov.uk/education/sqh
Wales: www.cardiffuniversity.net/socsi/npqh

Other training initiatives

For headteachers who have taken up post, the National College provides two programmes of development. The Leadership and Management Programme for New Headteachers (HEADLAMP) is designed for those in their first two years of leadership. The programme is designed to complement the NPQH and it is individually tailored to meet the needs of heads in different contexts. First heads undertake an analysis of their own training needs, on the basis of which they decide which aspects of training to buy from the various providers. The training can be either short courses, one-to-one coaching or mentoring schemes but the responsibility of accessing the specific courses lies with the individual head. The school can receive funding from HEADLAMP to support the training.

Revell (2002e) reports that 130 headteachers in England are currently taking part in a one-year pilot scheme 'New Visions Induction to Headship Programme' which may become a national training programme for existing heads.

The Leadership Programme for Serving Headteachers (LPSH) is designed for existing headteachers. Described in the publicity as an 'innovative programme', it is a course which involves four elements: Pre-workshop preparation, a four-day residential workshop, post-workshop opportunities and a follow-up day. The programme draws on the National Standards for Headteachers and research. It focuses on personal development, and encourages heads to share expertise. Again for this scheme, funding is centrally available. Details of these schemes can be found on the Web site of the NCSL (www.ncsl.org.uk).

For headteachers who have already gone through NPQH or who have been in post for some time, they might like to consider the range of masters (MA, MEd, MSc, MBA) and doctoral programmes (EdD, DBA, PhD) which are offered by the various HEIs around the country. The importance of continually developing the headteacher's knowledge of learning, teaching and leadership cannot be overemphasized.

Role of the headteacher

This section of the chapter takes a broader view of the role of the school headteacher. We look first at some of the research literature on headship and then focus attention on relevant key personal competencies of the Manager Charter Initiative, which has informed much of the NPQH thinking, as a framework for discussing some of the practical aspects of the role of headteacher.

Findings from research and the literature

In the literature the three aspects of leadership, management and administration are differentiated from each other. Everard (1986) (cited in Neil *et al*, 2001: 40), for example, describes the area of management as future-oriented, entrepreneurial, proactive, concerned with achieving change by working on people's values, beliefs and ideas to raise standards and define future goals. Administration, according to Everard, is present-oriented and reactive. Leadership, on the other hand, is the exercise of high-level conceptual skills and decisions; it should envision mission, develop strategy, inspire people and change culture. It has been well documented that leadership is one of the most observed and least understood phenomena on earth (Burns, 1978, cited in Campbell-Evans, 1993: 99).

It has also been suggested that the consequence of the legislation implemented in the 1980s for school management has resulted in a dichotomy for the headteacher who has to act both as the chief executive and the leading professional (McEwen *et al*, 2002: 147). Most importantly, however, it is the headteacher who is responsible for ensuring that the school community is a 'learning community' (Stewart, in press). According to Stewart (citing Campbell-Evans, 1993: 110), the headteacher is responsible for binding the various threads of 'values, leadership, vision and culture' together. Gunter (citing Young, 1971: 24) states that: 'Describing and understanding leaders and leadership in education is about knowledge production: who does it, what they do, how do they do it and why do they do it? The emphasis is not so much on the product of knowledge in the form of a fact or a theory, as the process by which there is a selection and organization from the available knowledge [...] which involves conscious or unconscious choices' (2001a: 5).

Two interrelated research projects have been carried out into school leadership among groups of primary and secondary headteachers in England, Northern Ireland and Wales, to identify what it was that school heads actually did and how these actions matched their professional values (Neil *et al*, 2001; McEwen *et al*, 2002). The headteachers were asked to keep an online time-diary of their activities over the period of a month; they were also required to record the value they placed on these tasks. Follow-up interviews were held with the headteachers to explore in greater detail the findings from their diary. The tasks they recorded in the online log could be divided into four categories, relating to administration, management, leadership and teaching and learning. Examples of tasks which fell into these categories are given in Table 7.1.

The general findings from the research revealed that in all schools most of the time was spent by the headteachers on low-level administration tasks, despite the fact that they attributed low value to such tasks. The headteachers were reluctant to delegate to middle management or to other members of the SMT, especially tasks to which they attributed higher value. Delegation was a particular problem in small schools, as one headteacher pointed out: 'That's fine when you've got someone to delegate to' (Neil *et al*, 2001: 50). Another headteacher stated that he would like to have delegated some tasks but was unable to, and as a result he was unable to spend time doing the aspects of his job which he thought were priorities: 'I have a vision of how I'd like to be a leader, but life doesn't actually turn out that way' (Neil *et al*, 2001: 51).

The fact remains, therefore, that the job of school headteacher is a complex one, which involves administration, management and leadership abilities. There are jobs which need to be done by the headteacher, or delegated by him or her to suitable colleagues, without which the school would cease to function. It is important, however, that the headteacher should not become so involved with the low-value housekeeping tasks that sight is lost of the fact that the headteacher is the main learner and the main instrument of change in the school. What is needed is some way of combining the routine and chief executive functions with the more highly valued focus on learning which is, after all, what the school's business should be about. The work of Stewart and colleagues at the New Zealand Principal

Table 7.1 Diary of headteachers' activities

Focus	Task in log-book	Examples
Administration	Routine administration	Routine phone calls, visits from parents and others
	Significant administration	Staff meetings, BOG, clergy, SMT, assembly
Management	Consulting with HoD	Discussion with HoD/subject co-ordinator about department's work
	Discussion with teacher	Discussion with a teacher outside the classroom
	Resolving conflict	Attempt to resolve conflict between individuals or groups of staff, parents or others
Leadership	Encouraging good management	Informal/formal meetings with management on progress/successes
	Identifying school's professional capital	Observation of or initiating discussion with management on the school's intellectual and professional capital and its use across the school
	Planning and reflection	Time alone to plan and reflect
	Disseminating good practice	Spreading and encouraging good professional practice
Teaching and learning	Assessment	Dealing with all aspects of assessment
	Teaching	Classroom teaching including cover for teacher absences
	Discipline/progress	A review of an individual student about discipline problems or their academic progress
	Classroom visit	Classroom visit including observation or obtaining information on students' progress or areas of the curriculum
	Addressing class/year/school	Speak to groups ranging from classes to whole school
	Discussion with class/year group	Formal/informal discussion with class or year group on future academic plans

and Leadership Centre at Massey University has been widely accepted in New Zealand as one way of combining management and leadership for learning. Stewart has developed a Digital Portfolio and a Conceptual Job Description as a process to encourage the linking of action and thinking. By being linked to the Standards for Principalship, the digital portfolio allows the headteachers to engage in reflective action as they engage in a reflective critique of their own work whilst meeting the required National Standards. This work is available for review in the publications (Stewart and Prebble, 1993; Stewart, 2000; Stewart, in press) and at the Web site www.edex.net.nz.

Practical aspects of the headteacher's role

In discussing the practical aspects of the job of headteacher, reference will be made interchangeably to the terms headteacher, manager, strategic manager, chief executive and leader. Some of the aspects relating to middle management already discussed in Chapter 6 will be of relevance for the senior strategic manager.

The MCI competences

As a framework for this section we will focus on the Manager Charter Initiative (MCI; 1998), which pioneered an approach to management development whereby the competent manager provides a portfolio of evidence to prove competence. Accreditation of prior knowledge and achievement as an assessment method prevents experienced and competent managers from going through unnecessary hoops. Gaps identified in knowledge and skill are incorporated into an action plan. Candidates do not fail as in a system of normal referencing but receive advice as to how they can achieve competence. Crediting competence in the workplace has proven to be cost and time effective, benefiting both the organization and the individual manager. The influence of the MCI on the approach developed in the NPQH is evident.

The knowledge requirements for senior managers are as follows: communication, continuous improvement, organizational context, delegation, information handling, involvement and motivation, leadership styles, legal requirements, meetings, planning, providing support, recruitment and selection and working relationships. The personal competencies, which complement the knowledge requirements relate to the skills and attitudes which are considered to be essential for effective performance. The relevant personal competencies we will deal with in the following sections are:

- acting strategically;
- behaving ethically;
- focusing on results;
- building teams;
- communicating;
- acting assertively;
- managing self (NEBSM: 7ff).

The knowledge requirements and personal competencies relate to each other as follows: The justification as to **why** a manager carries out a role in a particular way links to the knowledge requirements. **How** the manager feels that he or she achieved the results relates to the personal competencies. It is with the **how** that the following section deals with.

Acting strategically

The personal competency of 'acting strategically' (NEBSM: 7) is key since it is essential to the strategic manager and his or her organization for joint learning and progression. The NPQH standards define 'strategic direction and development of the school' as Key area 1 and that: 'The headteacher working with the board of governors develops a strategic view for the school and its community and analyses and plans for its future needs and further development within the local, national and international context' (DfES, 2001d: 12).

The MCI (1998) definition of strategy is 'long-term plans which will guide the organization in achieving its mission', the 'mission' being the long-term goal the organization seeks to achieve and 'vision' is the way you would like your organization to be in the future.

An example of how the knowledge requirement and personal competency 'acting strategically' fit together is taken from the unit of the MCI entitled 'Review the external and internal operating environments' (NEBSM: Unit A6). The competency 'acting strategically' is evidenced when the strategic manager:

- displays an understanding of how the different parts of the organization and its environment fit together;
- works towards a clearly defined vision of the future;
- clearly relates goals and actions to the strategic aims of the organization;
- takes opportunities when they arise to achieve the longer-term aims or needs of the organization (NEBSM, Unit A6).

Focusing specifically on the first indicator above, ie 'displays an understanding of how the different parts of the organization and its environment fit together', the manager may use the widely known benchmarking tools of PEST and SWOT analysis to determine the strengths and development issues of the internal aspects of the organization and to assess the status of the organization in relation to the environment in which it operates. In the case of a school, the external environment would be other local schools, the local, national and international community.

PEST analysis allows the headteacher to analyse the school with regard to external issues in terms of the following environments:

- political;
- economic;
- social;
- technological.

In order to benchmark, it is necessary for the headteacher to look at his or her operating external environment before focusing on the internal environment. We will take Northern Ireland as the context for this example. There has been widespread publicity in the national media of civil unrest in the locality of North Belfast which is a flashpoint between Catholic and Protestant neighbourhoods; protestors from one community created an environment which prevented school children from walking to school. The following issues arise:

- Political environment. A headteacher in this environment would have to consider how the context in which the school is located affects the short- and long-term planning in the light of these constraints. It could be pragmatic in the short term, for example, by hiring transport in order to convey the children safely to school. In the long term it might involve the headteacher taking advantage of a relevant government initiative, for example, Education for Mutual Understanding, by establishing a working relationship with a school in the other community.
- Economic environment. There is now a greater importance placed on knowledge which has an impact on the curriculum. In a locality where there is high unemployment, the headteacher would have to ensure that the curriculum has relevance for the students in the school and that appropriate provision was made in terms of training opportunities and careers guidance.
- Social environment. The social environment might relate to the socio-economic categories of the children in the catchment area. For the headteacher analysing the social external environment, there would be sensitive issues associated with this fact; for example there would be a high percentage of children on free school meals. This would impact on several areas of the school's pastoral care system.
- Technological environment. The technological changes which have emerged during the 1980s and 1990s have created an international environment whereby the swiftness of communication impacts on the leading educators. In the Northern Ireland context headteachers have to ensure that they and their staff are trained to use ICT in order to facilitate children's learning. The government initiative New Opportunities Fund contains certain measures which allow the Department of Education to allocate funding to schools specifically for staff training and development in ICT, student development and hardware.

Another benchmarking tool is SWOT analysis which is a method of helping the headteacher to analyse his or her organization from an internal perspective for strengths and weaknesses and a combination of internal and external with regard to opportunities and threats:

- Strengths;
- Weaknesses;
- Opportunities;
- Threats.

The successful headteacher must know him- or herself and the school. Internally, qualitative and quantitative evaluation instruments are used to determine an audit of current corporate competence. The findings subsequently inform the planning process which is an integral strategic aspect of the role of the strategic manager, particularly as he or she relates to the Board of Governors.

Findings for a school in Wales might be as follows:

- Strengths of the school might include: committed staff, who freely give of their time for extra curricular activities; well qualified staff with considerable subject expertise, who continue to be willing to support new government initiatives and related continuing professional development; an active PTA which recently raised, through sponsorship, finance for six new computers to support the Reading Recovery scheme; a new state of the art all-weather pitch; a Board of Governors actively involved in supporting the headteacher.
- Weaknesses might include: excellent individual teachers who comprise teams which are evidently not yet high-performing; administrative staff requiring ICT training; inadequate financial planning; lack of systematic reviewing; truancy; neighbourhood vandalism impinging on the school grounds.
- Opportunities identified might include: access to new measures allowing additional funding to inform the curriculum; interventions such as speakers and consultants to support curriculum development; twinning with a school in Austria; partnerships with local business; motivation to climb league tables.
- Threats might be: demographic shifts leading to falling numbers; 75 per cent of children taking free school meals; a deputy head responsible for pastoral care requiring CPD; a recently built competing local school with state of the art facilities.

The headteacher can use this method to best effect by recognizing and building upon the strengths of the organization, by considering the weaknesses as development issues and by turning threats into additional opportunities. In using these tools for benchmarking, however, the headteacher must have a clear strategy for the school.

Hargreaves and Hopkins (1991: 128) define a strategy as: 'the framework for solving problems in development planning and includes: a definition of the purpose or goal to be achieved; an outline of the main pathways for reaching the goal; a planned time frame for reaching the goal; an estimate of the costs'.

Evidence for a headteacher's strategy will include products or outcomes such as a business and corporate plan incorporating the development plan, consultative documents and discussion papers, agenda and minutes of effective governing body or senior management team meetings and annual reports. Specifically, the headteacher creates and implements a strategic plan, underpinned by sound financial planning which identifies priorities and targets for ensuring that students achieve high standards and make progress, increasing teacher effectiveness and securing school improvement. Acting strategically in the school context directly correlates with school improvement. The headteacher must first recognize that he or she is both the leading professional and the chief executive of the organization which is staffed by professionals, a dual role discussed in the research section above. The difficulty in working in both capacities has been mentioned in the research above (Neil et al, 2001; McEwen et al, 2002), but with the increased bureaucracy on schools dating from the Education Reform Act (1988), headteachers are responsible, for example, for the financial running of the school in addition to the curriculum and learning which are fundamental to schools. Fidler (1996) critiques the importance of the leader in a professional setting acting as chief executive in a managerial capacity and also as a leader in the symbolic and political sense. The headteacher as chief executive is also a manager of managers (the managers being the middle managers such as heads of department or curriculum leaders as discussed in Chapter 6). Above all, the headteacher must espouse professional values (Grace, 2000; McEwen et al, 2002).

The Scottish National Standards define the starting point for strategic thinking as: 'Thinks in the long term, has clarity of vision, actively generates ways of achieving aims, able to see and use opportunities and avoids threats, has ability to see the whole as well as the parts and is flexible and open to new ideas' (University of Edinburgh, 2001, Scottish National Standards 3.2.2).

The English National Standards for headteachers use seven performance indicators identifying how the headteacher turns strategic thinking into strategic reality. The headteacher must:

- create and implement a strategic plan;
- lead by example and embody the vision;
- create an ethos;
- provide enthusiastic direction;
- ensure that the management, finance, organization and administration of the school support its vision and aims;
- ensure that policies and priorities take account of national, local and school data, and inspection and research findings;
- carry out systematic monitoring and review (DfES, 2001d: 12).

When the headteacher as chief executive has agreed the plan with the Board of Governors, a plan which embraces SMART – specific, measurable, achievable, realistic and time related objectives, known and understood by all stakeholders – he or she can continue the process of empowerment and self-evaluation. Hargreaves and Hopkins list some advantages of development planning which are precise and convincing:

- A development plan focuses on the educational aims for all the students;
- A development plan covers all aspects: curriculum and assessment, teaching, management and organization, finance and resources;
- A development plan captures the long-term vision;
- A development plan relieves the stress of teachers by allowing them to exercise more control over change;
- Teachers receive recognition and their confidence grows;
- The quality of staff development improves;
- The partnership between the teaching staff and the governing body is strengthened;
- Reporting on the role of the school is made easier (1991: 30).

They emphasize the importance of building on early success, of building a general understanding of the process, of generating ownership and commitment and of focusing on priorities. The plan must identify roles and responsibilities and is essentially a creative process involving people. This very creativity includes a straight line from 'a' to 'b' and by its very nature must be reviewed regularly. The plan is a working document, which should not lie on a shelf gathering dust, but should be referred to and used. Planning is enhanced by the process of auditing the school's external and internal working environment, as discussed earlier; of turning priorities for development into SMART objectives towards implementation and evaluation. As the headteacher acts strategically and addresses each of the stages of planning he or she is involved in a cyclical process and can enter or leave the cycle at any point. See Figure 7.1 below.

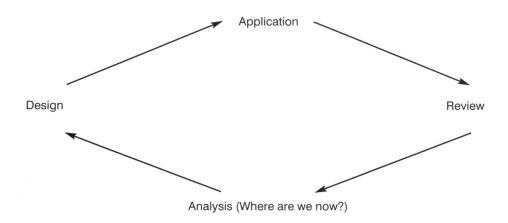

Figure 7.1 Planning stages

Related issues for the headteacher are:

- Where do we hope to be in three years' time?
- What help do we need to get there?
- How do we implement these?

The practical outworking of the plan hinges on the headteacher's policies and procedures, evidence that the school promotes quality issues which centre upon systematic reviewing.

School policies

The review, as contained in the school development plan, is spear-headed through school policies. The main issues for the headteacher regarding policies are how to organize and ensure confidence. There are some policies which are common to most schools: equal opportunities policy; health and safety policy; child protection policy; staff development policy; homework policy; assessment policy; disability awareness policy; drugs policy. The nature of a school's policies, in addition to being determined by external constraints, will also be dependent upon the sector which the school represents: a nursery school would consider a policy on play to be essential but not necessarily one related to drugs misuse.

Policies and related procedures should be a major influence on the work of a school. The headteacher as chief executive must be clear about those that are necessary for legal compliance, and not only as out-workings of his or her vision. For example, a Health and Safety Policy will always be needed to meet statutory requirements and this cannot be ignored. An example might be the need to install extra toilets because of European legislation.

This objective, as detailed in the school development plan, and linked to the Health and Safety Policy can be tested by asking if it is SMART. Reviewing is interim or final. Interim questions might be:

- Have I asked for planning permission?
- Does my budget allow for capital expenditure?
- Have I dealt with relevant child protection issues?

The final reviewing would indicate that the new facility is in place and 'fit for purpose'.

Other policies, for example the school homework policy, may depend entirely on the vision and values of the school. The commitment of all shareholders can be achieved by involving them in the process of creating policies. This, in a progressive school, might also include the opinions and recommendations of the major shareholder – the students. Pupil representation is one feature of the school as a learning organization.

The final accountability for the creation of policies and procedures is that of the headteacher in his or her role as chief executive and such an approach improves effectiveness and helps staff to cope with the many changes faced by education-alists.

Prior to empowering change in the organization, the headteacher must engender change in him- or herself.

The learning journal

As stated earlier, the headteacher is the head learner in the school. It is essential, therefore that he or she continues to learn and, learn in the role as headteacher and encourage the staff in the school to continue learning as professionals. It is through reflection on learning that self-improvement will take place and the development of all the personal competencies will be achieved to full potential through systematic reflective learning. Maintaining a learning journal for personal reflection is a very useful tool for measuring personal improvement.

The key for the use of this tool is to become aware of the learning opportunities that are present in most experiences. The processes involved in reflecting on the learning opportunities assists the headteacher in being more able to articulate what has been learned and, thereby, behave differently in the future. Various opportu-nities, both formal and informal, present themselves daily to the aware head-teacher – discussions with staff; meetings with parents; inspection findings; press releases; shadowing; conferences; Web site research. The research journal used in the project mentioned above (Neil *et al*, 2001; McEwen *et al*, 2002) is an online log which encourages headteachers to map their time. The journal recommended by Stewart (2000) focuses attention on learning both for the headteacher and the school as an organization.

The learning community

While reflecting on his or her learning and therefore optimizing improvement, the headteacher should also have a strategy for building learning into the organization. Lewin (1947) has contributed a number of techniques to analysing change. His assumption was that an organization was at equilibrium with its surroundings when forces for change balanced forces which resisted change. The headteacher might usefully employ this force field analysis model to identify the relevant forces resisting change. Earlier in this chapter we considered the necessity for the head-teacher as chief executive to analyse the external environment and the next stage in this process is to audit the internal capability of the school. This serves to measure the strengths and weaknesses of the school against the backdrop of the envi-ronment in which the school operates. Lewin's model complements the use of the other analytical strategies such as PEST and SWOT, discussed earlier in this chapter.

Lewin identifies three stages in the change process: unfreezing, moving and refreezing. The headteacher must first 'unfreeze' the school – staff must feel uncomfortable first before they are prepared to change. Refreezing involves changing organizational norms, procedures and policies. There are various interventions which the headteacher might employ to facilitate change:

- organizational learning;
- organizational development;
- school-based review;
- school inspections (see Chapter 8);
- consultancy;
- quality assurance initiatives;
- CPD;
- performance management (see Chapter 9);
- management competencies (discussed in this chapter).

Schools should embrace learning as a priority but this is not always self-evident. Consequently the CPD of staff and the challenges of a knowledge-based society are often low on the list of priorities. It can be argued that when a school focuses on improving teaching and learning, the essence of the remit of the chief executive officer as headteacher, this ultimately impacts on the whole school as an improving organization (Neil *et al*, 2001; McEwen *et al*, 2002). Performance management and assessing teachers against national criteria support this process, as will be discussed in Chapter 9.

For further information on quality schemes such as the Excellence Model, Investors in People and Charter Mark, refer to the Cabinet Office Web site: www.cabinet-office.gov.uk.

Moral communities

Sergiovanni (1991, 1996, 1998) argues that theories of management, motivation and control used in corporations do not make sense for schools. Sergiovanni's theory of school leadership has as its central premise that moral connections are grounded in cultural norms. He states that moral connections come from the duties teachers, parents and students accept and the obligations they feel toward others and towards their work (see also Grace, 2000).

Obligations result from common commitments to shared values and beliefs. Sergiovanni's schoolhouse theory is ideas-based. It emphasizes real connections; evokes sacred images; acknowledges the intrinsic motivation of humans; compels people to respond for internal rather than external reasons; acknowledges that people are motivated in part by self-interest but having the capacity to respond for internal reasons; reflects constructionist teaching and learning principles; strives for transformation. He emphasizes that it is only the inquiring teacher who will produce inquiring students. We might extrapolate that the inquiring headteacher will produce inquiring teachers. Sergiovanni stresses that real schools are loosely managed but culturally tight, hence allowing the chief executive to manage change through collegiality and shared values.

Behaving ethically

This second personal competency relevant to a school leader (NEBSM: 19) is defined as:

- showing integrity and fairness in decision making;
- setting objectives and creating cultures which are ethical;
- clearly identifying and raising ethical concerns relevant to your organization;
- working towards the resolution of ethical dilemmas based on reasoned approaches (NEBSM: 19).

Rendering account for stewardship of a school is a legal, professional and ethical requirement for headteachers. It is through the allocation of public funds and the financial support of parents and others, that a headteacher is enabled to maintain a school. Therefore it is essential that the headteacher is able to account for his or her decisions and policies. Accountability is the key word that separates the head-teacher from the deputy and from all other members of staff. They all have varying levels and degrees of responsibility but no accountability. To coin a phrase: the buck stops at the headteacher. The school's accountability, and therefore that of the headteacher, is determined by statute law on education.

The headteacher's ethical and professional responsibilities, however, are wider than those legal aspects. The caring tradition continues to be crucial to the role; care and consideration for all relevant stakeholders goes far beyond legislative require-ments. Headteachers are frequently the main channel of communication between the school and all stakeholders such as the local community, the LEAs, the Departments of Education, the media, and they are accountable for levels of communication. Headteachers are responsible to the Governing Body of the school to communicate responsibly with the external operating environment.

The headteacher must ensure that the school has:

- procedures for viewing performance or results: inspections, audits;
- mechanisms for bringing the organization to account: appraisal, reports, complaints procedures, feedback;
- formal investigative procedures: disciplinary hearings, procedures of civil and criminal law, appeals; sanctions, penalties and rewards;

- statements about roles and responsibilities: job descriptions, contracts, policies.

Public awareness has been raised through government intervention and the necessity of providing a high quality service. This high quality service is determined by the headteacher's accountability to raise standards. The White Paper *Excellence in Schools* (DfEE, 1997) links standards thus with accountability through recommending performance tables; challenging targets; improved school inspection by Ofsted; a more outward looking Department of Education; key focus on special educational needs and raising of achievement of ethnic minority students. Documents such as the school prospectus and the Governing Body's annual report have prescribed contents.

There is increasing willingness and opportunities for parents to seek legal redress for inadequate schooling of their children. The ethical headteacher will not only ensure that parents do not have cause for redress but will create an open forum for communication and dialogue with parents.

Focusing on results

The pressure on headteachers to obtain results at many levels has never been greater. The headteacher as chief executive shows why he or she performs competently in relation to the MCI Standards by:

- maintaining a focus on objectives;
- tackling problems and taking advantage of opportunities as they arise;
- prioritizing objectives and scheduling work to make best use of time and resources;
- focusing personal attention on specific details that are critical to the success of a key event;
- establishing and communicating high expectations of performance, including setting an example to others;
- monitoring the quality of work;
- minimizing barriers to excellence;
- setting goals that are demanding of him- or herself as chief executive and of others (NEBSM: 77).

'Managing for results' (MFR) and the related 'management by objectives' are practical terms used to describe successful management, although the former is more relevant to schools. Managing for results makes a clear statement as to the results which can be achieved from the system, not just in terms of task, but also in terms of motivation, well-being and development of people. There is no ambiguity or misunderstanding with managing for results. Results can be planned for and measured. MFR is a continuous process and must be flexible enough to cope with the changing needs of the organization, ie the school. Key result areas/analysis is a useful tool for the headteacher to analyse all aspects of the organization critically.

Since Local Management of Schools (LMS) devolved financial control to the school, one of the significant result areas for the headteacher is that of monitoring and control of budgets, with predicted expenditure matching actual expenditure as closely as possible and with all variances explained. Although the primary responsibility of a school is to provide the best education possible for its students, control over a delegated budget brings responsibility for financial stewardship. The standards for financial management identified by Ofsted cover:

- governance;
- financial planning;
- budget monitoring;
- purchasing;
- internal control;
- assets/security.

For further information on these standards, refer to the Ofsted Web site: www.ofsted.gov.uk/public/index.htm. For further guidance on financial management the Web site of the Audit Commission is useful: www.audit-commission.gov.uk.

Raising standards must also be at the core of a school's work and the headteacher needs to identify clearly the strengths and weaknesses of performance of students and to set targets for raising achievement. The statutory requirements for target setting should not be used to add to the bureaucratic burden of teachers. However, headteachers should expect teachers to be involved in setting targets and the target setting process should be kept simple and manageable.

Building teams

(See NEBSM: 59). In performing effectively the headteacher will build effective teams. In the MCI personal competency definition an effective team builder will:

- actively build relationships with others;
- make time available to support others;
- provide feedback designed to improve people's future performance;
- show respect for others;
- show sensitivity to the needs and feelings of others;
- keep others informed about plans and progress;
- use power and authority in a fair and equitable manner.

A useful starting point for the senior manager's approach to effective team building is to address why effective teams produce results (note the link to previous personal competency). After the various stages of team development have been completed: forming, norming, storming, performing teams operate efficiently and effectively and achieve results based upon collaboration. Research, particularly that of Belbin (1981) has shown that effective teams are made up of a variety of types of people. She identifies eight different characteristics or types of behaviour as follows:

- a person who prioritizes and motivates, leading to decision making;
- an ideas person;
- someone who actively listens and handles 'difficult' people easily;
- a details person focused on the task;
- an organizer whose plans turn into actions;
- a negotiator who networks effectively;
- someone who challenges and pushes others to their full potential;
- a consultant/analyst who provides a variety of choices (based on Belbin, 1981).

Effective teams have sound procedures, good communication systems, understood and known by all involved. Active listening is one of the essential skills which promote effective team management. Teamwork shares the workload, pools resources and sees speedier achievement of results. The headteacher has a key role in leading his teams and in creating an atmosphere conducive to learning.

Teams achieve results when all members are clear about roles, responsibilities, goals, timescales; when there are choices in pathways; when there is regular reviewing; when members feel that they are contributing; when the leader disallows scape-goating and collusion; when the leader creates an atmosphere of openness, precluding hidden agenda.

As a result of Belbin's research, a Self Perception Inventory was devised which is a useful tool in management development; it is also suggested in Chapter 4 that awareness of roles in a team could also be a useful area for staff generally. The headteacher should be aware of the types of behaviours and personalities in the senior management team and indeed those of the Board of Governors.

Communicating

(See NEBSM: 7). The headteacher is the main communicator both internally and between the school and the community, as discussed earlier in this chapter. Those people possessing this personal competency is defined as follows in the MCI standards as follows:

- identifies the information needs of listeners;
- listens actively, asks questions, clarifies points and rephrases others' statements to check for mutual understanding;
- adapts communication styles appropriate to learners and situations, including selecting an appropriate time and place;
- confirms listeners' understanding through questioning and interpretation of non-verbal signals;
- encourages listeners to ask questions and rephrases statements to clarify their understanding;
- modifies communication in response to feedback from listeners.

The headteacher is constantly using a variety of situational communication modes: use of interim or summative written or verbal reports, assemblies, meetings with teachers, meetings with senior staff, meetings with parents, conferences, staff development days, Board of Governor meetings, meetings with teacher union representatives, interviews, classroom teaching and many others. The methods of communication are both formal and informal and include internal and external channels. The written and verbal reports may be for Governors, parents, the LEA, the Department of Education or the press.

The headteacher's main channel of communication internally is through the school development plan, as discussed earlier in the chapter. The headteacher has, however, daily opportunities to communicate the vision of the school to all stakeholders, particularly staff and students through dialogue and discussions.

Chairing meetings is an internal aspect of the headteacher's role as communicator. It affords an opportunity to communicate vision and goals effectively; to influence; to set creative agendas and lead the organization forward; to make decisions and solve problems; to action plan towards setting short- and long-term goals. Ineffective meetings add to bureaucracy and waste time and resources. It is therefore essential that the headteacher use meetings to best advantage for the school.

The headteacher as effective communicator adheres to general rules:

- Know your audience.
- Know your message.
- Use appropriate methods and media for the listener.
- Check for understanding.
- Use empathy and feedback.
- Keep it short and simple (KISS).

Acting assertively

(See NEBSM: 69). The MCI standards detail the personal competency of acting assertively as follows:

- take personal responsibility for making things happen;
- take control of situations and events;
- act in an assured and unhesitating manner;
- say no to unreasonable requests.

It is a common observation that some people are better at getting their own way than others. Assertiveness, the ability to be firm, clear and personally powerful, is valuable to all managers, in this case headteachers, because energy is released and the headteacher feels more confident. It is easier for people to respect a confident manager. Assertiveness must be accompanied, however, by vision, good ideas and integrity, hence creating a more productive working environment. Headteachers can improve their assertiveness by attending specific training programmes which help them to examine their own backgrounds and any related 'baggage' which might prevent them from being assertive. Skills learned at these sessions include: being focused, communicating a clear and unambiguous message, repeating a point, emphasizing, reflecting, summarizing.

One of the essential generic skills in acting assertively is that of active listening. It is common to feel that the input of a colleague in a discussion is simply an irritating interruption of one's own train of thought or flow of ideas.

It is necessary to learn how to listen actively, creating a relaxed atmosphere which indicates that you are truly interested in the thoughts and ideas of the other person, that you are in fact willing to listen. Some special techniques are: reflecting, summarizing, clarifying, probing, use of body language, empathy as employed in a counselling setting. When there is an atmosphere of unconditional positive regard, the other person is encouraged to be open and creative. Active listening can provide the following for the headteacher:

- more data/access to additional information to help with thinking and taking decisions;
- more good ideas;
- better relationships;
- increased commitment;
- airing of feelings preventing pent-up resentment and aggression;
- support when dealing with difficult people (for further useful information on this sensitive issue consult Sutherland and Cooper, 1997).

These skills are particularly important in appraisal procedures as will be discussed in Chapter 9.

Some tips on behaving assertively:

- Own your own 'I' statements: rather than saying 'Everyone thinks', say 'I think'.
- Repeat what you heard the other person saying, that is reflect it back, which helps the speaker to realize that you were listening properly.
- Let the other person know that you know how he or she feels.
- Disclose your feelings at an appropriate level.
- Ask for more information and be prepared to say that you need time to think.

Covey (1992) recommends the preferred option is a win–win situation. Choosing to act assertively may mean not getting what you want but having to negotiate a compromise instead.

Managing self

The final personal competency we will look at is 'managing self' (NEBSM: 59) since the headteacher must continue to know him- or herself in order to be able to know his or her school and its stakeholders. It includes the following:

- accepting personal comments or criticism without becoming defensive;
- remaining calm in difficult or uncertain circumstances;
- handling others' emotions without becoming personally involved.

This is related to the section 'self-awareness' discussed in Chapter 6.

Self-evaluation is an essential approach to managing self. Evaluation may be as simple as knowing which questions to ask. According to Robbins, questions are the laser human consciousness and it is through questions that we learn: 'In fact, the entire Socratic method (a way of teaching that dates back to the ancient Greek philosopher Socrates) is based upon the teacher doing nothing but asking questions, directing the student's focus and getting them to come up with their own answers. Successful people are those who have asked better questions and, as a result, have got better answers' (1992: 188).

What are the questions that a headteacher might ask first in order to manage self? The following are possible areas of reflection. The answers of course are the responsibility of the reader:

- How well do I manage time?
- Do I have a healthy work life balance?
- Do I have strategies for handling stress?
- Do I plan effectively?

- Do I unlock my own creativity?
- Do I understand the difference between busy and effective?
- Do I have a generous nature?
- Do I know what is important?
- Am I comfortable with accountability?
- Are my relationships positive and productive?
- Do I know when to say 'No'?
- Do I recognize when I am becoming unwell and seek help?
- Do I value my mental health?
- How do I sabotage my own learning and hence the learning of my teams and organization?
- Do I know how to breathe properly?
- Does my life have a spiritual dimension?
- Do I really have a vision worth following?
- What is the most important thing I can do right now?

In the management of self, the questioner begins by asking firstly questions about himself as headteacher and subsequently about his school and all related stakeholders. However, this process must begin with managing self. Questions are the answer – How do I build my school on my vision?

This section has provided some insight into the roles and responsibilities of the headteacher. Within a book such as this it is not possible to cover in great detail every aspect of leading a school and the reader is referred to the reading list at the end of the chapter and to the references at the end of the book.

The following case study will set some of what has been discussed above in the context of one school and the work and vision of one school headteacher.

Case study of a headteacher

Dr Bobby Jennings is the headteacher of Slemish College, situated in the town of Ballymena in County Antrim, which is an integrated, co-educational sixth form college with over 600 students and 42 teaching staff and 18 support staff. The college has been running for over seven years and Bobby, its only headteacher, this year was winner of the Leadership Trust Award, having been nominated by a student in the school. He agreed to be interviewed on his perspectives of the life of a headteacher; in the interview the following aspects were discussed:

- professional profile;
- school priorities;

- the job of a headteacher;
- working with staff;
- managing CPD for staff;
- producing the school development plan;
- impediments to the job;
- advice for aspiring headteachers.

Professional profile

Bobby started his work in education as a teacher of PE, later training to teach RE, working as a subject leader of both subjects at some stage. He has taught in four schools, including the present one. For some years he was employed by one of the LEAs as an advisor and this brought him into contact with school headteachers. It was his work in the LEA that made clear to him the potential the job of headteacher offers to initiate change and to be able to influence the learning of children and which inspired him to apply for the job of headteacher in Slemish College. He has various academic qualifications including a degree, a masters in theology and a masters in educational management and a doctorate in philosophy.

School priorities

The headteacher is responsible for the vision of the school, according to Bobby; it is his vision, and the shared vision of the staff and students, that the focus in Slemish College should be on learning and teaching, ensuring that there is an ethos conducive to independent learning for the students. He believes that there should be transparency at all levels, from management to NQT and that the work for the school should be child-centred. Recently the school has undertaken a Quality Audit which focused on learning styles and multiple intelligences; this audit was carried out by teams in the school and validated by external school inspectors. The headteacher was one of those involved in the headteacher research discussed in an earlier section of this chapter.

The school has twice been awarded the Investor in People (IiP) award and they use Business Excellence (part of the European Foundation for Quality Management) as a tool to look at the work of the school as a whole. These initiatives are important for the staff and the students, but also for the Board of Governors and, in the competitive market, the parents and potential clients of the school. The school is also one of the London Institute's network schools.

The job of a headteacher

The job of headteacher can only be understood in the context of the school in which he or she is working. The feature which would distinguish the role in this case-study school is that the headteacher started off with a clean slate; there were no cynical staff in post whom he had to change to his way of thinking, no traditions which had to be continued and, in general, no 'baggage'. All staff were appointed on his approval and applicants for jobs in the school are left in no doubt about the ethos and direction of the school. The staff in the school are young, enthusiastic and of very high quality; in recent years two of the NQTs have been awarded Teacher of the Year, one class assistant was Class Assistant of the Year 2002.

The headteacher's door in the school is literally open most of the time. Staff, students, parents have access to him.

Leadership, management and administration

There is a degree of overlap from one to the other, according to Bobby. The commitment to leadership as opposed to the other two aspects of the job is revealed by the nomenclature of the senior staff structure; he is supported in his role by a deputy head, three assistant heads (senior teachers) and an extended leadership team of four (most of whom are subject leaders). Together the senior leadership team (SLT), which contains a good gender balance, age range, mix of personalities and breadth of experience, mutually support one other in order to ensure that all the tasks are undertaken.

'It is important to recognize the strengths and qualities of the members of the SLT. I can honestly say that I really trust my senior staff and therefore am able to delegate many of the tasks to them, that they do far better than I can. We have done the Belbin Inventory and therefore we are aware of each other's strengths and weaknesses. I like the strategy aspects of the job'.

Bobby admits that there are administrative tasks which he is either not interested in or that other staff do better than he can and he is more than willing to let the staff work to their strengths:

'I, for example, am more creative and am not really interested in sitting at a desk pushing papers. I want to get out there, to be involved in the life of the school. Delegation is vital and my SLT are very keen to free me up wherever possible to get on with the creative aspects of the job that I do best'.

There are, however, aspects of administration which, although others could do, Bobby, as headteacher, feels it important for him to be involved in, such as interviewing staff. Next year, it is in his plan to spend some time at lunchtimes eating with the students and finding out more about their views; he has done this in the past and it was successful. 'For me it is important to be visible in the school'.

Qualities of a headteacher

According to Bobby, from his own experience both as a current headteacher and having worked with several headteachers in his capacity as adviser, an effective headteacher has to have many of the following qualities:

- interpersonal skills;
- integrity;
- enthusiasm;
- commitment;
- sound judgment;
- capacity to be a role model.

Some of these things cannot be learned, but others can:

'It is important when you make mistakes to be open and honest about them. I think that the staff here would recognize that if I have made mistakes, it has been done with no malice aforethought and that they have been genuine mistakes. They are more likely to be forgiving if they feel that they can trust you and that you are a person of integrity. The staff here are very supportive'.

In addition to these qualities, it is important for a headteacher to inform him- or herself about the literature on learning, teaching and leadership. Bobby does this by attending and participating in international conferences and by reading widely. He has to remain *au fait* with developments for his input to a post-graduate course on Expert Teaching at one of the local HEIs.

Working with staff and CPD

It is vital to have the staff working with you as headteacher. Bobby admits that it is easier for him than for other headteachers in other schools since he has a very committed staff who share his vision. This cannot be taken for granted, however and efforts have to be made to keep staff on board. This is done by encouraging staff to express their views on aspects of the school, either at formal meetings with their line manager or informally. Each year all staff are involved in an induction which takes place in a hotel in June. At this induction views of staff are listened to and are considered for implementation.

'When the staff see that we are committed to listening to their views and putting them into practice, if they fit with the school development plan etc, they realize that they are important and that they have a say in the running of the school. I would say that we try to get away from a top–down model of management'.

The school has a number of initiatives to encourage staff participation in learning and teaching:

Critical appreciation scheme

All staff are involved in critical reflection by observing colleagues teaching once per year. This was done on a cross-subject basis where staff observed friends teaching, and is now consolidated into departments. Staff complete an observation schedule on the visits and have a post-lesson discussion. It has proved very valuable in opening the classrooms up but also for encouraging the staff to focus more on learning.

'Even during informal times, staff can be heard openly talking about the learning which is going on in their class. Our recent quality audit focusing on multiple intelligences has also created a discourse about learning in the staff. This has to be a positive thing for the whole school'.

Staff on committees

In order to encourage participation in the life of the school, there is an open policy on committee and team membership. That is to say, that any staff with an interest in a particular aspect of the work can opt to serve on a committee, such as the curriculum committee, learning support working party, health and safety committee, for example. The quality audit team contained membership from staff with differing levels of experience.

'It is vital that the staff feel that they can work to their strengths in this school. Many staff here are in promoted posts because of the excellent contribution they make to the work of the school. In other more traditional schools, I am sure that such young teachers would not be in these roles of responsibility. I think it is important for the general life of the school that the staff are given every opportunity to develop their professional portfolio'.

Staff CPD needs

Each year departments are asked to present their list of CPD requirements; these might be courses, visits, invitations to speakers, conferences. The leadership team looks at these requests and if they are in accordance with the school development plan, funding and opportunities are provided for staff to participate in them. In recent years some staff have attended conferences on learning styles, others have visited schools in the US which were integrating Gardner's multiple intelligence model. Speakers have been invited to hold seminars on, for example, management for aspiring subject leaders: 'We see it as our role to facilitate the professional development of our staff. I think we are fairly generous in the resources we provide for staff to get involved in CPD'.

School development plan

One of the main tasks of the senior leadership team is the writing of the school development plan (SDP). Again staff have an input to this document. In April all staff are involved in an internal audit. They are asked to consider each area of the school's work (such as leadership; pastoral dimension; equality, social justice; learning support, careers) and to rate it according to a three-point scale: strong, satisfactory or area of concern. These are collated and discussed by the SLT. If an area is noted as being of concern by more than four members of staff, this is considered as an area of priority for the SDP. Other issues identified by the SLT are also taken on board. In June of the year, the SDP is submitted to the Board of Governors for approval, although they may raise points or make a contribution before the SDP is finalized. 'I think that in this way the staff feel a certain ownership of the document and they are therefore more committed to being involved in carrying it through. It has to be a shared document'.

Challenges

'The main change which has emerged in recent years, despite government protestations to the contrary, is the increased bureaucracy. As an integrated college we have to supply various pieces of information both for the Department of Education but also for the Northern Ireland Council for Integrated Education (NICIE). Also, I agree that teaches in schools have to be accountable, but I am not sure whether we have got it quite right. The teachers do not have the freedom to teach that they should have'.

Another challenge to the work as headteacher is transportation.

'This might seem a strange impediment, but there are various things I would like to try out with the curriculum and the timetable, but we are constrained by transport. Our students come from a very wide catchment area and it is therefore not possible, for example, to start at 8.30 am. This would allow us much greater flexibility in adapting the curriculum and being creative. But we live in the real world and as a leader I have to find ways round it'.

Rewards

Ultimately Bobby gets great satisfaction from his job. He says that the one thing which he finds the most rewarding is seeing individual students succeed.

Recently the students obtained their GCSE results:

'Just seeing the expression of pleasure on the students' faces when they got their results was not to be missed. It is especially true of the students who had gained most 'value-added' from the school'.

From the point of view of staff in the school, again this headteacher would give priority to opportunity for development.

'A major part for me would be the thought that we have given young staff every opportunity to develop in the profession'.

Advice

In terms of advice, Bobby would highlight much of what has been discussed already:

- Don't do it if you are not committed and enthusiastic.
- Have a love for children and for children's learning.
- Familiarize yourself with the literature on learning, education and leadership.
- Avail yourself of every CPD opportunity.
- Find ways of communicating with young people.
- Be a role model.
- Believe in the individuality of each young person.

This case study has presented the work of a headteacher in the context of one post-primary school. For reasons stated at the beginning of the case study, it may present a more rose-coloured picture than will be the case in many schools. What it does present in addition, however, is the importance for the school leader to remain focused on leadership, on learning and teaching and to find ways of freeing the school leader up to carry on the vision. The management and administrative functions will still have to be carried out, but, as a member of a team, using the strengths of each member, these functions should not detract from the leadership of the school.

Key points

- The route toward headship is now clearly mapped out with National Standards and a qualification in headship (NPQH).
- There are conflicting aspects to the role of the headteacher.
- It is a demanding job, with many responsibilities, but it can be ultimately rewarding.

Self study

Key questions

For the headteacher:

- Is your school a learning community? What is your evidence?
- Do you:
  - agree personal development plans with your staff?
  - give regular feedback? – How?
  - benchmark? – How?
  - review systematically? – How?
  - encourage mentoring? – How?
- You are the headteacher of a school which has just been congratulated on its success in achieving targets in a recent report of the Inspectorate. How did you, along with your Governors, your staff and your other major stakeholders achieve this?
- How would you lead your school towards change?
- What are the practical out-workings for the headteacher who maintains that accountability is an ethical requirement?

For the Board of Governors:

- How are you supporting your headteacher in realizing the vision for the school?
- What could you do to alleviate some of the administrative pressure on the headteacher and the SMT?

Recommended reading

Gunter, H (2001) *Leaders and Leadership in Education*, Paul Chapman, London

Loader, D (1997) *The Inner Principal*, Routledge, London

Riley, K and Louis, K S (2000) *Leadership for Change and School Reform*, RoutledgeFalmer, London

Sergiovanni, T J (1996) *Leadership for the Schoolhouse: How is it different? Why is it important?* Jossey-Bass, San Fransisco

Stewart, D (2000) *Tomorrow's Principals Today*, Kanuka Grove Press, Palmerston North

Stewart, D and Prebble, T (1993) *The Reflective Principal: School development within a learning community*, ERDC Press, Palmerston North

8 The process of inspection

The role of inspection agencies

A high level of inspection and accountability has now become a fact of life for schools. Researchers talk of a 'culture of inspection' (Scanlon, 1999: 5) and the persuasiveness of 'Ofsted discourse' in schools (Ferguson *et al*, 2000: 5). Even though, as Strathern (2000) suggests, too much information can detract from understanding and trust, and inspection can often leave schools exhausted, nevertheless schools have little choice but to conform to the wishes of the government regulatory body in the cycle of inspections currently in place.

What is interesting is that the non-ministerial organization Ofsted, which undertakes inspections in England, has changed its ways considerably since it was set up in 1992 and is continuing to do so. It is quite clear that many of the problems identified in research are being addressed. At the time of writing it is possible to discern three different phases of Ofsted operation:

- the first round of inspection: 1993–98;
- the newer 'gentler' phase: 1997–2003;
- the proposed changes: post 2003.

Ofsted was set up to be a body where responsibility is devolved and regulated at different levels. Contractors bid for inspections and then employ inspection teams. These inspection teams contain many of the former Her Majesty's Inspectors (HMIs). The teams contain a registered inspector (RgI) who leads, other team inspectors and one lay inspector per team (to represent interests outside the school). Inspectors will receive training of varying levels (see Ferguson *et al*, 2000: 2–3). This organizational aspect has not changed, although the new proposals (Ofsted, 2001a) do recommend that more serving heads and teachers should be recruited as inspectors and also that arrangements for lay inspectors be changed. The problematic areas in particular relating to lay inspectors have been identified in research (Hustler, 1999), namely the lack of representation of minority groups and non-representativeness of a lay inspector of the local community if he or she becomes full-time or permanent. Both these issues are addressed in the new proposals with a 'more diverse pool of lay inspectors' and proposals for fixed-term contracts (eg 5 years) (Ofsted, 2001a: 10).

The first round of inspection

Between September 1993 and July 1998 all the state schools in England were inspected (more than 18,600 primary, around 1,000 special and over 3,600 secondary schools). There was considerable opposition to the initial mode of inspection with reports of devastating effects on schools and sometimes questionable approaches.

The second phase

Since 1997 there has been reported improved satisfaction with the way inspections are carried out. Chapman, for example, in his recent research comments 'many teachers noted an improvement in the interactions with inspectors compared to previous inspections' (2001: 64) and Ferguson *et al* report on improved levels (94 per cent) of school satisfaction in their recent research (2000: 44). This contrasts with earlier research where much more negative attitudes in schools were reported (Case, Case and Catling, 2000). Inspection findings too have become more positive with, for example, 25 per cent of teaching in Key Stages 1 and 2 deemed unsatisfactory in 1993/94 and only 4 per cent deemed unsatisfactory in 2000/01 (Ofsted, 2002a). This may mean inspections have become gentler or that schools have improved. There is though still at the time of writing a sizeable group of academics quite opposed to the current inspection process (see the articles in Cullingford (ed), 1999 for example).

The arrangements set up towards the end and after the first round of inspections contained several new changes, which are outlined in the Ofsted document *Inspecting Schools: The Framework* (1999b):

- Although all schools originally had a full inspection, this was changed from 1999. Where a school received a positive report in the first round of inspections and was doing well, then a short inspection was deemed sufficient. This short inspection would take less time, between 25–60 per cent of the former period and involve smaller inspection teams, would not include written teacher feedback or observation of all teachers, and would not require so much documentation to be provided by the school (Ofsted, 1999b).

- Feedback was to be given to all teachers observed. This was brought in during the period 1997–98 after dissatisfaction was voiced by teachers (Ferguson *et al*, 2000: 48).
- The role of the governing body is becoming increasingly well defined. In 1998 governors were graded (out of 7) and a recent publication mentions the need for governors to monitor and evaluate a school's work (Ofsted, 2001b).
- Schools are now to be inspected on a six-yearly cycle rather than the original suggested four-yearly cycle, unless they are schools who are on special measures or deemed to have serious weaknesses (announced in 1996).

By July 2003 all secondary schools and most primary and special schools will have been inspected at least twice (Ofsted, 2001a: 1).

Arrangements 2003 onwards

The proposals published in 2001 (Ofsted 2001a) have several further new suggestions:

- a short inspection for almost all primary schools;
- new arrangements for inspecting special schools;
- flexible inspection systems to accommodate different school contexts;
- less bureaucracy;
- more serving heads and teachers on inspection teams;
- different arrangements for lay inspectors;
- schools choosing an area for inspection;
- grades for individual teachers to be abolished;
- better feedback to teachers;
- better report writing;
- more contact with parents through reports and a post-inspection meeting;
- listening to the views of students through questionnaires;
- working in closer harmony with other outside agencies.

In the new draft framework of 2002 the 'short' inspection has been renamed 'standard' with a 'full' inspection being renamed 'enhanced' (Ofsted, 2002b). Many of the suggestions that have been made and criticisms that have been levelled are accommodated by these new proposals.

There are though some areas suggested by researchers which have not been addressed by the new proposals. These include:

- improving the follow-up by Ofsted in all schools not just for those who are weak;

- giving schools a greater sense of ownership by using schools' own self-evaluations;
- separating the roles of accountable reporting and school development which are not compatible;
- ensuring that primary inspectors have appropriate expertise (Ferguson *et al*, 2000; Millett and Johnson, 1998; Scanlon, 1999).

These possible improvements are discussed in more detail in the sections that follow.

Arrangements in the UK

Scotland, Northern Ireland and Wales have different inspection arrangements. In Wales, the body responsible for inspecting schools is called Estyn. The inspection framework is similar to that in England but Welsh as a second and first language is also included in inspections. In Scotland, Her Majesty's Inspectors (HMIs) are responsible for both inspection and curriculum development and there is direct feedback into policy-making (MacNab, 2000). Many features are similar to Ofsted inspections (see below) with a report published for each school inspected including a list of key strengths and recommendations. In MacNab's research there was some scepticism in schools about inspections helping teachers to develop professionally but suggestions for curriculum development had been welcomed. An interesting aspect of inspections is highlighted by MacBeath (1999: 96), namely canvassing insights from parents and students (a feature partially in place in Ofsted inspections and likely to become more developed in England post-2003).

Northern Ireland also employs HMIs for inspection purposes with a strong emphasis on developmental input (Gray and Gardner, 1999). The inspection service is called the Education and Training Inspectorate (ETI) and it provides inspection services for the Department of Education, the Department of Employment and Learning and the Department of Culture, Arts and Leisure. Five different types of inspection are possible (distinct and specialist, general, focused, follow-up and quality assurance inspections – see Gray and Gardner, 1999: 458). Although Gray and Gardner report some anxiety relating to inspections in general, the schools in the research that they undertook reported positive reactions to inspections: 'The majority in each sector [...] felt that inspectors' reports were fair and accurate [...] For the majority of principals [...] the most valuable aspect of the inspection was the external validation of good practice that it provided' (1999: 462 and 464).

For the independent schools in England and Wales, the Independent Schools Inspectorate (ISI) is responsible for inspection.

The role of an Ofsted team in England in a school is to report on the following:

- the educational standards achieved (students' attainment, progress, attitudes to learning, behaviour and attendance);
- the quality of education (teaching, curriculum, assessment, pastoral care and relationship with parents);
- the efficient management of financial resources and leadership;
- the spiritual, moral, social and cultural development of students. (Ofsted, 1999a: 4; Ferguson *et al*, 2000: 370).

In Scotland there is a similar emphasis on quality of education and standards but less specific focus on finance and spiritual moral welfare (MacNab, 2000: 86). In Northern Ireland there is a similar picture but with an interesting dimension offered by 'quality audit inspections', where schools invite inspections teams to audit their own self-evaluations.

Experience and process of inspection

Although arrangements in the different parts of the UK differ slightly it is likely that many aspects of the inspection experience will be similar. Insights here have been drawn from the considerable body of literature that has proliferated since inspection became more of a high-profile event.

The experience and process of inspection can be looked at in terms of the three different phases:

- pre-inspection;
- the inspection visit;
- post inspection.

The experience and process can also be considered in two further dimensions: the impact of inspection on personal professional development; and the impact of inspection on school development.

The pre-inspection phase

In an Ofsted inspection during this phase there are statutory activities which take place; and statutory documents which are completed. In addition schools will want to make their own school-based preparations.

Statutory activities and documents

Before all inspections:

- The registered inspector/team leader (RgI) will visit the school to help prepare for the inspection, by briefing the staff and making him- or herself familiar with the school.
- Ofsted provides both the Ofsted team and the school with information about the school and similar schools from their database. This is the *Pre-Inspection Context and School Indicator* (PICSI) annex which may need to be updated on the RgI's pre-inspection visit.
- Performance and assessment data (PANDAs) providing comparative information about similar schools will also have been sent annually to schools (Thomas, Smees and Elliot, 2000) describe how a school may use such data; the governing body and school must arrange a meeting between the RgI and parents, giving parents at least one week's notice; reports suggest that about 40 per cent of parents attend such a meeting (Mansell and Matthews, 2001). Before this meeting a parents' questionnaire needs to be distributed and returned to the RgI. Reports suggest 'high levels of parental satisfaction' here (Mansell and Matthews, 2001).
- The headteacher will need to complete a set of Ofsted forms (S1–S4) giving information on an evaluation of the school. Ofsted recommends that heads complete and update these forms on an annual basis (Ofsted, 1999a: 30). These forms are sent to the RgI together with the last inspection report, the current school development plan and the school prospectus. In addition the RgI will need to be given further documentation at the pre-inspection meeting (a timetable, a staff handbook, list of key people and a plan of the school).
- In addition, the following documentation will need to be given to the RgI:
  - the last annual report to parents;
  - minutes of governors' meetings;
  - evidence of progress towards targets set by governors;
  - curriculum plans, policies, guidelines and schemes of work;
  - school self-evaluations;
  - any interim external evaluations since the last inspection.

Three new suggestions for the pre-inspection phase have been proposed for post-2003. These are:

- A more transparent process for dealing with the opportunities for parents, the school or governors to demand an early inspection if they are worried about standards.

- Schools being able to choose a special area of focus for inspection from their own self-evaluation to be identified on the self-evaluation form.
- A questionnaire for secondary school students aged 11–16 (Ofsted, 2002b: 43).

The latter suggestion has raised some concerns (see Learner, 2001; Letters, 2001) suggesting that 'malicious' students might misrepresent their teachers. However, there is also evidence to suggest that student feedback can be helpful, as will be seen in Chapter 9 when appraisal and performance management are discussed.

School-based preparations

There is likely to be a high level of preparation, and attendant anxiety, in the pre-inspection phase. In order to use this period effectively and to cut down on stress it may be helpful to think about the following aspects:

- co-ordinating and focusing preparation;
- monitoring the level of paperwork;
- undertaking self-evaluation;
- using consultants;
- not envisaging major changes.

Co-ordinating and focusing preparation

Research in schools has shown that teachers are likely to invest a huge amount of time and energy in preparing for lessons that may be observed and providing documentation about their teaching. Teachers in an ethnographic study by Case, Case and Catling talk of 'an obsession with recording everything in writing so that you could prove that you'd done it' (2000: 616), and in research by Ferguson *et al* of 'preparation [… as] a very intense, almost frantic time' (2000: 30). It is very understandable that activity at this level takes place. However, there are likely to be opportunity costs. Ferguson *et al* suggest that the energy committed to the pre-inspection period comes from a limited additional supply that is not easily renewed. It is important therefore to ensure that this energy is used to advantage (2000: 34). One way of doing this can be to plan carefully and in advance what will be needed, to ensure co-ordination and accurate targeting. A key strategy used by some heads in the schools researched by Ferguson *et al* was to have a 'dry run' or mock inspection, although Ofsted itself has condemned this practice (2000: 24).

Monitoring paperwork

Ofsted state categorically that: 'Documentation should *not* be written specifically for the inspection as this puts an undesirable burden on staff (Ofsted, 1999a: 31, emphasis in the original). However this may be more easily said than done. Ferguson *et al*'s comments on a similar 1995 Ofsted statement suggest that such advice 'might seem (to headteachers who feel they have no choice in the matter) to be unrealistic and insincere' (2000: 38). It will be important for schools to consider all the documentation that will be needed, particularly given that a temporary snapshot is all that inspectors have access to. Schools requiring special measures are particularly likely to have to produce a large amount of paperwork (Scanlon, 1999). Ferguson *et al* report that 'good documentation' was seen as the most common reason given by primary heads for a successful inspection: 'many primary heads had decided that co-ordinators should be armed with files or "portfolios" of photographic and other evidence designed to demonstrate the quality and diversity of the curriculum. This was often felt to have been a good decision with beneficial effects in the outcomes of the inspection' (2000: 33). In the new proposals, Ofsted draw attention to their desire to reduce bureaucracy and point to their Web site (www.ofsted.gov.uk) and publication: *Reducing the Burden of Inspection* (Ofsted/DfES, 2001).

Undertaking self-evaluation

If schools have a strong culture of self-evaluation and development then the inspection experience may be less damaging. Chapman reports that schools who are 'moving' (ie self-evaluating/dynamic) felt more positive about their inspections because of confidence in their own work (2001: 66–68). Ferguson *et al* draw a distinction between 'self-evaluation' (where schools develop their own priorities) and 'self-inspection' (where Ofsted criteria are used) and they point to the particular value of the latter if this were to be audited by Ofsted. Ofsted itself in its earlier document points to the wisdom of using the Ofsted framework: 'Many schools now use the inspection framework for regular self-evaluation between inspections, and we have issued guidance and commissioned training to encourage this process' (2001a: 6). In this proposal the following comments are also made: 'The self-evaluation submitted by headteachers […] is still variable. We need to form a more productive relationship between the two [inspection and self-evaluation]' (2001a: 6). The focus on self-evaluation has become more prominent in the 2002 framework. Ofsted states: 'The school's self-evaluation should provide a strong focus for discussion with the registered inspector at the pre-inspection visit. If the school opts to nominate an area for particular attention in the inspection, it should stem from the self-evaluation' (Ofsted, 2002b: 43).

Using consultants

It appears that using a consultant in the pre-inspection phase has been a popular option: Ferguson *et al* (2000: 23–24) found that 70 per cent of primary schools had used consultants in some capacity as had 75 per cent of secondary schools in 1996 (rising from 25 per cent in 1993). These consultants may be LEA advisers, inspectors or other consultants. Many headteachers also considered it useful to have a trained Ofsted inspector on their staff (Ferguson *et al*, 2000: 33). The new proposal to include more heads and teachers on Ofsted teams will clearly be helpful here (Ofsted, 2001a).

No major changes

Advice from heads in the extensive research by Ferguson *et al* warned against undertaking major changes in the period preceding inspection (2000: 27–31). The shortened period of notice from Ofsted inspections (down from one year to five weeks) now also means this is less likely to happen.

The inspection visit

An enhanced Ofsted inspection visit is likely to last several days, although the whole inspection process lasts longer (given in the 2002 draft framework as 'a five-week "inspection window"', Ofsted, 2002b: 32). Standard inspections naturally last less time. As well as considering the designated inspection activities, it is also helpful to reflect on the process and experience of the inspection visit.

Designated inspection activities

In the framework for inspection appropriate until 2003 (Ofsted, 1999b), the following aspects are highlighted:

- 60 per cent of inspection time will be used to observe lessons, sample students work and teachers' records and talk to students (Ofsted 1999a: 6); after 2003 this is described as 'most of the time' (Ofsted, 2002b: 21).
- Those teachers who are observed will receive feedback and be graded in a full inspection, on a scale of 1–7. Sharing of grades was abolished after January 2002 and evaluations will feed back into general comments on quality of teaching (Ofsted, 2002b: 41–42).
- Discussions will be held with staff and governors (Ofsted, 1999b: 15).

- The team will have access to 'material that would normally be in the school' (Ofsted, 1999b: 32) including policy and assessment documents, attendance registers, lesson plans etc.
- At the end of the visit the RgI will provide oral feedback at a meeting with the head and governor(s).

These last three aspects have remained unchanged in the post-2003 framework.

Handling the inspection visit

It is useful to consider insights from research from schools undergoing inspection to identify key pointers in managing an inspection visit effectively. These pointers can either be of a practical nature or relate to the more personal issues of dealing with an experience which can range from unsettling to alarming.

Practical hints can range from the advisability of a head organizing daily contact with the RgI, to managing the stress involved in being observed. A useful course on coping with inspection stress is run by the Professional Association of Teachers (PAT). Part of this course deals with keeping your voice calm (avoiding coffee which dries the vocal chords, breathing deeply, relaxing and standing properly). In this connection it can also be useful to contact the Voice Care Network which is on www.voicecare.org.uk (see Ward, 2001c).

On a more personal level three particular areas emerge as priorities in the research on schools:

- responding to the inspectors in general;
- dealing with feedback from observations;
- discussing the school.

Responding to the inspectors in general

Schools in general appear to report a high level of satisfaction with inspection teams, although in some research there are more negative responses (Kogan and Maden, 1999; Cullingford and Daniels, 1999; Cuckle and Broadhead, 1999). In Ferguson *et al*'s wide-ranging research the team is able to report that 'the evidence suggests that inspections are conducted by teams of inspection who, in the main, prove to be sensitive and professional' (2000: 11). However, this is not always the case. Millet and Johnson focus particularly on the question of expertise in their research into inspection of mathematics at primary schools and they conclude that 'the assumption of subject expertise across the whole primary range may not be a tenable one' (1998: 512). Out of the nine inspectors they interviewed, expertise was sometimes only at the level of O-level Maths, raising queries as to the ability to comment on subject content. Silcock and Wyness (1998) interviewed 12 inspectors to consider their attitudes towards schools and reforms and found that only three were 'wholeheartedly in sympathy' with teachers' problems (with six balancing sympathy with the need for reform, and three having little sympathy and focusing on the need for reform and change).

There is likely then to be some variability between inspection teams and within them (commented on by Winkley, 1999 and by Fitzgibbon and Stephenson-Forster, 1999), and schools (and in particular the head) will need to take this into account in responses to an inspection. An interesting perspective is offered by Ferguson *et al*. Their research team organized for two senior staff from Ofsted to meet with their case study heads to discuss the inspection process. In response to criticism one of these inspectors advised that heads should learn to be 'more steely' (2000: 39); in other words to negotiate and act more as an equal partner in an inspection, defending the school's own priorities and ethos. This is an interesting suggestion although it may not be representative of Ofsted inspectors' attitudes in general (only one voice after all). One needs to remember too that the stakes are high in an inspection, so that headteachers may not feel safe in promoting their own agenda. However the research by Chapman on schools in their second round of inspections also showed that where schools were confident, they were more circumspect about the inspection findings and saw their own developmental agenda as more important (2001: 66; 70). There may be a case then for taking a strong line in an inspection. The notion of dialogue is certainly hinted at in some of the new post-2003 proposals (Ofsted, 2001a, 2002b).

Responding to observation feedback

Responding to feedback on one's own lessons may be a more problematic area. Case, Case and Catling, in their three-year study in schools undergoing inspection found that the sharpest area of conflict for teachers related to teaching methodology, since this was 'an issue with which teachers personally and emotionally identify' (2000: 613). The variability of inspectors' expertise identified in Millet and Johnson's research has already been mentioned. In addition to this there is the question of 'baggage', inspectors' preferred modes of teaching. This factor is mentioned by teachers and researchers in several projects and indeed is a factor recognized by Ofsted in its own guidance to inspectors (Ofsted, 1996: 4). This can also be a factor which may play a part in appraisal, with an appraiser unwittingly prioritizing their own preferred ways of teaching, as will be discussed in Chapter 9. It is then important to see any inspection judgements as an *interpretation*, as well of course as a source of additional insights. Winkley (1999) also points to the personal and variable interpretations of Ofsted teams (varying as much as 40 per cent in some cases between inspectors).

Another factor pointed out by schools and researchers is that inspectors are under great pressure when making their judgements. Ferguson *et al* (2000) provide a checklist of questions used by Ofsted inspectors in making judgements of a lesson. Of these 24 questions, 10 relate to teaching, 6 to students' response and 4 to students' progress. If inspectors only have a limited time to observe, then this means there is a wide range to cover, with snap decisions having to be made. The question of length of observations is also problematic and one which was identified as such by the House of Commons Select Committee evaluation of Ofsted (Alexander, 1999; see also Fitzgibbon and Stephenson-Forster, 1999). Ferguson *et al* document this debate, commenting that Ofsted and the Select Committee have simply agreed to differ on whether part or whole lessons should be observed (2000: 15).

Feedback too has been reported as variable. Millet and Johnson's research, for example, showed that inspectors with more mathematical expertise tended to give feedback which related to subject content, while those with less expertise produced comments relating more to general teaching approaches (1998: 513–15). It has also been the case that teachers have not been offered any feedback (Chapman, 2001: 70). The new proposals for post-2003 do recognize the need for improvement in this area by suggesting 'improved feedback for individual teachers' but without the contentious personally-fed-back gradings (Ofsted, 2001a).

Discussing the school

A delicate area of discussion is the extent to which headteachers and staff may wish to focus on weaknesses in their school. It has been suggested that if there was a higher level of confidentiality in inspections and these were focused on self-development, then the question of weaknesses could be an area where schools would really welcome feedback (Ferguson *et al*, 2000: 43–44). It is also possible that where there is a new headteacher in post (often the case in special measures schools), then there is much more willingness to talk about school's weakness for a variety of reasons, not least being able to use the inspection findings 'to take action which might not have been possible under other circumstances' (Scanlon, 1999: 54). Ferguson *et al*'s analysis of the difference in responses between new and experienced heads suggests 'that experienced heads are more circumspect and over one third of them, but only one-fifth of new heads, said that they had not volunteered any information about their school's weaknesses to the RgI' (2000: 73). Clearly then this is an area which deserves attention.

The post-inspection phase

Here it is useful to consider both the designated inspection activities, the Ofsted report and the range of possible responses.

Designated inspection activities

After an inspection a variety of documents will need to be processed, and some further activity may take place:

- The inspection team will send a written report and a summary six weeks after the end of the inspection to the school and governors and the school has five working days to comment on the accuracy of this report.
- The governors must ensure that an action plan is drawn up which addresses the key issues in the inspection report within 40 working days (eight school weeks) of the inspection and sent to Ofsted.
- Parents should also receive a summary of this action plan.
- Where schools are deemed to be failing they will be put on special measures and will have an HMI visit a few weeks after inspection to ratify the Ofsted decision. Six months after this a series of termly HMI visits will take place until the school is deemed to provide an acceptable standard of education. The LEA should provide extra financial support during this period.
- Schools deemed to have serious weaknesses are also subject to monitoring by the HMI.

An extra activity suggested in the post-2003 proposals is for an additional meeting between parents and the governors to discuss the inspection (Ofsted 2002b: 40).

The Ofsted report

There have been criticisms of the language of Ofsted reports being either so vague that the school cannot understand it (Cuckle and Broadhead, 1999), or so neutralized that it does not give much in the way of specific advice. Grubb, with his perhaps sharpened view as an outsider (from the United States), points to the wastefulness of a system where rich and generally informed comments (from inspectors with expertise) is transformed into numbers and then finally into the neutral language of Ofsted-speak: 'the expertise of the inspectors themselves is wasted' (1999: 80). In the post-2003 proposals (Ofsted, 2001a) Ofsted appears to have recognized this deficit and suggests new training for report writing and consultation with parents on format.

Responses to inspection

Schools will have a positive goal in the post-inspection period, but there is also likely to be (according to virtually all research) a negative reaction varying from a few weeks even up to a year in severe cases, the so-called 'post-inspection blues'. This dip in morale may make it difficult to implement the activities identified in the action plan.

Negative reactions may take the form of illness, absenteeism or resignation. In one research project a drop of 50 per cent in staff attendance was noted in some schools (Kogan and Maden, 1999). In special measures schools, for example, there is high level of difficulty reported in the recruitment and retention of teachers (Scanlon, 1999: 50ff). Teachers are also often likely to have a poor self-image, even where they had received good grades. Case, Case and Catling report that 'the fact that teachers... even where perceived as "successful" from the system's point of view made little difference to the poor self image that many developed during the inspection itself' (2000: 612). Scanlon also reports on teachers in special schools whose teaching was acknowledged to be good or very good who nevertheless were made to feel inadequate. One teacher pointed to this troubling disjuncture: 'you are made to feel that everything you've done for the last 20 years in teaching is absolutely useless [...] We knew that it was purely a management issue, that we had done everything we could and more and yet we still had to suffer the humiliation' (1999: 33). Scanlon also points out that such schools are not given credit for recognizing a problem even if they have not been able to solve it (1999). One study even suggested that an Ofsted inspection had a deleterious effect on GCSE results (Cullingford and Daniels, 1999), although Ofsted itself rejected the findings of this research (Ferguson *et al*, 2000: 35). However, as was mentioned earlier, it does appear that in inspections which are taking place after the first round and where schools themselves have a positive culture there seem to be more positive responses to the inspection process both during and after the inspection period.

If schools wish to complain about their inspection, there is a complaints procedure body (with the head of this now employed by the DfES, rather than by Ofsted as formerly). Details can be found on www.ofsted.gov.uk/about/complaints.

Inspection and personal professional development

As well as considering factors that relate to the three different phases of inspection it is also helpful to consider the overall impact of inspection on the level of both the personal professional development of the staff, and on the broader level of school development.

Ofsted claims that the inspection process improves both teachers and through them the standards of student achievement: 'It is teachers in schools who raise standards for students, and inspection feedback helps them to do so' (1999b: 28). The consultation document continues this theme of improvement (Ofsted, 2001a). Chapman's (2001) research into schools inspected in 1999–2000 is particularly revealing in this context. His research shows that teachers' perceptions of Ofsted's influence are much more limited: only 20 per cent of teachers reported that inspection feedback had prompted change, although 55 per cent considered the feedback useful. It is also important to remember that what is reported may not reflect what actually happens. Even if teachers suggest that they will change they may not actually do so; change may not mean improvement; and change may be revolutionary or just fine-tuning. It is clear that feedback from an outside source can be helpful and can help to overcome isolation that teachers may experience. However, it may be that an individual inspector's advice relates to a way of teaching that is not appropriate for or attractive to a particular teacher; or that the inspector may not have high levels of expertise in a particular subject (as reported earlier). In these cases it is understandable that teachers do not feel that the inspection advice is relevant or beneficial.

Inspection and school development

Ofsted also claims that inspection can is a 'potent catalyst for improvement' (Ofsted, 1999b: 1). Ofsted makes a specific claim in influencing school development: 'Good inspections provide vital management information on how good a school is and why. Thus they can help a school to improve' (Ofsted 1996b:30). The underlying assumptions here are that the priorities identified by Ofsted and by the school will be the same and that the Ofsted inspection is part of the mechanism to ensure the implementation of these priorities. This is further confirmed in Ofsted's advice to schools if they wish to carry out their own school evaluation: 'A common language has developed about the work of schools, expressed through the [Ofsted] criteria. Teachers and governors know that the criteria reflect things that matter' (Ofsted, 1998a: paragraph 18). There may though be a situation where the 'things that matter' to a school are different and here there may be a case for a head to be confident and 'steely' as was mentioned earlier.

A further complication with linking inspection and school development is that the two processes do not necessarily sit easily together. Inspection is summative with judgements made against standards in other schools, producing league tables and using standardized criteria for accountability purposes. This is part of the value-added process that the government is keen to promote, using amongst other things, PANDA information on similar schools (Thomas, Smees and Elliot, 2000).

School development is formative and a more 'in-house' affair with priorities drawn from particular circumstances of a school and the emphasis placed on understanding. Hopkins *et al* describe this as a difference between 'prove' and 'improve' (1999: 688).

An interesting factor here, which has been picked up in research, is the extent to which headteachers are able to predict the 'key issues' that will emerge in their inspection report, in other words in Ofsted terminology, how well heads know their school (cf. earlier comments on Ofsted's reactions to schools' self-evaluation). In the research done by Ferguson *et al* it appeared that heads were **not** able to predict very accurately what the key priorities would be. Thus the two key issues most frequently predicted by heads were 'standards' and 'information technology' whereas the two most included key issues in the schools' reports and included in general in inspection reports were 'assessment' and 'co-ordinators' role/monitoring' (2000: 58–59). There was some discrepancy here then in perceptions in Ferguson *et al*'s research, which may relate to heads' lack of knowledge or which may just point to different sets of priorities for schools and inspectors.

Another further helpful factor pointed out in Ferguson *et al*'s research is that inspection priorities are subject to change, with priorities identified by central government being likely to be influential. Ferguson *et al* (2000) suggest that 'management, leadership and strategic planning and provision for able students' are two key areas likely to feature in the future. Aspects related to management, leadership and strategic planning have been discussed in Chapter 7.

Clearly inspections can highlight issues usefully. They can provide helpful comparative information and will provide a *systematic* evaluation of a school in a way perhaps that has not been done internally. These aspects can all be useful pointers for schools in terms of working on their own self-evaluation and School Development Plan. The inspection process can thus provide a useful model and the inspection content can give helpful indicators. A school may then use these to confirm or establish its own priorities and identify these in readiness for further inspection.

Key points

- Ofsted arrangements have changed considerably.
- Schools need to consider how best to prepare and deal with the inspection experience.
- A strong culture of self-evaluation can be helpful here.

Self study

Key questions

For teachers:

- How can I sensibly and effectively prepare for inspection?
- How can I minimize personal stress?
- How can I benefit from inspection feedback?

For heads:

- How can inspection findings be helpfully integrated into the school development plan?
- What aspects of school performance should be highlighted?
- How can the school's own self-evaluation be brought up to speed to 'match' that of an inspection?

For governors:

- How can the governing body play a part in supporting and monitoring the school in its inspection experience?

Recommended reading

Chapman, C (2001) Changing classrooms through inspection, *School Leadership and Management*, **21** (1), pp 59–73

Ferguson, N *et al* (2000) *Improving Schools and Inspections: The self-inspecting school*, Paul Chapman, London

Ofsted (2001) *Improving Inspection, Improving Schools*, Ofsted, London

Ofsted (2002) *Inspecting Schools: The framework*, Ofsted, London

Scanlon, M (1999) *The Impact of OFSTED Inspections*, NFER and NUT, Slough

9 Performance management

Teacher appraisal has become an increasingly noticeable feature of school management procedures since the 1970s with varying levels of interest and participation. In 1991 the DES *Teacher Appraisal Regulations* and *Circular 12/91* were published, outlining a statutory requirement for schools of a two-year appraisal cycle (DES, 1991b). This was replaced by recommendations in the 1998 Green Paper: *Teachers Meeting the Challenge of Change* (DfEE, 1998b) which stipulated a yearly rather than a two-yearly cycle. Since then the regulations have been confirmed in further government publications: *Performance Management in Schools* (DfEE, 2000b), *Threshold Assessment* (DfEE, 2000c), *Learning and Teaching* (DfEE, 2001b) and *Schools Achieving Success* (DfES, 2001c).

It was recognized in the 1998 Green Paper that earlier systems of appraisal had been unsuccessful: 'The present statutory scheme of teacher appraisal has become largely discredited because in most schools it has been seen as a pointless additional burden rather than an integral part of the school's performance management arrangements' (DfEE, 1998b: 34–35). The renaming of appraisal (as 'performance management') with thus a stronger link to the school's management process has accompanied the introduction of incentives linking to pay – appraisal for threshold payments and the introduction of Advanced Skills teacher status. In the White Paper, *Schools Achieving Success* (DfES, 2001c), this is given legislative support (see below). The hope is expressed in the Strategy Document *Learning and Teaching* (DfEE, 2001b: 20) that: 'The introduction of performance management may make it easier to change understanding and attitudes for those teachers for whom [...] [professional development] would otherwise be low on their list of priorities'. It will be interesting to see if the desired improved standards of student achievement and teacher improvement will indeed result from these new initiatives.

Government regulations and recommendations

It can be seen from the statements taken from these government publications that the focus alternates between accountability and personal development objectives.

1998 Green Paper

Six key points are outlined in the 1998 Green Paper: *Teachers Meeting the Challenge of Change* (DfEE, 1998b) which relate to performance management. These are:

- including observation in the appraisal process;
- taking student progress into account;
- setting targets (including student performance targets);
- linking appraisal and pay;
- making 'performance information' available;
- requiring schools to have an up-to-date performance management policy including the impact of performance management systems on standards in Ofsted inspection frameworks.

Here there is a clear indication of a high level of accountability and linking performance management to improvements in students' performance and to pay. These ideas are confirmed in later government publications relating to teaching in general and also to performance management.

2001 strategy document

In the strategy document *Learning and Teaching* (DfEE, 2001b) there is a stronger focus on personal responsibility. Five key areas are mentioned in the section on performance management in this publication (2001b: 20–21):

- Setting one or more development objectives.
- Teachers having a duty to take responsibility for their own professional development.
- Consolidating Ofsted powers to identify development needs in order to evaluate how these needs have been accommodated in development activities, and to evaluate the impact on teacher effectiveness and student learning.
- Including in ITT programmes a focus on personal responsibility for CPD, the importance of CPD and effective forms of CDP.
- A general firming up of expectations of entitlement to a responsibility for individual professional development.

Here then there is a strong sense of performance management having a developmental role.

2001 White Paper

In the White Paper *Schools Achieving Success* (DfES, 2001c), there is a clear indication of the government's intention to bring in legislation to link appraisal to pay: 'We will update the 1986 Act provision empowering the Secretary of State to make teacher appraisal regulations so that there is an explicit power for schools to use appraisal data in pay decisions, as well as technical updating' (2001: 74).

There is a very clear message here that appraisal/performance management is seen in terms of accountability.

2000 Guidance for Performance Management in Schools

In the publications relating more specifically to performance management there is of course more detail in terms of expected priorities. The Guidance for *Performance Management in Schools* (DfEE, 2000b) contains three documents: a *Guidance Note*; a *Performance Management Framework*; and a *Model Performance Management Policy*.

The *Guidance Note* provides an overview of the new performance management arrangements and a summary of the two other documents, with answers to possible questions being given.

Key information includes:

- Funding arrangements: £20 million is to be made available annually to cover costs of performance management arrangements.
- Appraisal is identified as equivalent to performance management.
- Appraisers are identified as 'team leaders' or in the case of headteachers, appointed governors.

The *Performance Management Framework* is a much longer document which provides more detail and gives some examples of good practice. Benefits are identified for students 'because their teacher will have a more sharply focussed picture' of what they can achieve; and secondly for the teachers who 'will have a proper opportunity for professional discussion with their team leader' (DfEE, 2000b: 3).

Best practice is seen as:

- a commitment to the attainment and welfare of students;
- an appreciation of the crucial role that teachers play;
- an atmosphere of trust between teachers and team leaders, which allows them to evaluate strengths and identify areas for development;

- encouragement to share good practice;
- the integration of performance management with the overall approach to managing the school (DfEE, 2000b: 3).

Various key points are emphasized in the framework. Five of the six key points of the 1998 Green Paper are reconfirmed (the impact on standards in Ofsted frameworks is not mentioned). In addition the following points are highlighted:

- integrating performance management with overall school management, plans and policies;
- equity in policy and practices;
- using performance management to identify areas for further investigation where there is weak performance although 'performance management in itself is not part of the disciplinary or dismissal procedures' (DfEE, 2000b: 9).

The *Model Performance Management Policy* provides a model policy which schools may wish to copy. In this new guidance there is a reconfirmation of performance management leading towards measurable improvement in student achievement and integration into whole school objectives.

2000 Threshold assessment

The guidance document *Threshold Assessment: Guidance on Completing the Application Form* (DfEE, 2000c) provides information on:

- the Threshold standards (5 different standards);
- the application process (with the teacher applying, the headteacher assessing and an external assessor verifying);
- the presentation of evidence (on an application form, with supporting evidence kept available by the teacher);
- the assessment of evidence (by headteacher and external assessor).

The five standards stipulated are:

- professional knowledge and understanding;
- teaching and assessment;
- pupil progress;
- wider professional effectiveness;
- professional characteristics.

In this one-off appraisal linked to pay there is a clear emphasis on outcomes with teachers' effectiveness and student progress (in the immediate short term) being the focus.

Thus, although there is some emphasis on personal development in the CPD document *Learning and Teaching* (DfEE, 2001b), the main strategy for performance management in these government publications is linking development to other areas of development namely contributing to overall school development, and contributing to students' progress.

Judged against these measurable outcomes, effective teachers may then expect improved levels of payment.

Purposes of performance management

Appraisal or performance management then can be seen already in these government documents as having two functions: a **developmental** function focused on individual needs; and a **regulatory** function, providing information for senior management on performance, linking in some cases to reward and linking to overall school and student performance.

These two models can be broadly linked to the 'old' development model of appraisal – pre-1998 – and the new post-1998 regulatory model with its new terminology, although clearly vestiges of the old model still remain. However, the picture does not necessarily divide itself into two such clear separate alternatives, in that the functions can be seen as interactive and there can be the possibility that both can be achieved together.

Three other factors that emerge as important are:

- ownership of the appraisal process;
- linking school needs and personal needs;
- considering individual and collegial priorities.

The developmental model of appraisal

Day makes a useful comment which explains the usefulness of this kind of appraisal: 'Professional development is not something that can be forced, because it is the teacher who develops (actively), and not the teacher who is developed (passively)' (1999: 97). Day has worked particularly on developing personal development plans, which teachers prepare themselves. He believes that these plans overcome some of the problems of 'imposed' appraisal and that they also give rise to greater awareness of personal development. There is some link here then with the focus on personal responsibility in the latest thinking in the Government's approaches. Gunter (2001b) points to the research network supported by universities which underpins a developmental approach. (Day's work itself is a good example of this). Dadds (2001) also points to the value of focusing on teachers' inner knowledge as a source for professional development.

'Developmental' appraisal can be particularly helpful if teachers are unaware of their own needs or indeed their own strengths. Marriott, in her work as an adviser, inspector and senior manager, suggests that such lack of 'awareness is often because [...][teachers] have not been systematically observed and debriefed' (2001: 2), here also commenting on the usefulness of lesson observation.

In the research carried out by the National Foundation for Educational Research (NFER) into CPD activities during 2000–01 in a range of schools, the researchers found that developmental appraisal (where the process tended to comprise informal one-to-one staff reviews, discussions or interviews with someone from the senior management team) was seen as 'useful as it enables individual staff to focus upon their own CPD needs as well as the overall priorities of the school' (Brown, Edmonds and Lee, 2001: 56). Such interviews can also include the opportunity to review the career plans of the teacher and an opportunity to log aspirations (Fidler and Atton, 1999). An appraisal interview and classroom observation can both then be useful in a developmental approach.

Developmental appraisal is likely to be flexible and can thus perhaps also be helpful in accommodating different needs at different stages. An NQT, for example, is likely to have rather different developmental needs in an induction year compared to the needs of a more experienced teacher. A flexible approach can also take into account the different contexts in which teachers operate. Here then there would seem to be a strong argument for having some kind of flexible appraisal system in place alongside the more context-free standards which characterize the statutory performance management guidelines or regulatory framework.

However not all teachers welcome '"the soft option" of developmental appraisal... the college equivalent of the confessional!' (Middlewood, 1997: 175). Wragg and other researchers at Exeter University found in their extremely comprehensive survey of the pre-1998 appraisal system that the teachers, in both their wide surveys of 658 teachers and the 29 case studies, welcomed quite specific advice, and their research suggests the value of 'a sharper, more insightful focus on classroom transactions' (Wragg *et al*, 1996: 200). Fidler and Atton found in their analyses of poorly performing teachers that 'the purely developmental approach which was generally adopted for the first round of staff appraisals led to many such problems [of poor performance] being ignored' (1999: 28). Even the NFER research mentioned earlier found that a high proportion of their 18 case-study schools used **both** informal appraisal and more formalized performance management interviews to identify CPD needs (Brown, Edmonds and Lee, 2001: 35). Similarly Poster and Poster affirm the usefulness of having both casual drop-in observation and more formal observation (1993: 62–64). Many teachers and researchers then have confirmed the value of both a developmental and a regulatory model.

The regulatory model of performance management

A regulatory model of performance management differs from the developmental model in focusing more on evaluating teachers' performance against an expected set of standards. Bubb and Hoare's work based on Ofsted criteria (2001), is a good example of this. This can provide useful information for senior management as well as giving focused guidance to teachers, operating within the framework of a clear set of expectations (those provided in government guidelines plus any framework that the school may also have in place). Mahony and Hextall (in their research on the impact of standards on schools and on the TTA) talk of three different kinds of accountability: 'upwards' (to senior management), 'sideways' (to colleagues) and 'downwards' (to students) (2000: 144–45). The regulatory model of performance management certainly focuses more on accountability as was seen in the government publications. For threshold assessment, for example, evidence from teachers is scrutinized by external assessors. Here then there is clear accountability 'upwards' to the senior management in the school (and upwards again with head-teachers' judgements also being scrutinized).

The new performance management models also focus on 'downwards' account-ability in terms of impact on students' learning. This aspect of appraisal features strongly in official documentation although there is strong evidence to suggest that it is actually very difficult to **measure** impact on student progress. In the most recent research on CPD at the time of writing (Brown, Edmonds and Lee, 2001) the researchers point out that it was 'not always easy for teachers to supply tangible evidence of impact' (2001: iv). Flecknoe (2000: 439) (who looked specifically at student achievement with a group of teachers on a university course devoted to this) warns that it is difficult to show that student gains are related specifically to one teacher's classroom performance for several reasons: since there are many potential influences on student progress; because control groups are difficult to set up; and because those who are in projects usually perform better anyway, regardless of what approach is being taken (the so-called Hawthorn effect). Middlewood and Lumby also warn against directly linking student progress with specific teacher performance: 'The concept of value-added measures remains controversial in education' (1998: 80).

Even if we look at impact on teacher behaviour in classrooms rather than student progress, there is still some doubt about whether **short-term** gains are immediately visible. In Wragg *et al*'s 1996 research on early appraisal schemes, although 49 per cent of the teachers in the wider survey reported some gains in practice (still not a dramatic number), in the 29 case studies that were observed the researchers were quite definite about the lack of impact on teachers' practice: 'A frequent outcome [...] in the case studies was that appraisal had either not affected the appraisee's classroom teaching at all or [...] in a minor way, and this was confirmed not only by the interviews but also by the researchers' follow-up observations' (1996: 183, see also Owl, 2002). In recent research on the effect of threshold pay carried out by the Exeter University team the findings were that threshold payments had also made little difference to what teachers did in the classroom (Dean, 2001). However this is not to say that there are not **long-term** and more subtle benefits resulting from appraisals. There is a reference in many studies of appraisal to teachers' increased **confidence** being a result (Brown, Edmonds and Lee, 2000; Marriott, 2001). The Hay McBer report (2000), commissioned by the Government, provides a framework with three elements: professional characteristics; teaching skills; and classroom climate. This model is described in depth in Hartle, Everall and Baker (2001). Their suggestions for improving classroom climate are particularly interesting: namely that teachers could usefully concentrate on improving this 'classroom climate' in order to improve student progress, focusing on such elements as a pleasant physical environment and lack of disruption. School and classroom questionnaires for students to complete are available from www.trans-forminglearning.co.uk. There are suggestions here then that even in a more 'regulated' appraisal it can be helpful to go beyond a simple checklist approach.

Another view of 'downwards' accountability is for teachers to comment on their line managers, or for students to comment on teachers: so called 'reverse appraisal' or '360-degree appraisal'. Marriott comments that this is a feature of many effective departments that she has observed in her work as an adviser/inspector (2001: 5). Research by the Hay Group building on their earlier report shows that students may be extremely positive about their teachers (Ward, 2001b; Whittaker, 2001). However the leader of a major teaching union warns that where students are disaffected 'to allow those kids to appraise their teachers has the potential to wreak havoc' (Whittaker, 2001). A student evaluation form asking children to 'assess your teacher in seven important areas' is perhaps not a helpful model to follow here (Combes, 2002).

'Horizontal' or 'sideways' accountability mentioned by Mahony and Hextall (2000: 144) is a dimension that is less discussed. There is certainly emphasis on **learning** from others and this is a strong feature of government recommendations with Advanced Skills Teachers and Beacon Schools passing on good practice, and teachers generally sharing ideas. Beyond this though there can be the notion that teachers are accountable to each other as part of a team. Certainly in Wragg, Haynes and Chamberlin's investigations of failing teachers (2000), the team found that fellow teachers had little sympathy for under-performing colleagues: partly out of concern for children's welfare, partly because of potential damage to their institution as a whole, and partly because of the drain on their own time and energy. Here then is an important aspect of regulatory appraisal but one which is far less accessible to scrutiny.

A key factor in regulatory appraisal is linking successful teaching to improved pay. At the time of writing the first wave of threshold payments has been made but with harsh criticisms following in its wake. The multi-million-pound performance-related pay scheme has been criticized as reaping few benefits for improved practice (Dean, 2001), sapping teacher morale (Mansell, 2001a), being chaotically disorganized (Arkin, 2002b; Mansell, 2001b; Thornton and Mansell, 2001; Ward, 2001a) and being under funded (Mansell, 2002b; Slater and Mansell, 2002). A further refinement of this, such as the divisive ranking system used in industry, also seems very unlikely to be popular, although it has been warmly recommended by one headteacher after observing the system in action in his local Toyota factory (Hastings, 2001a). A study of teachers' views of performance-related pay (Dean, 2002) revealed a high level of negativity in terms of expected outcomes (divisiveness; resentment; increased bureaucratic control) and non-results (little impact on teacher recruitment or retention, or on student learning).

Regulatory appraisal then can be motivating for some and will undoubtedly furnish useful information for senior management but clearly carries considerable caveats as well.

Three overarching aspects of appraisal relate to the purposes of appraisal in a different way, in terms of:

- how teachers view themselves, namely considering how personal needs dovetail with those of the school;
- how they fit with the needs of a team;
- how ownership of appraisal can be facilitated.

If the appraiser is to consider how an individual teacher's development might dovetail into the school development plan, or into the needs of a school in general, then this will need skilful handling.

Another tension could exist in terms of developing individuals rather than considering collegiality. That is to say encouraging personal improvement may prove counter-productive for working and sharing within a team. Responses to the performance-related pay initiative have shown that measures promoting individuals can be divisive as suggested in the survey mentioned above. An interesting comment from one of the teachers in Mahoney and Hextall's research also points to the kind of problems that might occur: 'I just think it is going to be incredibly divisive, [...] people come into school and instead of sharing everything that you do, I think it is just going to end up with people keeping everything for themselves and feeling, well if I'm going to get good results then I'm going to get it for me' (2000: 75).

As well as considering how to reconcile the CPD needs of individuals with wider needs in the school community, there is also the question of ownership of appraisal. Research with teachers (Day, 1999; Mahoney and Hextall, 2000; Wragg *et al*, 1996; Wragg, Haynes and Chamberlin, 2000) has shown that success in initiatives, particularly those involving a deep level of change, needs to provide a sense of ownership. Given that the framework of standards in the statutory regulations is non-negotiable, it may be that this can be achieved within the **procedures** and **process** of appraisal. These are considered in the following two sections.

Management of appraisal procedures

Key procedures that deserve attention include the following:

- type of appraisal;
- choice of appraiser;
- choice of timing/lesson/focus;
- documentation;
- embedding appraisal in the school culture;
- training for appraisal.

Type of appraisal

There are three main types of appraisal:

- hierarchical appraisal;
- peer appraisal;
- self-appraisal.

Government regulations clearly indicate the first kind of appraisal as that most suited to their new performance management approach. In the *Performance Management Framework* (DfEE, 2000b) there is further guidance in terms of appraiser. This is usually a headteacher or line manager/team leader with the choice being guided by selecting 'the teacher who has the best overview of a teacher's work' (2000b: 9). Bubb and Hoare (2001) also point to the pivotal role of the headteacher who is likely to have the perspective of practices in other schools (2000b: 10). In the NFER research (Brown, Edmonds and Lee, 2001) it was the headteacher or someone from the senior management team who usually undertook the appraisals in their case-study schools. If teachers were being 'monitored' (ie their lessons were being observed) then this was usually done by subject co-ordinators or heads of faculty (2001: 36). Even in the early appraisal research (Wragg *et al*, 1996) the main appraisers (88 per cent) were of senior management or line manager status (1996: 65). This then is the most common appraisal set-up.

There has also been growing interest in peer appraisal and self-appraisal. As was mentioned earlier, self-appraisal can be highly successful in terms of motivation. It can also be integrated into a hierarchical approach, giving some sense of ownership. In other words if a teacher has already considered his or her own practice and needs, then conversation with an appraiser can feel more like an equal exchange of views (Horne and Pierce, 1996: 220). Jones provides six helpful examples of self-evaluation pro-formas (2001: 21–30). Horne and Pierce suggest that a period of self-appraisal can be useful after an initial meeting of appraiser and appraisee even though in early regulations this was not statutory (1996: 20).

Peer appraisal is likely to support a developmental approach and is championed by those critics who baulk against a more regulatory approach (Mahony and Hextall, 2000; Bartlett, 1998, 2000). Possibilities in this area are explored in greater detail in Chapter 3. Not all teachers though welcome peer appraisal. In Wragg *et al*'s 1996 research teachers commented that a peer system provided 'a more relaxed and non-threatening context for appraisal [...] even allowing teachers to tackle sensitive or difficult aspects of their teaching but that this might lead to the reinforcement of poor or inadequate practice, questioning whether it is possible for teachers who work closely together to offer objective feedback on classroom competence' (1996: 28–29). There was also some doubt as to whether peer teachers would have enough 'clout' to make sure that the necessary steps would be taken to follow up identified needs.

Choice of appraiser

As well as considering what type of appraisal is being undertaken, the choice of appraiser is also important in terms of successful outcomes. Again the skill of a headteacher will be called on in successful matching appraiser to appraisee. In Wragg *et al*'s research into early appraisal initiatives about half of the teachers had an imposed choice of appraiser, with the other half either choosing one themselves or negotiating the choice. The researchers note that 'the teachers whose appraisers were imposed were significantly more affected by their presence than those who had chosen or negotiated their own appraiser' (1996: 75).

Key features that teachers have identified as important in their appraisers are 'credibility' (ie respecting the appraiser's teaching ability) (Wragg *et al*, 1996: 66), someone who is not too 'self-focused' (Wragg *et al*, 1996: 70), 'subject and age-group expertise' (Wragg *et al*, 1996: 200; Poster and Poster, 1993: 81) and conversely the value of cross-curricular appraising, giving a 'wider perspective' (Horne and Pierce, 1996: 32). Owl (2002) has also identified the key need for 'trust' in appraisal situations. A headteacher will need to weigh up the importance of different factors according to the particular context of the teacher and the school.

Arrangements for appraising headteachers will need special consideration. Current regulations specify the appointment of governors and feedback in 2002 suggest that this was successful (Sassoon, 2002). Poster and Poster (1993: 24ff) comment on the difficulties in recruiting suitable appraisers who have sufficient up-to-date expertise (see also Horne and Pierce, 1996: 136–37). If an appraiser is dissatisfied with the appraisal process then there need to be arrangements in the school policy/procedures for an alternative appraiser to be found.

Classroom observation and interview – choices and planning

It is useful to note that classroom observation and reviewing can be helpfully augmented by other sources of information (Jones, 2001). Regulations in both early and late frameworks for appraisal (DES, 1991b; DfEE, 2000b) require both classroom observation and a meeting of appraiser and appraisee (although less than half of the case-study schools in the 2000–01 NFER research had used classroom observation to identify needs (Brown, Edmonds and Lee, 2001: 35) and very, very few classroom observations were undertaken by the external assessors for threshold payments (Dean, 2001).

Horne and Pierce (1996) provide a useful outline for an appraisal cycle:

- initial meeting;
- self-appraisal;
- classroom observation;
- collecting data from other sources, agreed by the appraisee;
- appraisal interview;
- appraisal statement, agreed by both parties;
- follow-up.

(One could perhaps also include 'evaluation' of the appraisal as a final stage).

Classroom observation can provide a useful source of information and opinion to underpin an appraisal interview. Planning this classroom observation will require skill and sensitivity on the part of the appraiser. It will be important to involve the appraisee in all aspects of the chosen observation focus to ensure some sense of ownership, mentioned earlier as a key feature of successful appraisal. Teachers may vary in terms of whether they want a 'difficult' or 'easy' class observed. MacDonald, as a school head of department, comments on the value of being seen with a favourite group (2002). Observation can be one long lesson or two shorter ones. Marriott points to the usefulness of being able to use observation from different occasions: 'When you have observed a teacher more than once, you can use comparative information and have an even more well-informed discussion' (2001: 62). However, time constraints may make this difficult. Horne and Pierce (1996: 13) calculate the appraisal process as three contact hours (30 minutes for initial meeting, 90 minutes observation and 60 minutes interview). If an appraiser has a maximum of four appraisees (Poster and Poster, 1993), then this is clearly a lengthy time commitment, once the writing up of the documentation has been taken into consideration. Headteachers, for example, in the threshold application spent on average around two hours on each application (Dean, 2001).

It will also be important to decide jointly on the focus of observation. It may be that a teacher wishes to have a particular aspect of teaching observed or an appraiser may have a particular focus linked to school priorities. There may also be a case for a more generally focused observation. Whatever the choice, observation processes and supportive prompt sheets are likely to be different.

This is investigated in more detail in the next section on the process of appraisal. It will also be important to identify a focus that is reasonable, observable and able to be evaluated. Fleming and Amesbury suggest that where an 'objective is difficult to measure then the question should be asked – is it worthwhile?' (2001: 139). This suggestion may appear too proscriptive. Horne and Pierce point to the teachers in their research having difficulty with selecting 'an appropriate focus that was both manageable and observable' (1996: 54). Mahony and Hextall question this still further, querying 'the extent to which certain key educational values are amenable in principle to conventional appraisal procedures' (2000: 79). The question of 'focus' thus needs delicate handling.

Two other aspects of setting up classroom observation worth mentioning are a further question of timing and the practicalities of the observation process. It may be useful to arrange for observation of a lesson **early** in the teaching year, where there are concerns over a teacher. In Wragg, Haynes and Chamberlin's analysis of 'failing' teachers, the teachers themselves point to the fact that criticism of their teaching had come late and that they were then unprepared for it (2000: 29). The practicalities of observation also need consideration. Appraisers should acquaint themselves beforehand with the content of the lesson, the type of students, the lay-out of the classroom and availability of suitable seating to avoid the embarrassment of a hovering adult presence. Marriott provides an excellent checklist of pointers to ensure a smooth accommodation of the observer figure into a lesson (2001: 30–31). When an appraisal interview is being set up it is also worthwhile considering environmental issues ensuring privacy and guaranteed non-interruption. In establishing procedures for appraisal it will be important then for the appraiser to liaise with the appraisee, and give consideration to the acceptability and feasibility of the arrangements.

Documentation

In an appraisal observation, as well as the 'checklist' of standards specified in the government framework (see Ofsted, 1999b), appraisers may wish to use priorities which have been highlighted in a school development plan. It can be useful to have a form with headings relating to these standards or priorities and Marriott provides useful examples of 12 different observation forms which are based both on government requirements and on individual schools' customized versions (2001: 47–61). Bubb and Hoare also provide exemplars of 11 observation forms (2001: 55–65), and an extremely useful table of the advantages and disadvantages of different types of observation (2001: 53ff). Included in the forms are schedules designed for both general observation and for more focused aspects of teaching.

Whatever documentation is used, this needs to be clear in its remit and shared beforehand with the appraisee so that there is a clear ground-plan for what the appraisal observation entails. Similarly, in an appraisal interview it will be helpful for appraisees to know beforehand the areas that will be discussed (providing a focus for the actual meeting) so that there will be an opportunity for self-appraisal in this area and the possible gathering of other relevant information. In terms of producing a final appraisal report it will be worth considering whether this works better as a list of bullet points (in the checklist mode) or a narrative. Again Marriott provides two useful examples of appraisal from an observation written up in these different ways (2001: 54–55).

Embedding appraisal into school culture

Linking individual teachers' continuing professional needs to the school development plan has already been mentioned and this is one way of embedding appraisal into the school culture. Several researchers have mentioned the usefulness of seeing appraisal as a 'normal' part of the business of a school – in much the same way as this is true in industry. Thus Wragg, Haynes and Chamberlin (2000), in their analysis of failing teachers, talk of the ideal model of performance management in large companies where 'objectives are set for the whole organization, for the departments within it and then for the teams and individuals who make up the department [...] [with] clarity of expectations and standards, backed up by frequent or continuous reviews of performance'. In such an environment there is a 'cultural acceptance of being assessed' (2000: 29). (See also Metcalfe, 1999).

If appraisal becomes an integral part of working practice rather than a 'bolt-on activity' then it is more likely to be acceptable. The headteacher mentioned earlier who has studied practices in a local factory had the following comment to make: 'if

[...][performance management is] seen as imposed by the DfES, it won't work. People have to be part of the process' (Hastings, 2001a). Middlewood also sums this up well: 'for appraisals of any kind to be effective, in both its developmental and evaluative aspects, it needs to be **embedded** within the culture of the organization' (1997: 178, emphasis in the original). It is helpful to think too of development, at both personal and school level, building on existing strengths. Jones mentions both 'cultural' and 'systemic' frameworks here (2001: 11–12).

Here then the issue of ownership resurfaces. It is not just a question of teachers experiencing a sense of personal ownership but also schools themselves taking on board the whole appraisal process as part of their normal practice.

Training for appraisal

It is clear from the points already covered that the process and associated procedures of appraisal demand a high level of skill. Marriott points to the fact that of the teachers she has encountered 'few [...] have had any training in observation, or have even given it much thought. This may stem from the widespread assumption that we all know good teaching when we see it' (2001: 20). Smith suggests from her experience as an adviser and HE tutor that 'an investment in the training and development of the mentor/appraiser in terms of their management education [...] can help schools to produce [...] "quality outputs"' (1996: 286).

Some appraisers in Wragg *et al*'s early study had received some training in appraisal but these courses were usually short, not more than a half-day (1996: 57). In seeking to support a stronger appraisal/performance management framework, this is clearly an area where government funding could be helpful and where schools may choose to invest. Marriott makes some useful suggestions about possible methods of training for classroom observation (2001: 69–73). These include watching a video or role play and discussing reactions, or using paired observations of a lesson where the two teachers will then compare their results. In INSET run by one of us, the SMT all watched a teacher who had volunteered to be appraised/observed and then discussed ways in which feedback might be given (comparing this with the actual feedback we had provided).

Management of the appraisal process

The two main features of the appraisal process are observation of classroom practice plus feedback, and the appraisal interview.

As well as ensuring that clear and negotiated procedures are in place for these two elements, as mentioned above, it is also important to consider the handling of the process itself in both instances.

Classroom observation and feedback

The appraiser must consider his or her presence in the classroom and how this will affect both the teacher being appraised and the students. For example, should the appraiser play an active role in the lesson or be a 'fly-on-the-wall' observer? Talking to students and looking at their work is likely to provide valuable insights but this will need to be weighed against an appraiser then not being able to observe the rest of the class at work. It will be important too to think of how to monitor effectively and differently particular aspects of teaching or more general aspects. As well as observing students' responses and general productivity it will be useful to consider the beginnings and ends of lessons and the transitions between activities. Handling these key moments in a lesson contributes considerably to the pace of teaching and the general sense of efficiency of learning – as in Hay McBer's 'classroom climate' (2000). It will be helpful too to look at the intended lesson plan to see how this relates to what is observed. Marriott provides an excellent range of different aspects of classroom behaviour that can be taken as indicators of successful learning (2001: 16–28; 34–40). She makes the additional point that it is important for an appraiser to recognize his or her **own** teaching preferences which are likely to act as a filter in observing the appraisee: 'You will have definite views on how things should be taught... remember that what works for you, with your level of experience, may not work as well for others. Be open-minded' (2001: 34).

When it comes to feedback there are many aspects to consider. Good practice is to start a feedback session with praising the 'best' aspects of the lesson(s) you have observed. This will break the ice in what can be a difficult situation. It is also helpful to focus on the students' learning and on teaching activities rather than on the teacher. In this way it is possible to establish more neutral ground.

It is helpful to allow the appraisee 'space' in a feedback session. If there has been an opportunity for self-appraisal beforehand then the appraisee can contribute his or her own ideas from this self-evaluation. Marriott suggests, for example, that 'at the start of the feedback give the teacher time to talk about his or her perceptions of the lesson. For a variety of reasons, the teacher may take a different view of the lesson from yours' (2001: 63).

It will be useful not to allow too much time to elapse between observation and feedback so that events remain fresh in the mind for both appraiser and appraisee. However, it may be helpful to have a short interval to allow for reflection.

The appraisal interview

Many of the same recommendations for effective lesson observation and feedback apply to the interview as well. It is good to set up the interview more as a dialogue than a one-way process. This can partly be facilitated by the kinds of question that are asked, for example, open questions are likely to give appraisees more scope to contribute their own ideas. It is important for an appraiser to develop good listening skills so that the appraisee's own viewpoint is understood. Horne and Pierce, in their comprehensive overview of the appraisal interview, suggest that: 'it is useful to use the person's [the appraisee's] own words to encourage them to give further information on a topic' (1996: 110). Jones similarly provides pointers for 'active listening' (2001: 55). This is also a signal to the appraisee that you are on the person's 'wavelength' and trying to see things from his or her point of view. Other useful suggestions are to offer a variety of options in an interview (Horne and Pierce, 1996: 108) and to avoid offering your own solutions to any problems identified (Poster and Poster, 1993: 124). Both these suggestions give more responsibility to the appraisee and can thus provide a greater sense of personal ownership in the interaction.

When it comes to identifying targets Horne and Pierce focus on being specific. They talk of targets that are SMART, as mentioned in Chapter 7.

Even though an appraisal interview will have overall long-term perspectives it is important to identify short-term objectives which can be the focus of immediate activity in order not to lose the momentum of the appraisal experience. It can also be helpful in both the appraisal interview and in feedback after observation to limit the number of developmental objectives set so that the teacher is not overwhelmed with things to do.

Responses to the appraisal experience

It is clear from the research that has been done and from responses documented in the media that appraisal attracts mixed responses. For some it can be seen as a positive experience leading to reward, for others it represents either a threat to 'the comfortable stability of practice' (Day, 1999: 99) or a necessary burden.

Negative responses to appraisal

Reported negative attitudes to appraisal can take the form of slight misgivings: in the NFER 2001 research it is noted that 'a few concerns were expressed that this process [the formalized performance management interview] would be tied to performance related pay' (Brown, Edmonds and Lee, 2001: 36). At the other end of the scale there seem to be stronger reactions: Wragg *et al* reported in 1996 that 'a common response [...] [amongst staff] was that there was an atmosphere of resignation that [...][appraisal] had to be done' (1996: 194). Bartlett (1998) in his survey of teachers between 1992–94 paints an even gloomier picture: 'the suspicions that appraisal aroused and how staff approached it, meant that for many it was an expensive tokenistic exercise. The schools in the study appeared to be "going through the motions". Appraisees were guarded about what they discussed. Appraisers were tentative about how to manage the process' (1998: 228). Even in 2002 MacDonald reports that a significant proportion of teachers hate being observed at work by adults. In addition we have also mentioned the considerable furore in 2001 which followed in the wake of threshold assessments.

Positive responses to appraisal

More recent research appears though to have also produced some more positive reactions to appraisal. The NFER research, for example, comments on the appraisal process being 'useful as it enables individual staff to focus upon their own CPD needs as well as the overall priorities of the school' (Brown, Edmonds and Lee, 2001: 36). Marriott points to the positive benefits of teachers' strengths being identified in appraisal:

> Many teachers, even those who are the most experienced and confident, may not be used to having their work praised on the basis of first-hand evidence. Experienced teachers can be surprised when their strengths are clearly identified; they may even think that what they do well is routine and not worthy of comment. However, praise and recognition are important for their self-esteem and job satisfaction as well as encouraging their continued professional effectiveness (2001: 2–3).

She also comments on the benefits that can accrue for the appraiser: 'It may be that the most recently qualified person in a department has skills that others don't have and should be shared' (2001: 5) and here quotes 'ICT' and 'identifying targets' as two skills likely to be demonstrated by NQTs. It is also likely that appraisers will experience professional development themselves in undertaking the responsibility of appraisal. An appraiser will need to reflect on what values and aspects of teaching are important, and this process can lead in turn to reflection on one's own practice (see Owl, 2002).

It is clear then the whole appraisal process is undergoing change and becoming a more focal aspect of teachers' daily lives. There are challenges for both the appraiser and appraisee and it will be important for CPD providers to rise to the challenge of supporting these new developments.

Key points

- Appraisal can be development or regulatory.
- Appraisee involvement and negotiation is important at every stage of appraisal.
- Priorities for individual teachers can usefully be integrated with school priorities.
- It may be difficult to assess immediate short-term impact on students' progress.

Self study

Key questions

For the appraisee:

- What do I want to improve in my own teaching and professional life?
- Do I keep a record of reflections on my own teaching?
- Am I open to change?

For the appraiser:

- Am I aware of my own preferred styles of teaching?
- Do I set up appraisal procedures clearly and sensitively?
- Am I sufficiently aware during observations and interviews of how my appraisee might feel?

For the manager of the appraisal process:

- Is a clear appraisal policy in place?
- Has this policy been discussed with and explained to staff?
- Are there robust procedures in place for supporting teachers' continuing professional needs?

Recommended reading

Bubb, S and Hoare, P (2001) *Performance Management: Monitoring teaching in the primary school*, David Fulton, London

DfEE (2000) *Performance Management in Schools*, DfEE, London

Horne, H and Pierce, A (1996) *A Practical Guide to Staff Development and Appraisal in Schools*, Kogan Page, London

Jones, J (2001) *Performance Management for School Improvement: A practical guide for secondary schools*, David Fulton, London

Marriott, G (2001) *Observing Teachers at Work*, Heinemann, Oxford

Wragg *et al* (1996) *Teacher Appraisal Observed*, Routledge, London

Appendix

Useful Web site/e-mail addresses

All Saints Educational Trust www.aset.org.uk.

Audit Commission www.audit-commission.gov.uk

British Council www.britishcouncil.org

British Ecological Society
    www.britishecologicalsociety.org/grants/research/index.php

Cabinet Office www.cabinet-office.gov.uk/

Centre for British Teaching www.cfbt.com

Chartered Teacher project www.ctprogrammescotland.org.uk

Churchill Fellowships www.ovcont.org.uk

Classroom climate questionnaires www.transforminglearning.co.uk

Culham Education Foundation grant www.culham.ac.uk

Data protection www.dataprotection.gov.uk

Department of Education and Learning www.deni.gov.uk

Department of Education and Skills www.dfes.gov.uk

Farmington Fellowship www.farmington.ac.uk

Fast Track teaching www.fasttrackteaching.gov.uk

General Teaching Council for England www.gtce.org.uk

General Teaching Council for Scotland www.gtcs.org.uk

General Teaching Council for Wales www.gtcw.org.uk

Goldsmiths www.thegoldsmiths.co.uk

Heads and deputies performance www.cea.co.uk/reform/govern.htm

HMSO www.hmso.gov.uk

Hockerill Education Foundation grant hockerill@surfaid.org

Keswick Hall grant a.m.miller@uea.ac.uk

Learning in Wales www.learning.wales.gov.uk

Manchester Metropolitan University www.mmu.ac.uk

National College for School Leadership www.ncsl.org.uk

National Grid for Learning www.ngfl.gov.uk

NFER www.nfer.ac.uk

NI network for education www.nine.gov.uk

Northern Ireland www.class-ni.org.uk

NPQH England www.ncsl.org.uk

Nuffield www.nuffieldfoundation.org

NUT grants www.teachers.org.uk

Ofsted www.ofsted.gov.uk

Primary resources site www.primaryresources.co.uk

QCA www.qca.org.uk

Schoolmanager www.schoolmanager.net

Scotland www.scotland.gov.uk/education/sqh

Scottish Executive Education Department www.scotland.uk

Sergiovanni's work on leadership www.nsdc.org/library/developer/dev12–96.html

Socrates/Comenius www.socrates-uk.net

Stewart's work on digital portfolios www.edex.net.nz

Support sites www.classroomsupport.com, www.teachingideas.co.uk

Teacher network www.teachernet.gov.uk

Teacher Training Agency www.canteach.gov.uk

Teacherline www.teachersupport.org.uk

Teacherline www.teachersupport.org.uk

Teaching in Scotland www.teachinginscotland.com

Threshold www.deni.gov.uk/teachers

Times Educational Supplement www.tes.co.uk

University of Edinburgh www.ed.ac.uk

University of Leicester www.le.ac.uk/se/centres/emdu

Voice care network www.voicecare.org.uk

Wales www.cardiffuniversity.net/socsi/npqh

Welsh Assembly Government www.wales.gov.uk

References

Abdelnoor, A (2001) Five days that shaped the world, *Times Educational Supplement*, 17 August

Acker, S (1999) *The Realities of Teachers' Work: Never a dull moment*, Cassell, London

Alexander, R (1999) Inspection and education: the indivisibility of standards, in ed C Cullingford *An Inspector Calls: Ofsted and its effect on school standards*, Kogan Page, London

Andy–91 (2001) Welcome to the 2000, *Times Educational Supplement*, 9 November

Arkin, A (2002b) You've been barred, *Times Educational Supplement*, 15 March

Atkinson, A (2000) Teachers or managers? An evaluation of a Masters degree in education module linking change management to learning theory, *Journal of In-service Education*, **26** (3), pp 459–73

Aubrey, C (1997) *Mathematics Teaching in the Early Years: An investigation of teachers' subject knowledge*, Falmer, London

Banks, F, Leach, J and Moon, B (1999) New understandings of teachers' pedagogic knowledge, in eds J Leach and B Moon, *Learners and Pedagogy*, Paul Chapman in association with the Open University, London

Bartlett, S (1998) The development of effective appraisal by teachers, *Journal of In-service Education*, **24** (2), pp 227–38

Bartlett, S (2000) The development of teacher appraisal: a recent history, *British Journal of Education Studies*, **48** (1), pp 24–37

Bates, T, Gough, B and Stammers, P (1999) The role of central government and its agencies in the continuing professional development of teachers: an evaluation of recent changes in its financing in England, *Journal of In-service Education*, **25** (2), pp 321–35

Beauchamp, G (1997) In-service education and training in the classroom, *British Journal of In-service Education*, **23** (2), pp 205–18

Belbin, R M (1981) *Management Teams: Why they succeed or fail*, Heinemann, London

Bell, L (1991) Approaches to the professional development of teachers, in eds L Bell and C Day, *Managing the Professional Developments of Teachers*, Open University Press, Milton Keynes

Brace, G (2002) Training? They're biting our hands off to get more, *Times Educational Supplement*, 17 May

Brice Heath, S (1982) What no bedtime story means: narrative skills at home and school, *Language and Society*, **11**, pp 49–76

Brookes, G (2002a) Aggressive parents, *Times Educational Supplement*, 3 May

Brown, S, Edmonds, S and Lee, B (2001) *Continuing Professional Development*: *LEA and school support for teachers*, LEA Research Report, 23, NFER, Slough

Bubb, S and Hoare, P (2001) *Performance Management*: *Monitoring teaching in the primary school*, David Fulton, London

Budge, D (2002) Good in theory, *Times Educational Supplement*, 12 July

Bush, T (1995) *Theories of Educational Management*, Paul Chapman, London

Bush, T and Foreman, K (1998) National Standards and the training and development of headteachers, Paper presented at MBA students' day, University of Leicester, School of Education, Leicester. Web site www.le.ac.uk/se/centres/emdu

Busher, H (1988) Reducing role overload for a head of department: a rationale for fostering staff development, *School Organization*, **8** (1), pp 99–103

Busher, H and Harris, A (1999) Leadership of school subject areas: tensions and dimensions of managing in the middle, *School Leadership and Management*, **19** (3), pp 305–17

Busher, H and Harris, A (2000) *Subject Leadership and School Improvement*, Paul Chapman, London

Campbell, J and Neill, S (1997) Managing teachers' time under systematic reform, in eds T Bush and D Middlewood *Managing People in Education*, Paul Chapman, London

Campbell-Evans, G A (1993) A values perspective on school-based management, in ed C Dimmock, *School-Based Management and School Effectiveness*, Routledge, London

Canovan, C (2002a) Technology going to waste, *Times Educational Supplement*, 12 April

Canovan, C (2002b) Training fails to hit the spot, *Times Educational Supplement*, 19 April

Carnell, E and Lodge, C (2002) *Supporting Effective Learning*, Paul Chapman, London

Case, P, Case, S and Catling, S (2000) Please show you're working: a critical assessment of the impact of Ofsted inspections on primary teachers, *British Journal of Sociology of Education*, **21** (4), pp 605–22

Chapman, C (2001) Changing classrooms through inspection, *School Leadership and Management*, **21** (1), pp 59–73

Chartered Teacher Project (2001) Chartered Teacher Programme: Consultation Paper 1, SEED, Edinburgh

Clancy, J (2002) Excellence no bar to doing even better, *Times Educational Supplement*, 17 May

Clarke, J (2002) Where angels fear to tread, *Times Educational Supplement*, 1 March

Cole, G and Johnston, C (2002) Teachers must sing for their laptops, *Times Educational Supplement*, 14 June

Combes, A (2002) Let your class be the judge, *Times Educational Supplement*, 11 January

Comiskey, B and Buckle, K (1996) Two steps forward; teachers' professional development using Open College materials, *British Journal of In-service Education*, **22** (1), pp 55–65

Convery, A (1998) A teacher's response to 'reflection-in-action', *Cambridge Journal of Education*, **28** (2), pp 197–206

Cook, T (1998) The importance of mess in Action Research, *Educational Action Research*, **6** (1), pp 93–108

Covey, S (1992) *7 Habits of Highly Effective People: Restoring the character ethic*, Simon and Schuster, London

Crawford, M (1997) Managing stress in education, in eds T Bush and D Middlewood, *Managing People in Education*, Paul Chapman, London

Creese, A, Daniels, H and Norwich, B (1997) *Teacher Support Teams in Primary and Secondary Schools*, David Fulton, London

Crozier, G (1999) Is it a case of 'We know when we're not wanted'? The parents' perspective on parent–teacher roles and relationships, *Educational Research*, **41** (3), pp 315–28

Cuckle, P and Broadhead, P (1999) Effects of Ofsted inspection on school development and staff morale, in ed C Cullingford, *An Inspector Calls: Ofsted and its Effect on School Standards*, Kogan Page, London

Cullingford, C and Daniels, S (1999) The effect of inspections on school performance, in ed C Cullingford, *An Inspector Calls: Ofsted and its Effect on School Standards*, Kogan Page, London

Dadds, M (1998) Supporting practitioner research: a challenge, *Educational Action Research*, **6** (1), pp 39–52

Dadds, M (2001) Continuing professional development: nurturing the expert within, in eds J Soler, A Craft and H Burgess, *Teacher Development: Exploring our own practice*, Paul Chapman in association with the Open University, London

Dawkins, R (1989) *The Selfish Gene*, Oxford University Press, Oxford

Day, C (1997) In-service teacher education in Europe: conditions and themes for development in the 21st century, *British Journal of In-service Education*, **23** (1), pp 39–54

Day, C (1998) Working with the different selves of teachers: beyond comfortable collaboration, *Educational Action Research*, **6** (2), 255–73

Day, C (1999) *Developing Teachers: The challenges of lifelong learning*, Falmer, London

Dean, C (2001) Damning verdict on performance pay, *Times Educational Supplement*, 13 July

Dean, C (2002) PRP applicant wanted cash for son's Manhatten dream, *Times Educational Supplement*, 11 January

DENI (1998a) *The Teacher Education Partnership Handbook: Integrating and managing partnership-based teacher education in Northern Ireland*, DENI, Bangor

DES (1989) *Discipline in Schools: Report of the Committee of Enquiry* chaired by Lord Elton, HMSO, London

DES (1991a) *Education (School Teacher Appraisal) Regulations* No 1511, HMSO, London

DES (1991b) *School Teacher Appraisal, Circular 12/91*, DES, London

Desforges, C and Lings, P (1998) Teaching knowledge application: advances in theoretical conceptions and their professional implications, *British Journal of Educational Studies*, **46** (4), pp 386–98

DfEE and Department of Health (2000) *Fitness to Teach: Occupational Health Guidance for the Training and Employment of Teachers*, Stationery Office, London

DfEE (1997) *Excellence in Schools*, DfEE, London

DfEE (1998a) *Requirements for Courses of Initial Teacher Training*, DfEE Circular 4/98, DfEE, London

DfEE (1998b) *Teachers Meeting the Challenge of Change*, DfEE, London

DfEE (2000a) *National Standards for Headteachers* (DfEE 0195/2000) September 2000, DfEE, London

DfEE (2000b) *Performance Management in Schools*, DfEE, London

DfEE (2000c) *Threshold Assessment: Guidance on completing the application form*, DfEE, London

DfEE (2001a) *Good Value CPD: A code of practice for providers of professional development for teachers*, DfEE, London

DfEE (2001b) *Learning and Teaching: a strategy for professional development*, DfEE 0071/2001, DfEE, London

DfEE (2001c) *Schools Building on Success*, The Stationery Office, London

DfES (2001a) *Continuing Professional Development: Video case studies*, DfEE, London

DfES (2001b) *The Induction Period for Newly Qualified Teachers*, DfES 582/2001, DfES, London

DfES (2001c) *Schools Achieving Success*, The Stationery Office, Norwich

DfES (2001d) *National Standards for Headteachers*, DfES 0195/2000, DfES, London

DfES (2002a) *Best Practice Scholarships*, DfES, London

DfES (2002b) *NPQH Consultation: Proposals to introduce a mandatory requirement for first-time headteachers to hold the NPQH*, DfES/0249/2002, DfES and NCSL, Nottingham

Dunham, J (1978) Change and stress in the head of department's role, *Educational Research*, **21** (1), pp 44–48

Egan, D and James, R (2002) *An Evaluation for the General Teaching Council for Wales of the Professional Development Pilot Projects 2001–2001*, PPI Group for GTCS, Cardiff

Egan, D and Simmonds, C (2002) *Review of CPD in Other Professions in the UK and Teacher CPD in Other Countries*, GTCW, Cardiff

Elliott, J (1991) *Action Research for Educational Change*, Open University Press, Milton Keynes

Evans, J, Lunt, I, Wedell, K and Dyson, A (1999) *Collaborating for Effectiveness: Empowering schools to be inclusive*, Open University Press, Buckingham

Farrell, T (2001) Critical friendships: colleagues helping each other develop, *ELT Journal*, **55** (4), pp 368–74

Ferguson, N, Earley, P, Fidler, B and Ouston, J (2000) *Improving School and Inspections: The self-inspecting school*, Paul Chapman, London

Fidler, B (1996) *Strategic Planning for School Improvement*, Pitman Publishing, London

Fidler, B and Atton, T (1999) *Poorly Performing Staff in Schools and How to Manage Them: Capability, competence and motivation*, Routledge, London

Fitzgibbon, C and Stephenson-Forster, N (1999) Is Ofsted helpful? An evaluation using Social Science criteria, in ed C Cullingford *An Inspector Calls: Ofsted and its Effect on School Standards*, Kogan Page, London

Flecknoe, M (2000) Can continuing professional development for teachers be shown to raise pupils' achievement? *Journal of In-service Education*, **26** (3), pp 437–57

Fleming, P (2000) *The Art of Middle Management in Secondary Schools*, David Fulton, London

Fleming, P and Amesbury, M (2001) *The Art of Middle Management in Primary Schools: A guide to effective subject, years and team leadership*, David Fulton, London

Foster, P (1999) 'Never mind the quality, feel the impact': a methodological assessment of teacher research sponsored by the Teacher Training Agency, *British Journal of Educational Studies*, **47** (4), pp 380–98

Friedman, A, Davis, K and Phillips, M (2001) *Continuing Professional Development in the UK: Attitudes and experience of practitioners*, Professional Associations Research Network, University of Bristol

Frost, D (1999) Developing primary MFL: a teacher-led community-focused approach, in eds P Driscoll and D Frost *The Teaching of Modern Foreign Languages in the Primary School*, Routledge, London

Ginns, I, Heirdsfield, A, Attweb, B and Watters, J (2001) Beginning teachers becoming professionals through Action Research, *Educational Action Research*, **9** (1), pp 111–33

Glover, D, Gleeson, D, Gough, G and Johnson, M (1998) The meaning of management: the development needs of middle managers in secondary schools, *Educational Management and Administration*, **26** (3), pp 279–91

Grace, G (2000) Research and the challenges of contemporary school leadership: the contributions of critical scholarship, *British Journal Educational Studies*, **48** (3), pp 231–47

Gray, C and Gardner, J (1999) The impact of school inspections, *Oxford Review of Education*, **25** (4), pp 455–68

Grubb, W N (1999) Improvement or control? A US view of English inspection, in ed C Cullingford *An Inspector Calls: Ofsted and its Effect on School Standards*, Kogan Page, London

GTCE (General Teaching Council for England) (2001a) *General Teaching Council Working for Teachers: The first corporate plan of the General Teaching Council 2001/02*, GTCE, London

GTCE (2001b) *Draft Professional Learning Framework: The General Teaching Council's Professional Learning Framework: a draft for discussion and development*, GTCE, London

GTCE (2002) *Speaking Up for Teaching: Corporate plan 2002–2003*, GTCE, London

GTCS (General Teaching Council for Scotland) (2002a) *The Standard for Full Registration* SEED, GTCS, Edinburgh

GTCS (2002b) *Standard for Full Registration Self-evaluation*, GTCS, Edinburgh

GTCS (2002c) *Standard for Full Registration Portfolio*, GTCS, Edinburgh

GTCS (2002d) *Achieving the Standard for full registration: Guidance for schools*, GTCS, Edinburgh

GTCW (General Teaching Council for Wales) (2001a) *Professional Development Pilot Projects: Information booklet and application forms*, GTCW, Cardiff

GTCW (2001b) *Continuing Professional Development An Entitlement for All The General Teaching Council for Wales' Advice to the National Assembly for Wales*, 2nd draft, GTCW, Cardiff

GTCW (2002a) *Professional Development: A Whole School Initiative: Information booklet 2002–2003*, GTCW, Cardiff

GTCW (2002b) *Professional Development Pilot Projects: Information booklet 2002–2003*, GTCW, Cardiff

Gunter, H (2001a) *Leaders and Leadership in Education*, Paul Chapman, London

Gunter, H (2001b) Teacher research networks, 1980–2000, *Educational Review*, **53** (3), pp 241–50

Haigh, G (2001a) Good will hunting, *Times Educational Supplement*, 30 March

Haigh, G (2001b) Take my advice, *Times Educational Supplement*, 30 November

Haigh, G (2002) Five steps to heaven, *Times Educational Supplement*, 8 March

Hammond, P (1999) How can a head of department affect the quality of teaching and learning? Final report on a TTA Teacher-Researcher Grant Project 1997–9, pp 1–31, www.leeds.ac.uk/educo/documents/

Hancock, R (2001) Why are classroom teachers reluctant to become researchers? in eds J Soler, A Craft and H Burgess, *Teacher Development: Exploring our practice*, Paul Chapman in association with the Open University, London

Hargreaves, A (1994) *Changing Teachers, Changing Times: Teachers' work and culture in the postmodern age*, Cassell, London

Hargreaves, A (1996) Revisiting voice, *Educational Researcher*, **25** (1), pp 12–19

Hargreaves, A and Fullan, M (1998) *What's Worth Fighting for in Education?* Open University Press, Buckingham

Hargreaves, A and Fullan, M (1992) *What's Worth Fighting for in Your School?*, Open University Press, Buckingham

Hargreaves, A and Hopkins, D (1991) *The Empowered School*, Cassell, London

Harland, J, Ashworth, M, Atkinson, M, Halsey, K, Haynes, J, Moor, H and Wilkin, A (1999) *Thank You for the Days? How schools use their non-contact days*, NFER, Slough

Harris, A (1998) Improving ineffective departments in secondary schools, *Educational Management and Administration,* **26** (3), pp 269–78

Harris, A (1999) *Effective Subject Leadership in Secondary School: A handbook of staff development activities,* David Fulton, London

Harris, A (2001) Running to stand still, *Times Educational Supplement,* 14 September

Harris A, Jamieson, I and Russ, J (1995) A study of effective departments in secondary schools, *School Organization,* **15** (3), pp 283–99

Hartle, F, Everall, K and Baker, C (2001) *Getting the Best out of Performance Management in Your School,* TES/Kogan Page, London

Hastings, S (2001a) Lessons from the production line, *Times Educational Supplement,* 14 September

Hastings, S (2001b) When little means a lot, *Times Educational Supplement,* 19 October

Hastings, S (2002a) Hoarse sense, *Times Educational Supplement,* 1 June

Hastings, S (2002b) Sabbaticals, *Times Educational Supplement,* 19 April

Hay McBer (2000) *Research into Teacher Effectiveness,* Research Report 216, DfEE, London

Health and Safety Commission, Education Service Advisory Committee (1998) *Managing Work Related Stress: A guide for managers and teachers in schools,* 2nd edition, The Stationery Office, London

Higgins, S and Leat, D (2001) Horses for courses or courses for horses: what is effective teacher development? in *Teacher Development: Exploring our own practice,* eds J Soler, A Craft and H Burgess, Paul Chapman in association with the Open University, London

Holloway, K and Long, R (1998) Teacher development and school improvement: the use of 'shared practice groups' to improve teaching in primary schools, *Journal of In-service Education,* **24** (3), pp 535–45

Holmes, E (2001) *Teachers' Guide to Successful, Professional Development,* School Managernet, The Stationery Office, London

Hopkins, D, Harris A, Watling, R and Beresford, J (1999) From inspection to school improvement? Evaluating the accelerated inspection programme in Waltham Forest, *British Educational Research Association Journal,* **25** (5), pp 679–90

Horne, H and Pierce, A (1996) *A Practical Guide to Staff Development and Appraisal in Schools,* Kogan Page, London

Howson, J (2001) Uneven spread of a rare breed, *Times Educational Supplement,* 30 November

Hustler, D (1999) The Ofsted lay inspector: to what purpose? in ed C Cullingford *An Inspector Calls: Ofsted and its Effect on School Standards,* Kogan Page, London

Johnson, C (2002) NOF 'naff' says Ofsted, *Times Educational Supplement, Online* 26 April

Johnston, C (2001) Heads must have an understanding of how ICT can improve learning, *Times Educational Supplement,* Online, 12 October

Jones, J (2001) *Performance Management for School Improvement: A practical guide for secondary schools*, David Fulton, London

Jones, P and Sparkes, W (1997) *Effective Heads of Department*, Network Educational Press, Stafford

Kerschner, R (1999) The role of school-based research in helping teachers to extend their understanding of children's learning and motivation, *Journal of In-service Education*, **25** (5), pp 423–46

Kogan, M and Maden, M (1999) An evaluation of evaluation: the Ofsted system of school inspection in ed C Cullingford *An Inspector Calls: Ofsted and its effect on school standards*, Kogan Page, London

Lacey, P (1996) Training for collaboration, *British Journal of In-service Education*, **20** (1), pp 67–80

Leach, J (2001) Teaching's long revolution: from ivory towers to networked communities of practice, in eds F Banks and A Shelton Mayes *Early Professional Development for Teachers*, David Fulton, London

Learner, S (2001) Soft-touch style but tough on standards, *Times Educational Supplement*, 14 September

Leask, M and Terrell, I (1997) *Development Planning and School Improvement for Middle Managers*, Kogan Page, London

Letters (2001) Don't let children assess teachers, *Times Educational Supplement*, 14 September

Lewin, K (1947) Frontiers in group dynamics: concept, method and reality in social science, social equilibrium and social change, *Human Relations*, **1** (1), pp 5–41

Lieberman, A and Grolnick, M (1996) Networks and reform in American education, *Teachers College Record*, **98** (1), pp 7–45

Little, J (1990) The persistence of privacy: autonomy and initiative in teachers' professional relations, *Teachers College Record*, **91** (4), pp 509–36

Lloyd, C and Draper, M (1998) The LID (Learning Interactively at a Distance) project: supporting learning, teaching and continuing professional development using information and communication technology, *Journal of In-service Education*, **24** (1), pp 87–97

MacBeath, J (1999) *Schools Must Speak for Themselves: The case for school self-evaluation*, Routledge, London

MacDonald, I (2002) Are you looking at me? *Times Educational Supplement*, 21 June

MacNab, D (2000) Curriculum development and HM Inspection of Schools: a Scottish case-study, *Oxford Review of Education*, **27** (1), pp 85–102

Mahoney, P and Hextall, I (2000) *Reconstructing Teaching Standards, Performance and Accountability*, Routledge, London

Mansell, W (2001a) Call to scrap super teachers, *Times Educational Supplement*, 31 May

Mansell, W (2001b) Performance pay saps teacher morale, *Times Educational Supplement*, 21 September

Mansell, W (2002a) Ministers face up to red tape defeat, *Times Educational Supplement*, 14 June

Mansell, W (2002b) Pay rises break the school bank, *Times Educational Supplement*, 19 July

Mansell, W (2002c) Quartet fine-tune school's revival, *Times Educational Supplement*, 25 January

Mansell, W and Matthews, A (2001) Inspections all ears as parents speak out, *Times Educational Supplement*, 7 September

Mansell, W and Shaw, M (2002) Morris puts standards before staff workload, *Times Educational Supplement*, 10 May

Mansell, W and Ward, H (2002) Ministers fear heads will hijack extra cash, *Times Educational Supplement*, 26 July

Mansell, W, Slater, J and Ward, H (2002) Record cash deal tied to new targets, *Times Educational Supplement*, 19 July

Marland, M (1971) *Head of Department: Leading a department in a comprehensive school*, Heinemann, London

Marriott, D (2001) The chance to feast upon shared ideas, *Times Educational Supplement*, 26 October

Marriott, G (2001) *Observing Teachers at Work*, Heinemann, Oxford

McEwen, A, Carlisle, K, Knipe, D, Neil, P and McClune, B (2002) Primary school leadership: values and actions, *Research Papers in Education*, **17** (2), pp 147–63

McNiff, J (1988) *Action Research: Principles and practice*, Routledge, London

MCI (Manager Charter Initiative) (1998) *Management Standards: MCI senior management: adding value*, MCI, London

Melrose, M and Reid, M (2000) The Daisy Model for collaborative Action Research: application to educational practice, *Educational Action Research*, **8** (1), pp 151–65

Metcalfe, C (1999) Developmental classroom observation as a component of monitoring and evaluating the work of subject departments in secondary schools, *Journal of In-service Education*, **25** (3), pp 447–60

Middlewood, D and Lumby, J (1998) *Human Resource Management in Schools and Colleges*, Paul Chapman, London

Middlewood, D (1997) Managing appraisal, in eds T Bush and D Middlewood *Managing People in Education*, Paul Chapman, London

Miller, C, Smith, C and Tilstone, C (1998a) Action, impact and change: developing classroom practice through distance education, *Journal of In-service Education*, **24** (1), pp 111–22

Miller, C, Smith, C and Tilstone, C (1998b) Professional development by distance education: does distance lend enhancement? *Cambridge Journal of Education*, **28** (2), pp 221–30

Millett, A and Johnson, D (1998) Expertise or 'baggage'? What helps inspectors to inspect primary Mathematics? *British Educational Research Journal*, **24** (5), pp 503–18

Moran, A, Dallat, J and Abbot, L (1999) Supporting NQTs in post-primary schools in Northern Ireland, *Research Report Series*, **14**, DENI, Bangor

Morgan, C (1998a) Cross-cultural encounter, in eds M Byram and M Fleming *Foreign Language Learning in Intercultural Perspective: Approaches through drama and ethnography*, Cambridge University Press, Cambridge

Morgan, C (1998b) The role of the native speaker in EAC and bilingual initiatives, *English Language Teaching News*, **36**, pp 102–08

Morgan, C (1999) The process of transfer from primary to secondary in a bilingual schooling context, *International Journal of Bilingual Education and Bilingualism*, **2** (4), pp 233–51

Morgan, C and Feyertag-Pressel, B (in press) Learning skills across the curriculum in a bilingual schooling context

Morgan, C and Neil, P (2001) *Learning to Teach Modern Foreign Languages: A handbook for teachers*, Kogan Page, London

NEBSM (National Examination Board for Supervisory Management) (undated) *NVQ/SVQ in Strategic Management Level 5*, *MCI endorsed*, NEBSM, London

Neil, P, Carlisle, K, Knipe, D and McEwen, A (2001) Principals in action: an analysis of school leadership, *Research in Education*, **66**, pp 40–53

Nicholls G (1997) *Collaborative Change in Education*, Kogan Page, London

Nicholls, G (1999) Continual professional development, in G Nicholls *Learning to Teach*, Kogan Page, London

NITEC (Northern Ireland Teacher Education Committee) (2002) The Continuing Professional Development of Teachers in Northern Ireland – a proposal presented to the Minister of Education, June 2002, DE, Bangor

NPQH/CPCP (2001) *The National Standards for Headteachers in Wales* (http: www.cf.ac.uk/socsi/npqh/)

O'Hara, L and O'Hara, M (2001) *Teaching History 3–11 The Essential Guide*, Continuum, London

Ofsted (1996) *Training of Independent Inspectors Prep 01: Introduction to the Course*, HMSO, London

Ofsted (1997) *Subject Management in Secondary Schools: Aspects of good practice*, Ofsted, London

Ofsted (1998a) *School Educational Matters*, Ofsted, London

Ofsted (1998b) *Secondary Education 1993–97: A review of secondary schools in England*, The Stationery Office, London

Ofsted (1999a) *The Annual Report of Her Majesty's Chief Inspector of Schools: Standards and quality in education 1997/98*, The Stationery Office, London

Ofsted (1999b) *Inspecting Schools: The framework*, Ofsted, London

Ofsted (2001a) *Improving Inspection, Improving Schools*, Ofsted, London

Ofsted (2001b) *School Governance: Making it better*, Ofsted, London

Ofsted (2002a) *The Annual Report of Her Majesty's Chief Inspector of Schools: Standards and quality in education 2000/2001*, The Stationery Office, London

Ofsted (2002b) *Inspecting Schools: The framework for inspecting schools in England from September 2003*, Ofsted, London

Ofsted/DfES (2001) *Reducing the Burden of Inspection*, Ofsted, London

Owl, J (2002) Why the watchword is trust, *Times Educational Supplement*, 29 March

Palmer, S (2001) Too much target practice, *Times Educational Supplement*, 7 December

Parkin, J B (1984) *School Self-Evaluation and the Management of Change*, Department of Education and Management, Sheffield

Parkin, J (2002a) After-hours thinking, *Times Educational Supplement*, 8 March

Parkin, J (2002b) They're only trying to help after all, *Times Educational Supplement*, 19 April

Poster, C and Poster, D (1993) *Teacher Appraisal: Training and Implementation*, 2nd edition, Routledge, London

Poulson, L (2001) Paradigm lost? Subject knowledge, primary teachers and educational policy, *British Journal of Educational Studies*, **49** (1), pp 40–55

Purdon, A (2001) New teachers' perspectives on continuing professional development: accountability or professional growth? *Scottish Educational Review*, **33** (2), pp 110–22

Reed, J and Learmonth, J (2001) Revitalising teachers' accountability: learning about learning as a renewed focus for school improvement, *Journal of In-service Education*, **27**, (1), pp 11–27

Revell, P (2001) Sabbatical for staff in the poorest schools, *Times Educational Supplement*, 7 September

Revell, P (2002a) Get me off the treadmill, *Times Educational Supplement*, 22 March

Revell, P (2002b) Let off steam in the hot seat, *Times Educational Supplement*, 8 March

Revell, P (2002c) Log on for help, *Times Educational Supplement*, 19 April

Revell, P (2002d) Take your partner by the hand, *Times Educational Supplement*, 8 February

Revell, P (2002e) First steps for new leaders, *Times Educational Supplement*, 26 April

Reynolds, D (2002) Misuse of computers unplugged, *Times Educational Supplement*, 11 January

Robertson, J (2000) The three Rs of Action Research methodology: reciprocity, reflectivity and reflection in reality, *Educational Action Research*, **8** (2), pp 307–26

RTU (Regional Training Unit) (undated) *Professional Qualification for Headship in Northern Ireland PQH(NI) Overview*, RTU/NPQH, Belfast

Ruiz, M, and Parés, N (1997) The professional developments of teachers by means of the construction of collaborative thinking, *British Journal of In-service Education*, **23** (2), 241–52

Sarland, C (2001) 'Becoming our own experts': lessons from the past, *Educational Action Research,* **9** (2), pp 171–85

Sassoon, D (2002) Face up to making the head better, *Times Educational Supplement,* 5 July

Scanlon, M (1999) *The Impact of Ofsted Inspections,* NFER and NUT, Slough

Schulman, L (1986) Those who understand knowledge: growth in teaching, *Educational Researcher,* **15** (2), pp 4–14

SEED (Scottish Executive Education Department) (2000) *A Teaching Profession for the 21st Century (The McCrone Report),* SEED, Edinburgh

SEED (2001a) *A Teaching Profession for the 21st Century: Agreement reached following the McCrone report,* SEED, Edinburgh

SEED (2001b) *Teaching in Scotland: It's the making of us,* SEED, Edinburgh

Sekules, V, Tickle, L and Xanthoudak, M (1999) Seeking art expertise: experiences of primary school teachers, *Journal of In-service Education,* **25** (3), pp 571–82

Selwyn, N (2000) Creating a 'connected' community? Teachers' use of an electronic discussion group, *Teachers College Record,* **102** (4), pp 750–78

Sergiovanni, T J (1991) *The Principalship: A reflective practice perspective,* Allyn and Bacon, Boston

Sergiovanni, T J (1996) *Leadership for the Schoolhouse: How is it different? Why is it important?* Jossey-Bass, San Fransisco

Sergiovanni, T J (1998) Leadership as pedagogy, capital development and school effectiveness, *International Journal of Leadership in Education,* **1** (1), pp 37–46

Shaw, M and Mansell, W (2002) Only the chancellor can take the load off, *Times Educational Supplement,* 10 May

Silcock, P and Wyness, M (1998) Strong in diversity: primary inspectors' beliefs, *The Curriculum Journal,* **9** (1), pp 105–27

Slater, J and Mansell, W (2002) Salary awards take large bite out of budgets, *Times Educational Supplement,* 22 February

Smith, P (1996) Collaborative models of developing competence, *British Journal of In-service Education,* **24** (2), pp 285–92

Smith, A and Langston, A (1999), *Managing Staff in Early Years Settings,* Routledge, London

Solomon, N (2001) Whose lesson is it anyway? *Times Educational Supplement,* 14 September

Stewart, D (2000) *Tomorrow's Principals Today,* Kanuka Grove Press, Palmerston North

Stewart, D (in press) What does a reflective principal do?: Being an educational leader, *SPANZ, the Journal of the School Principals' Association of New Zealand* (August 2002)

Stewart, D and Prebble, T (1993) *The Reflective Principal: School development within a learning community,* ERDC Press, Palmerston North

Strathern, M (2000) The tyranny of transparency, *British Educational Research Journal*, **26** (3), pp 309–22

Sutherland, V and Cooper, C (1997) *30 Minutes to Deal with Difficult People*, Kogan Page, London

Thomas, S, Smees, R and Elliot, K (2000) Value added feedback for the purpose of self evaluation, in ed S Askew *Feedback for Learning*, Routledge Falmer, London

Thornton, K and Mansell, W (2001) Threshold losers give vent to anger, *Times Educational Supplement*, 20 September

Thornton, K (2002) Fast-track training firm under fire, *Times Educational Supplement* January 18

Tricoglus, G (2001) Living the theoretical principles of critical ethnography in educational research, *Educational Action Research*, **9** (1), pp 135–48

TTA (Teacher Training Agency) (1998) *National Standards for Qualified Teacher Status, Subject Leaders, Special Educational Needs Co-ordinators*, HMSO, London

TTA/DfES (2001) *Qualifying to Teach: Professional standards for qualified teacher status and requirements for initial teacher training*, TTA/DfES, London

TTA (2002) *Review of the Induction Standards*, TTA, London

Turner, C K (1996) The roles and tasks of a subject head of department in secondary schools in England and Wales: a neglected area of research? *School Organization*, **16** (2), pp 203–217

Turner, C K (2000) Learning about leading a subject department in a secondary schools: some empirical evidence, *School Leadership and Management*, **20** (3), pp 299–313

University of Edinburgh (2001) *The Standard for Headship in Scotland: The Scottish Qualification for Headship* (Standard version of 5/4/01), University of Edinburgh

Vincent, C (2001) Researching home-school relations: a critical approach, in eds J Collins and D Cook *Understanding Learning*, Paul Chapman in association with the Open University, London

Wallace, W (2002) Made in Sheffield, *Times Educational Supplement*, 18 January

Ward, H (2001a) Get paid for putting your lessons on-line, *Times Educational Supplement*, 14 September

Ward, H (2001b) Inspiring lessons win pupil praise, *Times Educational Supplement*, 19 October

Ward, H (2001c) Keep cool when an inspector calls, *Times Educational Supplement*, 28 September

Ward, H (2002a) Advanced skills staff eager to get out more and share wisdom, *Times Educational Supplement*, 12 April

Ward, H (2002b) Alarm at surge in use of ready-made lessons, *Times Educational Supplement*, 20 June

Ward, H (2002c) Work for us, get your life back, *Times Educational Supplement*, 14 June

Welsh Assembly Government (2002) *Induction and Early Professional Development in*

Wales – from competency to proficiency. Draft 1, Welsh Assembly Government, Cardiff

Whittaker, M (2001) So class, how am I doing? *Times Educational Supplement*, 12 October

Wikeley, F (2000) Learning from research, in ed S Askew *Feedback for Learning*, Routledge Falmer, London

Wilkins, R (2000) Practitioner research in LEA-directed INSET, *Journal of In-service Education*, **26** (1), pp 99–113

Willard, C (2001) Heads logging on to online lifeline, *Times Educational Supplement*, 12 October

Winkley, D (1999) An examination of Ofsted, in ed C Cullingford, *An Inspector Calls: Ofsted and its Effect on School Standards*, Kogan Page, London

Wisdom, P (2001) I'm on your side, *Times Educational Supplement*, 5 October

Wolff, J (2002) It only takes a minute, *Times Educational Supplement*, 19 July

Woods, P, Jeffrey, B, Troman, G, Boyle, M and Colchin, B (1998) Team and technology in writing up research, *British Educational Research Journal*, **24** (5), pp 573–92

Wragg, E, Wikeley, F, Wragg, C and Haynes, G (1996) *Teacher Appraisal Observed*, Routledge, London

Wragg, E, Haynes, G and Chamberlin, R (2000) *Failing Teachers?* Routledge, London